Gardening with Shape, Line and Texture

Gardening with Shape, Line and Texture

A Plant Design Sourcebook

Linden Hawthorne

Timber Press
Portland | London

For Freya and Ellen, Richard and Virginia

Front cover
The complementary shapes, lines and textures of
verbascums, eremuruses, poppies and alliums contribute
to the success of Beth Chatto's Gravel Garden in Essex,
England. Photo by Andrew Lawson

Frontispiece
The restored woodland and water garden designed by
Harold Peto exploits a device that Pope and Kent would
have known as 'calling in the country'—borrowing
the wider landscape as a focal point. (Wayford Manor,
Crewkerne, Somerset) Photo by Nicola Stocken Tomkins

Text copyright © Linden Hawthorne. All rights reserved.
Photographs copyright © Jonathan Buckley, Torie Chugg, Liz
Eddison, Sam Eddison, Derek Harris, Linden Hawthorne,
Andrew Lawson, Marie O'Hara, Gary Rogers, Jane Sebire,
Derek St Romaine, Nicola Stocken Tomkins and Mark Taylor.
Illustrations copyright © Catriona Stewart. Credits appear on
page 280.

Published in 2009 by Timber Press, Inc.

The Haseltine Building	2 The Quadrant
133 S.W. Second Avenue, Suite 450	135 Salusbury Road
Portland, Oregon 97204-3527	London NW6 6RJ
www.timberpress.com	www.timberpress.co.uk

Design by Dick Malt
Printed in China

Library of Congress Cataloging-in-Publication Data
Hawthorne, Linden.
  Gardening with shape, line and texture : a plant design
sourcebook / Linden Hawthorne. -- 1st ed.
      p. cm.
  Includes bibliographical references and index.
  ISBN 978-0-88192-888-4
  1. Gardens--Design. 2. Landscape gardening. 3. Landscape
plants. I. Title.
  SB472.45.H388 2009
  712'.6--dc22
                          2009022652

A catalogue record for this book is also available from the
British Library.

Contents

Acknowledgements

Special thanks are due to Erica Gordon-Mallin and Anna Mumford at Timber Press, for faith and patience, and for acquiring the services of the fabulous photographers at the Garden Collection: Andrew Lawson, Derek Harris, Derek St Romaine, Gary Rogers, Jane Sebire, Jonathan Buckley, Liz Eddison, Marie O'Hara, Nicola Stocken Tomkins, Sam Eddison, Mark Taylor and Torie Chugg. Special thanks also to Catriona Stewart.

Preface

As gardeners we take enormous pleasure in simply strolling through the garden, head down, enjoying the individual beauties of plants. Yet when we sit back to view the combined effect—the whole planting, the whole garden—we sometimes feel that something is missing: something more is needed if the garden is to be a finer thing than just a plant collection.

Many of us want to create a garden that is truly our own work of art. This book is for the garden-maker whose ambitions extend beyond copying another's style; however elegant and covetable the original, that approach leads to pastiche, and never gives the satisfaction of a work with its creator's own stamp.

In my experience, it is exactly when we do treat a garden as a work of art that we create the most beautiful and unique of plant compositions. To this end, we can benefit from learning a pattern language—a basic design vocabulary that, once grasped, allows us to confidently express our taste with style.

In the first chapter, I describe principles common to other art forms, such as architecture, painting, photography, graphic art and all sorts of design, and I suggest how to apply them in gardens. Grouping plants according to their shape and line is central to my approach, and the plant directories in the chapters that follow are organized this way. The focus will be on their shape, line, texture and form—and how they can be used to best effect in your plant compositions.

As with all systems of classification, there are always things that don't fall neatly into line. This is not a book about painting by numbers—it is about painting with plants. The groups outlined in this book's plant directories are a simple aid to placing plants in a composition. Any plant that you grow or buy can be ascribed loosely to one of these categories, which allows you to place it well rather than cramming it in.

Aesthetic elements alone, though, are not the complete picture in good garden design. All good design—in any field—demands that structural and functional elements are integrated to meet the practical needs of the user to the best aesthetic advantage: in other words, utility with beauty. And although human needs are paramount in the garden, it is essential to consider other living materials, the plants, among the intended users of the space. If their needs are not met, they do not thrive, and your palette is compromised, which is not ultimately conducive to gardening joy.

Good garden design is never simply a visual art, but a craft that marries the earthy practical skills of the gardener with the eye of an artist, and there are many similarities, I think, in the desires and imaginations of both. After all, if gardening didn't engage heart, soul and brain, it would just be so much hard labour.

Painting with Plants

◀ Clipped balls of box, holly and privet and mirrored plantings of *Phlomis*, *Nepeta* and *Stachys* echoed by the upswept branches of *Mahonia* lend unity and a strong underlying rhythm.

The idea that one can create a garden or landscape in much the same way as an artist composes a picture is by no means new. Many of the great garden designers including William Kent, Gertrude Jekyll, Russell Page, Roberto Burle Marx and Thomas Church were trained in visual arts, and the principles of good composition are seen in all of their gardens, whether traditional or modern.

The principles were consciously expressed in the eighteenth-century English landscape. During his Grand Tour of Italy in the early eighteenth century, William Kent, architect, painter and progenitor of the English Landscape style, studied architecture and became familiar with the work of the Landscape painters Claude Lorrain, Nicolas Poussin and Salvator Rosa. His friend, the poet Alexander Pope, commended the principle that you "paints as you plant" and coined the dictum that "all gardening is landscape painting"—a maxim that Kent made his own. Kent's landscape work, in which he created three-dimensional pictures from a palette of woods, lawn, water and the contrasts of light and shade, has been described as that of a purely visual artist, rather than the work of a gardener. Put crudely, with this pictorial sensibility he placed garden buildings in an idealized landscape, drawing inspiration from...

whate'er Lorrain light-touched with softening hue
Or savage Rosa dashed, or learned Poussin drew.

J. Thomson, *The Castle of Indolence* (1748)

And, like them, he adopted a formulaic approach, composing in the three planes of the near, middle, and far distance:

Three marked divisions we shall always find: Not more, where Claude extends the prospect wide.

Richard Paine Knight, *The Landscape* (1794)

Gertrude Jekyll, too, trained as a painter. In the introduction to one of her best-known books, *Colour Schemes for The Flower Garden*, 1914, she writes:

It seems to me that the duty we owe our gardens... is so to use the plants that they will form beautiful pictures.

My aim isn't to provide a historical treatise (fascinating as that would be); rather, my point is that many designers, including Kent in the wider landscape, and Thomas Church and Gertrude Jekyll in more intimate settings, have used compositional skills to create their gardens, and the principles familiar to them can be applied on a macro-level to the creation of a whole garden, and on a micro-level in borders and other planting schemes.

Composition and Divine Proportion

Let me expand on the idea of compositional skills. Composition is, by definition, the arrangement of elements to produce a satisfying whole—and perhaps the most important principle of composition, that of Divine Proportion, has been used in European works of art and architecture at least since the Renaissance, although its origins are far more ancient. Its use can be seen in the proportions of the Pyramid of Giza and the Parthenon. Divine Proportion, also known as the Golden Ratio, Section or Mean, was a concept as familiar to Palladio as to Le Corbusier, to Leonardo da Vinci as to Mondrian.

To apply Divine Proportion in gardens may imply an esoteric approach, but far from it. In

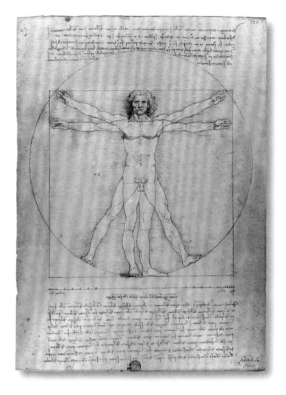

▶ Based on Vitruvius's *De Architectura*, da Vinci's *Vitruvian Man* (c. 1487) illustrates the Divine Proportions of an idealized human form.

practical terms, the principle provides a framework for the elements of a composition and gives a good indication of where focal points should be placed. Rather than pencil or paint, the primary materials in the palette are plants.

Perhaps the most famous expression of Divine Proportion lies in Leonardo da Vinci's fifteenth-century Vitruvian Man, which Leonardo based on theories expounded in *De Architectura*, Marcus Vitruvius Pollio's first-century BC treatise on architecture. It illustrates the relative proportions of the human body, which, Vitruvius stated, should be reproduced in all architecture and building. Leonardo's drawing not only symbolizes connections between the material and spiritual worlds, but it also illustrates practically the units of measurement such as the foot, cubit and yard—derived from the idealized human form—which were physical measurements used in building. In the drawing the proportion of one side of the enclosing square to the diameter of the circle was deemed Divine, as was the ratio between the measurements from foot to navel and navel to crown.

The simplest expression of Divine Proportion is the Golden Ratio of 1:1.618, shown in the drawings opposite. The definition of the Golden Ratio as the Divine Proportion was first seen in *de Divine Proportione* (1509), by Luca Pacioli, on the subject of the relationship between mathematics and artistic proportion and particularly on the appearance of the Golden Ratio in architecture. That Luca and Leonardo were collaborators, and indeed that Luca tutored Leonardo in mathematics, links the two Renaissance theorists in a way that has permeated our appreciation of beauty ever since.

Divine Proportion was used explicitly in the sixteenth-century architecture of Andrea Palladio. In the seventeenth century it was revived by Inigo Jones, and yet again in the eighteenth by Lord Burlington, patron of William Kent, informing all matters of taste in architecture, particularly the architecture that graced gardens in the eighteenth century and beyond. In the twentieth century the idiom was more modern, but the proportion still evident in the works of Mies van der Rohe, Frank Lloyd Wright and, most famously, Le Corbusier. It is considered to be aesthetically superior to all other proportions, and compositions that use it the most pleasing to the eye. It is the echo of the human form that makes Divine Proportion so appealing to the human eye, and so easy to use when applying it to compositions with plants.

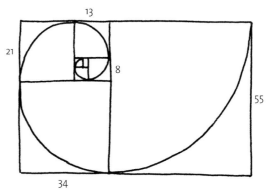

The Golden Ratio is the only way in which a simple line can be divided into two sections with perfect harmony. It represents the ideal balance between symmetry and asymmetry, or unity and variety. The Golden Ratio is one in which 1.618, the Golden Number, or phi (Φ), is a constant.

The sections of a line are in Divine Proportion when the ratio between the lengths of the two sections (AB:BC) is the same as the ratio between the longer of the sections and the sum of the two sections (BC:AC). If AB is 1, then BC is 1.618 (1 × 1.618, the Golden Number). When BC is 1.618, AC is 2.618 (1.618 × 1.618).

If the mathematics is boggling, look at it this way: the line AC is divided approximately into one third (AB) and two thirds (BC).

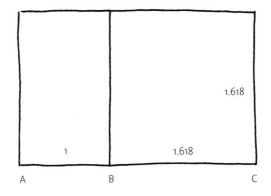

The Golden Rectangle, which can form the imaginary frame for a composition, conforms to the same proportions. Beginning with a square, the longer side of the rectangle is equal to the length of the square multiplied by the Golden Number, phi, 1.618. This is true whatever the size of the original square. But note again how the subdivision of the rectangle falls into approximate thirds.

The Fibonacci Series and Spiral

For centuries, philosophers, mathematicians and biologists have been exploring the Golden Ratio's appearance in natural structures, in the arrangement of sunflower seeds, the protuberances on pineapples, and the spiralling arrangement of leaves and branchlets on plant stems. At the root of this mystical spiral lies the Fibonacci Series, in which each consecutive number is the sum of the two preceding numbers: 1, 2, 3, 5, 8 and so on. The ratio of each

▼ Sunflower seeds and the form of ammonite are both arranged in a spiralling pattern.

successive pair of numbers is Golden. If a square is subtracted from the Golden Rectangle, another Golden Rectangle always remains. If the side of the square is used as the radius for an arc, the arcs in each successively smaller square form a spiral.

Whether appreciation of Divine Proportion—seen in natural *and* manmade structures—is innate or culturally imposed, I don't know for sure. But it's clear that at its simplest, it is an expression of perfect harmony. In many of its appearances, it is seen only in approximation. When you begin to look, you notice Divine Proportion everywhere: in Georgian windowpanes, in the page layout of a well-designed book and even, approximately, in paving slabs or copy paper. It is what an artist or photographer might deem the Principle of Thirds, using it to compose a picture by dividing the frame into three approximately equal parts in the vertical and horizontal planes. Such a framework gives a pleasing balance that is made dynamic by the placement of incidents—accents or focal points—at the intersections of imaginary lines marking the coincidence of thirds in the vertical or horizontal planes.

In terms of arranging elements in a garden composition, there are only a few things that need be grasped. First, Divine Proportion can underpin the spatial division of a plot, of a surface, or of a line, in both formal and informal designs. Second, the simple application of the Golden Rectangle is a perfect framework for a composition and guides the placement of your focal features. Third, the use of the Golden Ratio unifies a design and its recurrent use provides an underlying sense of rhythmic continuity within a composition.

Playing with Golden Numbers

The Golden Rectangle is the imaginary frame that I use when drawing up a planting scheme. In terms of living material, I consider there to be three natural layers of planting in a border: ground to knee, ground to navel, and ground to

▲ The universally familiar Japanese footbridge and waterlily pool in Monet's garden at Giverny was a recurrent theme in the artist's paintings throughout the late 1800s. Here the composition is divided into thirds, with all the visual strength of line lying across the second third. That the photographer, Andrew Lawson, has captured the composition in almost exactly the same way may be artifice, but is surely irresistible given the composition of the original. You can see this division of a canvas according to the Golden Ratio in works as diverse as those of Dali, Turner, Matisse and Mondrian.

the crown of my head. This does not necessarily mean that short plants go at the front and tall at the back, for this is too obvious a ploy. The layers billow and curve in three dimensions, not two, and can be made to ascend or descend, flow forwards or back, or lead the eye to the reward of a focal point or accent planting.

I also use the idea of thirds as a rough guide to the laying out of hard or soft landscaping— one third of the space taken up by paths or patios in proportion to two thirds of the mass of plantings, for example. And in wilder areas such as woodland gardens, I use it to create a ground flora, a shrub layer and a canopy: the expression of thirds exactly as they occur in a natural woodland.

Proportional ratios, however engaging, are never an end in themselves, but rather one of a range of useful tools in achieving a satisfying composition. If they're allowed to override practical requirements in terms of, for example, cost, function and maintenance, the end result doesn't qualify as good design.

Expanding the Vocabulary

In the designer's vocabulary, there are other elements needed to finesse the canvas, as described by these terms: scale, unity, variety and contrast, rhythm and repetition, and balance of mass and space, complemented by strategically placed focal points, with the overall picture sketched in by purposeful lines and distinctive forms. And no painting is complete without the overlay of texture and colour. These overlapping elements are the inseparable warp and weft that weaves the fabric of the finished scheme together.

Scale

Scale is similar to proportion, and the two terms are often confused. Scale refers to the relative size of elements within the whole scheme, while proportion refers to the relative dimensions of objects within themselves. It's self-evident that in the Landscape garden it's appropriate to use stately trees in grand avenues and bold naturalistic plantations, and that conversely these would be impossibly out of scale in the small garden.

Nevertheless, one frequently sees the suburban villa dwarfed by the mature copper beech, weeping willow or cedar of Lebanon. At the other extreme are the narrow ribbons of borders confined at the margins of a vast expanse of lawn. Not only are these features out of scale, but they also cause practical problems: huge trees in confined spaces are voracious consumers of light, water and nutrients, which makes life desperate for other plantings—and in the border that's too narrow, there is never enough room for the variety needed for satisfying compositions.

The human eye perceives scale differently indoors and outdoors. In the open, dimensions appear reduced by the comparison with the wider horizons outdoors. Observe the foundation walls of a new house, which appear to outline rooms too small to inhabit; the eye is tricked because the dimensions are judged against the larger outdoor scale. Consequently, features designed for outdoors need to be on a bolder scale, with walkways wider and steps broader and shallower. Planting designs need to be simpler and bolder to be in scale in larger areas, but can be more intricate and complex in more intimate areas.

▲ At the stone-tiled gazebo at York Gate in Leeds, the concord between millstone, setts and gravel creates the unity that underpins the repeated box topiary elements and herbs—framed and given perspective by a plain dark hedge.

In gardens, scale must also take account of time; there is often a long delay before plants reach their mature dimensions and one must plan so that they will be in scale once fully grown. This is one of the few advantages of planting semi-mature trees, and is a good reason for leaving existing specimens in place, at least until new plantings of your own choosing reach approximately the right scale.

Unity

Unity is the harmonizing quality that ties a design together. It describes the use of linking elements that flow through the design to create a unified whole, and it implies a clear dominance of certain features with the subordination of minor elements.

There are many ways of achieving unity. In terms of a whole garden design, unity can be ensured where the style of hard landscaping accords with the architecture of the house or garden buildings, and where the materials used in both are similar.

All parts of the house and garden should be in harmony, linked by unifying elements so that nothing appears misplaced. It would be nonsensical, for instance, to use Westmoreland slate in a garden surrounding a house built in the Cotswold vernacular style in soft golden sandstone, or to use London brick in conjunction with the soft, silvered cedar shingles of the Oregon vernacular.

The style of the garden itself—formal or informal, for example—is another way of tying things together. At one extreme is the formal and geometric unity of the great French gardens; these disciplined compositions in woods, stone and water, with allées, avenues and vistas framed by crisply shaped plantings, are ruled by the straight line. In contrast, though using the same basic materials, the designs of William Kent and Lancelot (Capability) Brown were unified by a succession of purposeful, sweeping curves, rounded copses and serpentine water features, with contrast and variety

provided by the strong geometric lines of Classically inspired architecture. Incidentally, by citing gardens of such considerable size, I don't assume that you have limitless acres at your disposal; I am merely saying that great landscape gardens are good examples of principles that can be adapted to much smaller spaces.

Living Unity

Unifying themes might include natural plant associations—combining plants of similar habitats, such as woodland plants, rock plants and alpines, aquatics and marginals. William Robinson's unifying themes famously included adherence to definitive plant associations—the woodland garden, the herbaceous garden, the wild garden. Beth Chatto's use of denizens of dry or damp habitats, or Piet Oudolf's disposition of prairie plants among ornamental grasses, are more modern examples.

Unity might also be expressed in colour-themed plantings, by using blue flowers or silver foliage to weave a scheme together, for

◀ A cameo of blue and silver, with discrete drifts of *Eryngium giganteum* and *Verbena bonariensis* spangled with alliums and agapanthus, is part of Beth Chatto's dry garden in her garden in Essex. There is unity of colour here, but above all the planting is held together by the carefully selected drought-tolerant plants—chosen based on an intimate understanding of the dry habitats in which they originate.

▲ This streamside composition at Marwood Hill Gardens, Devon, is unified by a collection of moisture-loving perennials. While all originate in damp habitats, success lies in the details: conditions range from margins where roots are totally submerged, which suits *Iris pseudacorus*, through permanently moist soils for candelabra primulas and osmundas, and well above water level for *Iris sibirica* and hostas, which enjoy consistently moist but drained soils.

▼ Horticulturists in the Netherlands have long been sensitive to the aesthetics of ecological associations. Although it seems obvious that plants from similar habitats should go together, it takes critical observation and sensitive placement to get it right. The plant communities of grasslands, savannas and prairies inspire many of Piet Oudolf's influential naturalistic designs (here at Bury Court in Hampshire).

◀ The herbaceous borders at Miserden Park in the Cotswolds convey unity of colour, with golden yellows, white and silver—an appropriate scheme since the garden overlooks the Golden Valley in Gloucestershire.

▶ Unity of form and materials at Prieuré de Notre-Dame d'Orsan is emphasized by an arched cloister in hornbeam, which evokes the medieval monastic origins of the garden. (Design: Sonia Lesot and Patrice Taravella)

instance. On a micro-scale, a delicate and elegant example of colour unity might be glaucous-leaved *Galanthus* (snowdrops) in verdigris copper planters, with a unifying theme of blue-greens, grey-greens and pure whites repeated with iris, crocus and cyclamen.

A similar sense of unity is achieved through the use of the same plant materials throughout a garden for hedging, barrier plantings or other living-space dividers—traditionally clipped yew, beech or box, or even something as simple as turf used continuously throughout the space.

Where a design lacks underlying unity, the result is usually a discordant conglomeration

◀ The use of the same material throughout a design is one of the simplest of unifying themes, and very often it is a sweep of green lawn that fulfils the brief. Chamomile, especially the non-flowering form *Chamaemelum nobile* 'Treneague', is a perfect alternative—here infiltrating paving crevices, where it releases its fruity scent when brushed by passing feet.

of unrelated elements that as a whole is not visually cohesive. It will also appear obviously contrived and (heaven forbid) suggest that the designer lacks discipline, or worse, is trying too hard. One of the beauties of unity as a concept is that it simplifies and prevents you from creating a muddle that will obliterate your original intention and desire. Extreme unity, however, is also undesirable—it is just too boring. In short, unity can be achieved by:

- using similar materials throughout the design
- using paths, paving and turf as to link garden features together
- repetition of a pattern, colour, shape or texture
- using recurrent strong shapes, decisive lines, or sweeping curves to form the design's architectural skeleton or backbone
- using definite planting themes in character with the surrounding vegetation
- choosing colours, in both hard and soft landscaping materials, that blend harmoniously, avoiding those that clash or conflict.

▶ An unremarkable brick path is made beautiful by the contrasting patternwork of clipped chamomile.

▶ The uncompromising heat and glare of vast paving expanses has been avoided by sinking slabs to a level where they can be easily mown over. Along with being practical, elegant and beautiful in itself, the delineation draws the eye on to a series of views and planting compositions that surround the villa. (Design: Mr and Mrs Cesare Settepassi, Casa Nova, Italy)

▲▲ The silver parterres at Holker Hall, Cumbria, are an almost monochromatic study in form and textural counterpoint, but it is the rich contrast provided by the leavening of indigo, violet and purple flowers that removes the risk of monotony.

▲ Even where fine textural compositions in shades of silver and grey can be appreciated close up and on a small scale, the added colour contrasts of intense reds maximize impact.

▶ A simple patternwork of contrasting brick and cobble is unified by a natural overlay of moss.

Variety and Contrast

That there can be too much of a good thing is a certainly a cliché, but it is patently true when applied to unity. An adequate seasoning of contrasting features is essential to maintain variety and interest, and contrasts are sharper when set against an underlying theme that is clear and uncluttered.

A scheme that is short on variety is without essential character; a single note does not constitute a piece of music, nor does a single colour constitute a piece of art. Imagine running your eye through a grey border, composed of all shapes, shades and textures of grey, grey-green and silver foliage. However skilfully these neutral hues and rich textures are composed, the eye will hunger for the punctuation of rich contrast—a deep indigo, a shining magenta—and without that visual satisfaction the scheme will never be truly beautiful.

The same applies to, say, a uniform expanse of paving; it may be utilitarian, but it will probably evoke the dismal architectural experiments of the 1960s and it surely won't be appealing. Practically, it will also be glaring in sunlight, and will quickly become too searingly hot and dry for human comfort.

On the other hand, too much variety is disturbing because the sense of unity that satisfies the human desire for order is lost. The result is chaotic and restless, and instead of feeling gently guided through a series of deserved rewards, the eye flickers uncomfortably from one item to the next. The classic examples might be the small garden replete with wishing wells, bird baths, gnomes, fountain spouts and the rest, set against a background of multicoloured paving that matches nothing else in the arrangement; or the garden designed using every available material in the builders' catalogue, or the space crammed with individual specimens of every available plant.

Don't be afraid of simplicity. The simplest solution is usually the most elegant—and the most practical. Less often really is more.

▶ The simple lines of the pergola at Prieuré de Notre-Dame d'Orsan deliberately evoke a rhythm, with repeated lines at ground level and above the head, the patterning of light and shade, and the regular placement of cross allées. Patrice Taravella, architect and co-creator of the garden, described it as the rhythm of deep meditative breathing: "You exhale and inspire…" He meant "inhale", but it's an appropriate slip.

Rhythm and Repetition

As in music, rhythm provides an underlying pattern to a scheme, giving it visual order and flow. Whereas unity and variety concern the nature of the building blocks, rhythm is concerned with the way the blocks are linked together. The aim of rhythm is to encourage the eye to follow through from one element to the next, creating a sense of progression. As I move through the rhythm of a garden or a planting scheme, I want to feel that it is akin to breathing in and breathing out. My preference is for gentle, soothing transitions that have the effect of deep breathing, rather than the more edgy, staccato beat that you might choose for a more modern layout, which feels to me more like hyperventilation. But it's a matter of taste.

Rhythm is imposed naturally by the repetition of elements like an avenue of trees, repeated spires of eremurus or verbascum in a border, or in architectural features, such as a pergola, by the rhythmic placement of the series of strong verticals that form the essence of the structure. In a succession of similar curves in a layout, or the overlapping and interlocking of a series of

◀ Repeated vertical lines of crisply defined spires of eremurus and verbascum in the gravel garden draw the eye along the backbone of the planting as they rise above the neatly delineated mounds and clumps of other plants. Note, incidentally, how the natural form of almost every plant here has been given space to develop. (Beth Chatto Gardens, Colchester Essex)

◀ Clipped lollipop oaks at Hatfield House, Hertfordshire, create a rhythm of verticals and spheres that guides the eye and offers an invitation to sit, surrounded by echoing topiary spheres.

▲ In the private garden at Whichford Pottery, Jim Keeling uses arches in the structure of the summerhouse, their repeated pattern underscored by a moving pattern of light and shade through each day and season.

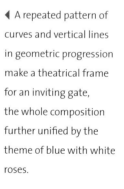

◀ A repeated pattern of curves and vertical lines in geometric progression make a theatrical frame for an inviting gate, the whole composition further unified by the theme of blue with white roses.

◀ Repeated soft curves, clothed in roses, honeysuckle and clematis, serve as a romantic frame to the rustic gate which acts as both focal point and enticing invitation.

geometric shapes in paving, the rhythmic effect is the same. In the gardens of Burle Marx, for instance, a succession of freeform, amoeboid shapes are rhythmically interlinked to draw the eye forward through the design, often echoed in the reward of a terminating vista or view of the landscape beyond.

Balance

Designers use the term balance to describe the distribution of impact and visual weight throughout a design. Elements of similar importance, size, form or colour interest are carefully positioned so that the overall effect is not lopsided. When a design lacks balance—when a single object has too great a presence—it's like the television-in-the-room syndrome; the attention is drawn to the exclusion of everything else.

In a border or planting scheme, for example, dense masses of strong colour carry too heavy a weight—but as points of intensity balanced against a calmer background of neutral greens or greys they create much more impact. So also can strong vertical lines be balanced by diagonals and horizontals, or dense, mounded plants balanced against the punctuation of plants with a more airy, transparent character. In a garden as a whole, areas of substantial planting are balanced against areas of open space.

Balance between mass and space has both visual and psychological elements. A well-designed garden provides a generous amount of open space in visual contrast and balance with its furnishings—the plantings, hard landscaping and other, perhaps architectural features, such as a seat or summerhouse. You can use the Golden Ratio as a guide to allocating areas to become your mass or your space, but most of us possess good instincts in this respect, if we're prepared to take note of them. You'll know it's right when it *feels* right for you; what's cosy for one can be suffocating for another.

When open spaces are too large, most of us feel vulnerable and exposed; conversely, too little space generates a claustrophobic feeling

▶ A tiny patio has been given an intimate sense of enclosure, confined and sheltered by lush architectural planting of an exuberance well balanced by the plainness of flooring and furniture. (Design: Penny Smith)

▶ A small terrace surrounded by low structural planting of clipped box hedging strikes the balance between a sense of enclosure while being sufficiently open to avoid being claustrophobic. (Design: Mirabel Ostler)

▶ Beech hedging provides total screening, but the enclosure is sufficiently spacious that the height of the hedge does not overwhelm. Plantings on either side are lower and softer in outline, giving shelter that can be overlooked.

▶ "Don't fence me in" might well have been the brief for this open terrace; there are views to the garden all around but nevertheless the whole feels secure because the site is walled.

▶ The voluptuous curves of a glazed urn are a focal point glowing in the striking shafts of brilliant Brittany light. (Tim and Isabelle Vaughan, Crech ar Pape)

▲ That the gardener Helen Dillon embraces the virtues of an offset focal point in bringing a dynamic sense of movement is clearly illustrated, as Diana is captured here striding out of the frame stage right. (The Dillon Garden, Dublin.)

▶ A Classical focal point—a graceful statue with a backdrop of dark yew—terminates a vista in the formal Casita at Iford Manor, Harold Peto's own Italianate garden in Wiltshire. Nevertheless, the same statue is the focus for several compositions in the Casita garden; it is seen across low plantings from various view points.

▶ The primary structural planting of clipped beech at East Ruston Old Vicarage, Norfolk, is multifunctional, providing the opportunity for a succession of framed focal points throughout the garden, each individual focus being one of a series of compositions.

▶ A focal point of a simple hurdle at Prieuré de Notre-Dame d'Orsan may look effortless, but it makes for a composition of Divine Proportions when viewed through its flanking hedges.

of being hemmed in. When it's just right, you'll have enough room to see and admire all you want to see freely, and you'll feel relaxed in the space without feeling either uncomfortably cramped, or dwarfed and intimidated. The ideal balance in a domestic garden might be to create a sense of enclosure, privacy, shelter and safety without a sense of restriction and confinement. At least that's what I aim for, and I think that the ideal division of mass and space is the one that makes you feel glad to be part of it.

That is the principle underlying the humane sense of intimacy generated by the enclosure of garden rooms (as at Hidcote, or Newby Hall in Yorkshire, for instance) in which each room, brought down to a human scale, is the locus for a series of beautiful planting compositions.

Focal Points

Focal points draw the eye; it's that simple. As satisfying endpoints, they reward the eye that has travelled the vista. They may take the form of urns, statues or temples, terminating a single, symmetrical view. On a more domestic scale, a seat or a specimen plant may serve that function. Sometimes, such singularity is all that's wanted, but it doesn't exploit the focal device to its fullest potential.

If a focus is offset, it lends a sense of dynamism and movement to a design. A succession of foci can do that, too; planted obelisks, for instance, or a well-spaced succession of architectural plants through a border—and with the added benefit of a flow of visual punctuation and inherent rhythm. The eye's desire for a focus is independent of scale: a tiny, upright specimen of *Juniperus communis* 'Compressa' would serve in an alpine trough. Alternatively, think of a cardoon (*Cynara cardunculus*) in a mixed border, a specimen tree in a smooth expanse of lawn or a mausoleum on a mount.

To broaden the picture, where a focal point is visible from more than one position, the ultimate being from 360° around, it illuminates and draws in every other element in the design,

▶ While we refer to this arcade as "a glorified plant stand", it also functions to link together wood and pasture, and brings a constantly changing rhythmic play of light and shade along its course. Here it frames a succession of focal points, the well head and an urn beyond, the latter luring the observer into the shady depths of wild woodland.

▶ Framing the focal point of a Lutyens seat is only half the story here, for it also serves as enticement to explore and an invitation to sit and stare.

▶ A perfect focal device that apparently extends the bounds, a clairvoyée permits a view and frames a vista of borrowed landscape beyond the garden.

▶ The moon gate permits a glimpse of a sanctuary, furnished with pool and seat. It could be called the Zen View, but also acts as a device to draw the observer in.

and then forms the highlight of a range of compositions from a variety of view points: maximum value.

Gradual Revelation and Surprise

The concepts of gradual revelation and the element of surprise were as well understood in ancient Chinese and Japanese gardens as in eighteenth-century English Landscapes or Edwardian gardens. The idea is not to show a garden's beauties all at once, but to reveal a little at a time as the visitor moves through the space. The traditional Japanese moon gate is a perfect example of what is sometimes called the Zen View. There is an element of restraint, so that one never sees all of the view, all of the time. Instead, the moon gate frames a composition—whether composed of plants, or of a distant view of landscape beyond the garden—which is seen in passing so that it never palls through over-familiarity.

With a less profound and perhaps more Western perspective, the concept often has overtly theatrical overtones. The creation of a succession of areas of space and enclosure, which is fundamental to the concept of revelation and surprise, can be thought of setting the stage, wherein the ultimate sign of success is to extract an audible exclamation of delight as the final set is revealed. The source of delight might be a sequence of focal points, views or plant compositions, the element of surprise ensured by having screens between them and the viewer. As Alexander Pope put it,

He gains all points, who pleasingly confounds,
Surprises, varies, and conceals the Bounds.

This was a trick exemplified in the eighteenth century by the ha-ha—an exclamation of "a-ha!" being desired on the discovery that an apparently uninterrupted Arcadian vista came to an abrupt halt in a spine-tingling vertical drop.

Parcevall Hall, an early-twentieth-century garden in Yorkshire, takes the technique to the brink. Here a gently meandering path through

▲ There can be no clearer invitation to progress through a garden than a half-open gate.

▲ Even the closed rustic door plays a role in drawing the observer through a garden, for the temptation to open it and explore beyond is irresistibly alluring.

▶ A sinuous line of stepping stones draws the eye into the garden beyond; that the way through is obscured by strategic planting is a sure means of charming the viewer into exploration.

◀ The oak gate is a two-way device for inviting exploration, here clearly framing a deserved endpoint to the journey: a focal point seating on terrace amid relaxed planting.

an orchard meadow strewn with wildflowers and fallen blossoms brings you to an inviting little wicket gate. As you lift your eyes on passing through it, the sharp intake of breath is involuntary—you're on the dramatic edge of a precipitous drop where the hills are cleft by a geological fault line almost sixty metres (two hundred feet) deep.

It may be walls, gates or windows that are used as screen and frame, or colonnades and pergolas, which offer the potential of surprises at both ends, with a rhythm of slightly different vistas through the fenestration formed by their columns. Plants are also equal to the task, whether used structurally in the form of hedges or other barriers, as specimens so that they might form a focal point from one standpoint, while simultaneously blocking the sightline beyond.

Line

The meaning that designers ascribe to the term line differs from the more common definition of the line made in drawing. To designers, line describes a course or direction that the observer can 'read', and it usually implies a desired effect on the observer.

As a garden designer, I interpret it so: the horizontal line might be perceived as placid; it plays the supporting role at the base of a composition, evoking the psychological sensation of being at rest. The vertical line, in contrast, evokes the tension of resistance to gravitational pull. The human eye exaggerates the vertical dimension and sees things as being taller than they really are, so it's usually necessary to over-emphasize horizontals in opposition to the verticals to achieve a balanced composition.

When they're in balance, the horizontal and vertical represent a visual stability that resolves the eye's desire for completeness. As in life, though, complete stability is a state that inevitably becomes tedious. It is the intermediate line—the diagonal, the sloping, the arching, the falling line—that brings movement and

▲ Through the gate lies another area to explore, its extent tantalizingly disguised by foreground planting that obscures a view of the whole garden at once.

◀ A slow, sinuous curve of a path is given rhythm by simple crossbanding as it draws eyes and feet to the reward of a gate with a clairvoyée—an inviting glimpse of the wider landscape beyond. (Goulter's Mill, Wiltshire.)

◀ Hidden by a tall beech hedge and swathed in summer roses, the glimpsed roof of a gazebo signifies the presence of a secret garden, that beguiling foretaste being the universally understood persuasion to seek and find.

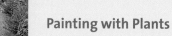

Painting with Plants

◀ The radiance of light and silk: a halo of gold illuminates the textures of *Hordeum jubatum* and *Lagurus ovatus*. (Sticky Wicket, Dorset)

◀ The fine gauze of *Stipa tenuissima* is embroidered with *Allium sphaerocephalon*.

◀ *Gunnera manicata* is an architectural giant with the intricate texture of vitreous prickles, and a downy network of venation when seen up close.

◀ The palmate and deeply impressed leaves of *Rodgersia aesculifolia* give off a metallic gleam.

dynamism to a composition. These are also the lines that weave together the vertical and horizontal to form the backcloth of the composition.

The curve is a softening, restful line, while a series of angular lines produce a sense of restless movement. The straight line, which forms the backbone of formal designs, evokes control and discipline. It's worth experimenting with the length and direction of lines to effect the visual rhythms and flows you desire. (Or perhaps I should say: I usually have to.)

When you draw up a plan, of course, the marked lines on paper delineate your spatial divisions, paths, beds, borders and all other features you choose to have. Whatever the form or course of a line, make it strong and decisive. The long, sinuous or voluptuous curve is more purposeful than the line that wobbles hither and thither; the eye is drawn to follow the sweeping and bold, but is fussed by the wiggle that lacks conviction. And in practical terms, the simpler your lines, the easier the features they represent will be to maintain.

Texture

The tapestries woven by the contradistinction and counterpoint of contrasting and harmonious surfaces can be the most rewarding element of plant associations. Foliage is the primary textural feature of nearly all plants; it is the predominant mass in a planting, the backcloth against which the floral display shines, and it far outlasts the period of bloom.

While foliage texture often does excite the sense of touch, it is the visual stimulation derived from its interaction with light and shade that carries more weight when standing back to admire. Contrast the filigree of tiny or finely divided leaves with the smooth and plain, the delicate with the robust. Exploit the glitter of rain-wet, small leathery leaves, or the light-filtering translucence of thin-textured leaves in conjunction with matte, light absorbing ones. Play the rough against the smooth:

the rugose, bristly, wrinkled, crumpled and undulating surfaces, with sheened leaves coated with microcrystalline waxes or clothed in hot-pressed silky hair that makes them gleam with collected moisture.

Colour

Whole books, even libraries full of them, are devoted to the study of colour theory. Has Gertrude Jekyll's *Colour Schemes for the Flower Garden* (1914) ever been bettered? Probably not; it's an engaging study and I recommend it. But I use a pared-down, rough guide to colour, in the form of a nine-point plan based on the colour wheel.

1. The primary colours, red, blue and yellow, are pure hues unadulterated by other colours. They lie equidistant from each other on the colour wheel.
2. Secondary colours are a mixture of two primaries: red plus yellow gives orange, red plus blue gives purple, yellow plus blue gives green.
3. Tertiary colours combine a primary with a secondary colour, thus creating intermediate graduations around the colour wheel: yellow-orange, red-orange, red-purple, blue-purple, blue-green and yellow-green.

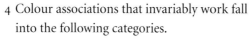
4 Colour associations that invariably work fall into the following categories.

- Complementary: any two colours that are diametrically opposite each other on the colour wheel.
- Close complementary: the main hue associated with one of the hues adjacent to the complementary.
- Divided complementary: the main hue associated with those on either side of the true complementary.
- Triads: any three hues equidistant from each other on the colour wheel, with one dominant and its companions subordinate.

5 Fine tuning. Equal masses of complementaries won't give a pleasing colour balance. Any complementary association works best when...

- one hue is dominant in mass and brightness, and the complementaries subordinate; and
- the dominant is a paler tint and the complementary more intense.

6 Tones, tints and shades are infinitely more interesting when painting with plants, because of their almost infinite subtlety and because few colours in your floral palette are pure hues. The tone of a colour refers to its depth, from the palest almost-transparent wash to the darkest and most intense. A tint of a hue is lightened by the addition of white; a shade is rendered deeper by the addition of black.

7 Monochromatic associations are difficult to pull off successfully. Essentially they comprise associations of the same hue in its varying tints, tones and shades. They nearly always work better with a smattering of complementary colour.

8 Strong, hot and bright colours look best in warm brilliant light; cool, soft and pale colours are more outstanding in shade.

9 Strong, bright and deep colours appear to advance towards the viewer; cool and pale colours recede. They allow you to play with perspective.

The Theory in Practice

I will gratefully plant whatever lovely thing I can grow, buy or receive. This used to mean cramming them into any available space, which seldom displayed any plant at its best; it is too random, and to compose randomly is to not compose at all. But when I was first taught landscape design, I resisted seeing plants as functional elements in a design; I thought the approach impersonal, restrictive and unappreciative of plants' special beauties: no soul, no passion.

Looking at a plant's function in a scheme, however, turns out to be a useful technique; its limitations in practice are usually the result of a narrow plant knowledge—too restricted a palette. Classifying plants by form and function is simply a tool, whereby all of your favourite, beloved plants, and even ones that are new to you, can be placed to their (and your) best advantage. They can be grouped into two major subdivisions.

Primary Plantings

Primary plants are those that can be used as structural elements in outdoor architecture. While they may be ornamental in their own right, more often they have the qualities of a good suit—they don't shout, but they're hard-wearing and well cut. When used as structural plantings their main function is to define space.

Many plants can fill the role, provided that they withstand regular clipping to keep them in shape. The classic primary plants are yew, beech, hornbeam, holly and box, but other less restricted forms can also be used as primary plants. They're exploited in various ways:

- to create shelterbelts, essential in exposed and coastal areas
- to create screening, enclosure and privacy at the perimeters of the garden

▲ In this narrow urban garden, hedges and freestanding shrubs and trees screen the garden and separate room-like enclosures. (Design: Mirabel Ostler)

▲ A sheltering and screening high hedge that divides a garden into separate areas need not be simply functional. Just as certainly, this white gate in a yew hedge will lure the observer in. (House of Pitmuies, Tayside)

▲ A clairvoyée penetrates the enclosing clipped yew hedge to permit a glimpse of the potager, and the intricately clipped hedge opposite, which echoes the line of the building's fenestration at Prieuré de Notre-Dame d'Orsan.

▶ A plump, undulating cloud hedge of box screens a 'chocolate box' thatched cottage from prying eyes (but induces longing to see over the other side).

▶ A buttressed hedge functions as shelter, backdrop and stage for a display of dahlias at Biddulph Grange.

▲ Piercing the hedges to allow cross-vistas—literally windows onto the potager—has reached a high art at Orsan.

- to enclose room-like spaces within the garden
- to separate areas of different use within the garden
- to define, guide or restrict access within the garden
- as a neutral, unobtrusive backdrop that shows off more intricate plantings
- as a unifying element
- as a frame for views or focal points, as clairvoyées, or by creating rhythmic gaps in the planting that overlook features or landscapes beyond.

Secondary Plantings

This term describes all the other plants in the garden, which are used for their decorative virtues, on and within the outdoor architecture of primary plantings; they provide the living fabric that clothes—*adorns*—the framework of structural plants. Secondary doesn't, therefore, imply second rate, or that they will be the second thing you think of. This is the type of planting that is most valued and enjoyed in gardens.

They can be grouped into several orders delineated by height, as described later, but while described as discrete units, in practice, the layers they form are fluid entities that blend into each other.

Plant layers form the broad brushstrokes that lead the eye to accent plants, the major source of variety and impact in the scheme. Usually sculptural or architectural in outline, accents contrast with the mass of the planting in size, shape, line, texture and colour; they are plants of strong character and substantial presence. They are focal points.

Some plants are so striking that they are planted singly to be admired in all of their glory. Their virtues must be multiple to justify the space; think of flowers and fruit, attractive foliage and, if deciduous, good autumn colour and a pleasing habit to grace the winter months. A specimen can make a grand focal point, decorating a space formed by structure planting or standing sentinel in a paved, gravelled or turfed area.

The most dynamic effects are obtained if the dominant focal points or accents are offset, and dominance is accented most effectively when less flamboyant plants surround it. Underlying planting layers might taper gradually up to the accent, so that their lines guide the eye towards it from one or several vantage points. Plants of mounded or horizontal form are useful here; they act as a visual anchor.

In a simple composition in which strong vertical lines are balanced against horizontals, the main accent plant might be set directly into a low layer of uniform height. Picture a clear-stemmed white-barked birch like *Betula utilis*, with a sweep of fine green turf beneath it. The visual lines of turf and tree resolve the tension between the horizontal and vertical in the most elementary form. For more sophistication, imagine the pristine creamy brilliance of the trunks of *B. utilis* var. *jacquemontii* 'Doorenbos' rising above *Viburnum plicatum* f. *tomentosum* 'Mariesii', its tiers outlined with pure white lace-cap flowers, the meadow turf beneath spangled with the late-flowering pheasant's eye, *Narcissus poeticus* var. *recurvus*, and white ox-eye daisies, *Leucanthemum vulgare*.

Depending on the size and nature of the scheme, there may be several accents, but clearly the number must be limited or their impact will be lost. Secondary accents are often used to maintain balance and interest while reinforcing a rhythm, but it's important that these lesser accents are subservient. If the primary accent doesn't speak clearly, or if there are too many accents, the composition is difficult to read and becomes unintelligible.

Planting in Order of Height

When asked by another gardener "How big does it get?" the first instinct is to say, "Oh, about so high", indicating knee, navel, chest or head height by hand, as the case may be. I indicate spread like a fisherman exaggerating his catch. I bet you do, too. Even when talking about tree heights, I make a mental approximation in terms of multiples of my own height. It's so much easier to visualize an approximation of knee, navel and crown, than to envisage sixty, ninety or one hundred fifty centimetres (that's two, three or five feet). Plants have little respect for heights given in reference books since dimensions are so strongly influenced by growing conditions. In broadly similar conditions, most plants tend to respond in the same way, so their relative sizes remain in due proportion. In any case, there are few instances where an exact height is critical; in these cases, get out the pruning shears.

The First Third

This is the base layer of a composition, and these are the plants that reach from the ground to knee high, anchor the scheme to the ground and, in essence, provide the foreground of the picture. These plants can also be used to create perspective, for instance where low-level plantings sweep towards the middle or back of the border, enhancing an impression of depth. Foreground plantings might also include plants of a transparent nature; they may be taller than knee-high but they are airy and translucent, as with *Molinia caerulea* subsp. *arundinacea* 'Windspiel' or *Stipa gigantea*.

You might choose low-level plants with similarities of colour and texture so that, from a distance, they provide a neutral foil for taller, more exuberant plants in the mid-ground. It is, however, the case that this planting will usually be viewed at close quarters, too, and it would be remiss not to take the opportunity to exploit interesting detail of texture and form where it can be most easily appreciated. Up close, plants such as the filigreed *Artemisia schmidtiana* 'Nana' or woolly-leaved *Stachys byzantina* present their beautiful textures; from a distance, they are an elegant, neutrally coloured foil. At several steps removed, the massed blooms of,

say, *Geranium pyrenaicum* 'Bill Wallis' creates a horizontal band of hazy colour; close up, the intricacies of tiny flowers, their satin textures and their intense colours are a joy.

The Second Third

This is the intermediate layer of planting, which fills the layer between knee and navel. Depending on the depth of the border, this height of planting usually forms the bulk or major mass of the design. I think of this layer as a matrix, the zone of soft, mounded cushions that supports plants of more emphatic form, greater stature or more individual beauty, and the plump pillows upon which shorter plants rest their heads.

The Third Third

The tallest zone of decorative plantings, from navel to crown or above, includes those plants that can be used to create the most striking effects, especially as they should, ideally, be chosen for their strong form or colour. Many plants in this group will be accent plants; since they rise above the main bulk of the scheme, they introduce the most telling contrasts into the composition. Against the backdrop of a hedge or wall, the plants' outline, foliage detail, branchwork tracery and flowers are seen with maximum clarity. At the same time, they may rise above smoothly mounded plants that give emphasis to contrasts of stronger line and form.

Three thirds don't make the whole picture when you're painting with plants; they are lines or layers that will form the main spatial divisions of the design. They're analogous to the framework that you would sketch out as the foreground, mid- and background on the canvas before you begin to paint. In living compositions, as in a painting, the next step is to fill in the detail with line and form, colour and texture.

Visualizing plants by line and form works in composing arrangements whatever the style you choose, whether traditional or modern, informal or formal, large or small in scale. Once it becomes a habit, you'll find that you have your own visual dictionary of plants, with your own ideas of how and where to place them. It will be a flexible vocabulary by means of which, as in any language, you express individuality in your planting schemes.

Organizing the Plant Palette

How do I identify the lines of the plants I use? I don't demand a line as clear as a pencil mark on paper. It's not a study in trigonometry; it's about seeing a line of beauty and using it in a composition as I would if sketching or painting. Systematic observation is a counsel of perfection, but frankly rather soulless. With age and experience, observation does become habitual for the gardener, though sometimes it's a serenely meditative process. Simply standing and staring reveals lines you had previously registered only subconsciously. So does sitting back on your heels as you take a breather from weeding. Repeating the exercise at the turn of each season is a pleasure. The slanting light of low sun or the clear light of summer illuminates different aspects of once-familiar plants. And since you need to see a bigger picture, lifting your eyes from the intimate enjoyment of the close-up and personal is imperative. The key to individual expression is to build a palette of your own.

I describe a collection of plants in the directories in the following chapters, but I use many more. And my search for the perfect plant is always continuing: whenever I find a line, form or colour that I quite like, I know that there is nearly always a close relative or cultivar that I'll positively love.

Horizontals and Tiers

Of course, few (if any) plants grow in a perfectly horizontal mode, not even those with the botanical specific epithets *horizontalis, prostratus* or *decumbens.*

By 'horizontal', I'm invoking a plant whose mass lends a linear, horizontal outline.

As in a painting, a horizontal line draws the eye across the scene, but is boring if uninterrupted. It's unlikely to sustain interest without punctuation somewhere along it, or a visual reward at its endpoint.

When building up a composition, I use plants with horizontal lines to balance verticals and diagonals. I might use them as a visual underscore to clipped cones, or the rounded forms of mounds, or exploit them as a baseline beneath plants of arching or weeping habit, where the horizontal line works to anchor their curves into a composition.

Visualize a swathe of wrinkled, grey-leaved *Geranium renardii,* forming a low linear mass beneath diagonal fans of tall bearded irises, or the verticals of *Veronicastrum.* In the botanical sense these plants may not have a horizontal habit; rather, it is the *line* that the mass of plant contributes to the overall composition that is horizontal. Low-level horizontals are analogous to flooring in an interior design; the foundation or foreground on which everything else sits, and which you will want to be beautiful as well as durable. Some call them carpet plants.

In some cases, as with many achilleas, with flat-topped flowerheads on tall stems, the botanical structures of a plant and its horizontal line *are* one and the same. Achilleas, and others like them, bring horizontal elements to a composition at some height, to punctuate a flow of rounded forms, or form a secondary line that sets off towering spires of hollyhocks or verbascums at the back of a border.

Plants that form tiers are horizontals with rhythm and repetition built in. Often shrubs or trees, these can be plants of considerable mass with a horizontally tiered branch framework, as with *Viburnum plicatum* f. *tomentosum* 'Lanarth' and *Cornus alternifolia,* the pagoda dogwood. In both, the tiered habit is reinforced by the poise and disposition of the flowerheads along the upper sides of the branches. With *Cornus,*

◀ Flattened heads of *Achillea* 'Fanal' form horizontal drifts beneath the upright stems of *Monarda* 'Cambridge Scarlet' and *Echinops ritro* 'Veitch's Blue'. (Design: Matthew Wilson, RHS Harlow Carr, Harrogate, Yorkshire)

▲ *Geranium* ×*cantabrigiense* underpins the ascending verticals of *Allium* 'Globemaster' and digitalis. (Design: Karl Foerster)

▼ The espaliered apples lend a series of horizontals to a strongly tiered form, bounding a potager at the Old Rectory, Sudborough.

▲ A horizontal ribbon of *Sedum spectabile* 'Stardust' anchors the arching and vertical lines of cortaderia.

▲ A horizontal carpet of *Convolvulus sabatius* and creeping thyme.

▼ Cloud-like tiers of *Cornus controversa* 'Variegata' with *Hosta sieboldiana* at Glen Chantry, Essex.

▶ Resolutely vertical spires of *Digitalis ferruginea*, the rusty foxglove.

the leaf patterning of the variegated forms, as with *C. controversa* 'Variegata', gives the tiers a light and airy aspect, not quite see-through but casting only light dappled shade beneath.

There are several ways to magnify the effect of tiers: restricting underplanting to plants that form a low, linear mass which allows a vertical length of trunk to rise above it before branching out into tiers is one. Other elements can provide a foil for a strong habit—try placing tiered plants to echo hard landscaping in the form of steps or terraces, or against a distinctive brick bonding pattern; this repeats the lines to give a backbeat to the composition, and gives enormous visual satisfaction. If it has happened by accident, you need only smile and nod graciously when complimented.

Verticals and Diagonals

The plants that most obviously lend strong vertical lines are those whose flowerheads take the form of spikes, racemes or narrow panicles. They may have inflorescences that spire skywards, like the veratrums and *Perovskia* 'Blue Spire'; in others, the whole plant aspires to the vertical, as with many of the verbascums, eremurus, and the Elatum Group delphiniums.

I will be first to admit that you might quarrel with my definition of some of the strongly diagonal plants. For instance, I include yuccas, *Phormium tenax*, bearded iris in general, and *Iris pallida* 'Variegata' in particular, as especially useful for the diagonal lines presented by their fans of basal leaves. Of course the flowering spikes are strongly vertical, but the fans persist much longer, before and after flowering time.

So plants that lend more than one line are multi-taskers. It's nearly always the case that the foliage mass of a plant makes a longer-lasting contribution to its line of beauty than do the flowers themselves. That's a benefit, not a detraction—so do let's be relaxed about it; visualizing by line is a tool, not a rule.

That trunks of trees make a vertical line is stating the obvious (unless you have in mind the

▶ Held on leafless stems, the inflorescences of *Eremurus robustus* give almost disembodied vertical lines at head height or above.

▼ The fans of bearded *Iris* 'Indian Chief' and the slender leaves of *Cordyline* punctuate a border with a succession of diagonal lines. (Design: Paul Kelly)

medlar, or mulberry, which, as they say, become increasingly gnarled and picturesque with age). The less obvious point is if you are going to use a tree's main stem as a vertical element, it needs to be more than just a straight dull grey or brown line, especially in smaller spaces. So let its bark give it the bite. The birches (*Betula*) abound in species with stunning bark. The snake-bark maples, such as *Acer capillipes*, *A. davidii* and *A. rufinerve*, reinforce the line with bark striations in variations on a theme of greens and grey-whites. Several cherries have splendid bark, such as *Prunus serrula*, banded in polished, mahogany red that only the most unfeeling gardener can pass without stroking. The tactile element is unsurpassed in the madroña, *Arbutus menziesii*, with curls of chestnut that flake to reveal smooth golden-olive skin beneath, likened by some to the skin of a maiden's thigh (though I wouldn't know about that).

Arcs and Fountains

This category of plants bring the curving, arching, falling line to the picture. They echo rounded forms and serve as the dynamic link between horizontal and vertical lines. The term arching has the same meaning in the botanical as in the visual sense; it's what the stems of, say, *Exochorda* ×*macrantha* 'The Bride', or *Dipelta floribunda*, do naturally. When burdened with the full weight of flowers, the complete stem, from base to tip, forms an arc.

In plants described as fountains, the stems ascend almost vertically then arch at the top. Many of the taller grasses like stipas and molinias do this, as do a number of cane-forming species, such as *Rubus thibetanus*. It's an outline also seen in shrubs such the beauty bush, *Kolwitzia amabilis*, or cultivars of *Buddleja davidii*.

Pendent or pendulous are the botanical terms that describe plants of weeping habit; they have branches that fall gracefully from a stem of some height, and if they do so almost vertically, the overall effect is like a cascade. It's

▶ The strong line of *Pyrus salicifolia* 'Pendula' is crisp and sinuously arching when leafless in winter—perfect when outlined by snow and echoing snow-dusted box domes.

▶ At Rosemary Verey's iconic arch at Barnsley House, Gloucestershire, the ascending verticals of alliums rise to meet the descending chains of laburnum.

▶ Ascending golden fountain of the giant feather grass, *Stipa gigantea*.

a good bet that 'Pendula' or 'Pendulum' will appear in their name.

In some cases, as with wisteria, *Garrya elliptica*, or *Laburnum* ×*watereri* 'Vossii', it may be the cascading chains of bloom that give the weeping effect. It's a moot point as to whether you might group them with the verticals. I often do; Rosemary Verey's famous laburnum tunnel uses laburnum chains like that, the vertical line reinforced by the upstanding stems of alliums that rise to meet them.

Clumps and Mounds

Plump, pillowy, rounded forms are the essence of mounds. A certain density of foliage is part of the package, and I take the opportunity when deadheading or clipping to reinforce a mounded, billowing form. Mounded plants are the usually the predominant mass in borders, their unassuming outlines unify a scheme and provide a low-key matrix against which plants of stronger line become outstanding.

That doesn't mean they're dull. I want them to have good colour in flower, and fine colour and a range of textures in leaf, before and after flowering. If they are evergreen, or semi-evergreen, so much the better, because then they give long-term structure to successive layers in a scheme. With a winter presence, they'll frame the early bulbs which begin the season, then mask fading bulb foliage as new spring growth gets underway.

Clumps have the functional qualities of mounds, but are of less regularly rounded outline, since many clump-formers produce multiple stems from the crown; hemerocallis, peonies, poppies and agapanthus belong here. Some mounds and clumps are chameleons, they may take on a fountain like or vertical line when in flower.

Clouds and Transparents

Clouds and transparents are the plants that breathe air and light into a scheme. Hazy, shimmering, and ethereal are words that describe their virtues; *Gypsophila paniculata*, *Stipa gigantea*, *Nepeta govaniana*, *Salvia candelabrum* and *Dierama pulcherrimum* are classic examples. These are essentially see-through plants, either with airy and graceful inflorescences on slender stems that rise well above a basal mass of foliage, or with foliage that is itself delicate in form and insubstantial in heft, as with the fennels (*Foeniculum* species). Regardless of height, transparents can be placed as accents near the front of borders, where their apparent fragility can be enjoyed close-up, without the plantings behind them being obscured.

Filler Plantings

There are several reasons why gaps appear in plantings. Some are inevitable, and are remedied by patience, forward thinking or clever combination planting. Others are the result of greed, impatience and bad planning; I speak for myself here.

The first in the inevitable category is that new plantings take time to mature. Don't succumb to overplanting unless you are prepared to be absolutely ruthless and thin out before it's too late. If you have chosen plants for their natural form, they must have sufficient space to achieve that. Plants set too closely will grow into each other—you may want them to—but the lines of the more vigorous will win out. Rely on mulches to suppress weeds in the interim; a loose organic mulch will improve growth by reducing weed competition, retaining soil moisture and keeping soil structure in good condition. And any weeds that seed into it are thrillingly easy to pull.

Nevertheless, patience can be limited in even the most conscientious planter. Prompted by an aversion to the look of bare soil (or even mulch), I am usually seduced into filling gaps and was led to believe that annuals and biennials are the solution. Bitter experience reveals that the most careful selection of them is critical.

I once inadvertently created voids that took two whole seasons to remedy; I lost entire drifts of young lavenders, perovskias and *Caryopteris ×clandonensis* on account of the unchecked, brutish behaviour of a batch self-sown *Verbena bonariensis*. Greedy for a see-through swathe of vibrant purple aloft strongly vertical stems, I didn't thin the seedlings enough. I've also had colour schemes compromised by self-sown foxgloves, *Digitalis purpurea,* which would have been the desired white-flowered variants if only I had been ruthless with the babies; young plants that will have purple flowers have pink-tinged midribs, those of the white are pure palest green.

In essence, you need to be as picky with temporary fillers as with permanent plants, and have a realistic idea of their fighting weight. You also need to be ruthless with thinning and selection of self-sown seedlings. I now choose fillers with known behaviour patterns, of a colour that will always suit the main scheme, and a semi-permanent if mobile presence. For instance, in a blue-themed border, I might use the amber-yellow *Polemonium pauciflorum,* or *Digitalis grandiflora* 'Carillon'. Both are moderate in size and vigour; both are short-lived but willing self-seeders, and readily identifiable as seedlings—good choices, which I can live with.

Seasonal Fillers

Seasonal gaps also fall inevitably into categories. There are those that occur early in the season before the rise of the masses is underway, and others that occur with plants such as oriental poppies, *Papaver orientalis,* that feature highly in early summer and then either die back to leave lamentable voids or become shamefully shabby. For the first category, planting lots of early flowering bulbs in drifts through the scheme is a good solution. There are a several approaches to those in the second category, depending on whether the plant concerned disappears completely or whether it resprouts if cut back as soon as the flowers are done. In the latter case, rapid intervention will give a fresh crop of leaves that are pristine rather than tatty, and there may even be a later crop of flowers. In the former, where the plant is completely airbrushed out of the picture, do two-for-the-price-of-one in the same drift. I often put one

early bloomer and one late bloomer shoulder to shoulder. It works as long as you don't forget to deadhead the earlies.

Which Style?

The design vocabulary generally groups garden styles into broad 'families': formal, semi-formal, informal, or wild. This is style shorthand, for although wild and formal stand distinct at opposite ends of a spectrum, there can be overlap in between, if you so choose. Nor must you commit to a single style, unless space is very confined. You can either find some means of separating areas of different style; you can place different styles to make a statement of strong contrasts; or you can meld different styles together by treating them as a continuum. Whichever approach you choose, do it decisively and with deliberation.

The concept of garden rooms, wherein each room features a different composition, is a recurrent design theme that is eminently adaptable for the stylistically imaginative (or indecisive) gardener. It's a concept as ancient as the Paradise garden of Persia, as medieval as the *giardino segreto*, and as modern as you care to make it. Famous examples can be found at Hidcote Manor in Gloucestershire, at Newby Hall in Yorkshire and in Beatrix Farrand's designs for Dumbarton Oaks in Washington, D.C.

In many long-admired gardens, such as Sissinghurst in England, the plan on paper would imply a highly formal scheme—in contrast to the soft and exuberant planting on the ground that would surely be classified as informal. A strongly architectural plan or layout is analogous to a sharply angular catwalk model; it's the clothes that cover the bones that define the style.

Formal Style

The formal style is briefly described by words like crisp, geometrical and above all symmetrical, often with divisions into compartments,

which may comprise hard landscaping or highly controlled, clipped or pruned plants. It can be classic or modern. Techniques such as planting through mulch matting to suppress weeds reduce maintenance phenomenally, but inevitably this style requires annual or biennial clipping to keep formal lines crisp. The more extensive the living structures, the more work it takes to keep them in shape. And if you rely on living plants for infrastructure they must be absolutely bomb-proof—bone-hardy, disease-

▲ The symmetry of the knot garden at Bourton House demands great attention to detail in its maintenance, for without the detailed crispness of line the essence of formality is lost.

◀ Deceptively artless informal planting reveals great sensitivity to the site, and solves the universal rural gardener's question of how to sit the garden comfortably in its surroundings: not so much 'calling in the country' as becoming part of it. (Design: Dan Pearson)

◀ The strongly formal architecture of this urban garden's layout is softened by the encroachment of lush informal planting upon its hard edges.

resistant and tolerant of hard clipping. It will break your heart if half of the design is consumed by pox, blights, plagues or vengeful acts of weather.

Informal Style

The informal style is altogether more relaxed, usually with softer, curving outlines and a more pliable, less regular approach to planting. Where hard edges exist, they are softened by gracefully spilling plants. The impression is rather *laissez-faire*, and this *can* be a lower-maintenance style of gardening than the formal, with the proviso that plants are well chosen in three respects. The first condition is that they make dense, light-excluding cover to suppress weeds. The second condition, corollary to the first, is that you can plant closely enough without compromising the eventual form of the plants.

The third is that the chosen plants can either stand on their own feet, or jostle shoulder to shoulder and support each other. The old-fashioned methods of supporting floppy plants with twiggy pea sticks and the like are time consuming to set up. They test the patience; it can seem an age before plants grow up sufficiently to disguise them—unless, of course, you find or make supports that you like and make a feature of them. These might include willow or hazel pyramids or cones, for example. I use bamboo, freshly cut when thinning clumps; the canes are then flexible and bend to my will.

Wild Gardens

The term wild garden is open to several interpretations, most of which imply a re-creation

of habitat type, such as the meadow garden, prairie garden, woodland garden or the gravel garden (the last mimics dry areas, such as the stony mediterranean garrigue, which abounds naturally in associations of drought-tolerant plants). Broadly, wild gardening means choosing plants that are adapted to a chosen habitat and providing conditions in the garden that approximate those found in the wild.

Don't be deceived into believing that giving Mother Nature a free hand allows the gardener to be a free spirit, and involves minimal input by letting nature take its course. In the wild—in their natural habitat—wild plants are kept in check by environmental and climatic conditions, and reminded of their social responsibilities by competition from their neighbours. Take wildlings out of context, give them a taste of luxurious living, and they rapidly become brutish and the lives of those around them short.

All wild gardens demand a basic understanding of the habitat you want to recreate and of the management techniques to keep things as you want them. In the woodland garden, full light and moisture reaches the ground only when the trees are leafless. This is why nearly all woodland natives are early flowering; they need to reproduce before the leaf canopy fills in by early summer, bringing shade and a degree of dryness to the woodland floor. In woodland or similar shaded conditions, it is the compositions of foliage form, colour, and texture that extend the interest through summer. If you want later flowers, you need to increase light and moisture levels by lifting or thinning the crowns of surrounding trees; improving the soil with plentiful organic matter; or creating open, sunny glades and rides to accommodate light-demanding species.

I also look after several meadows and they are a joy. The most successful is an ancient one subject to the same management technique since time immemorial: one cut in late summer, then bale and cart away. It's very rich in species, and low-fertility soil is key to success. I

◀ Beneath a canopy of high-pruned trees, foxgloves, dicentras, aquilegias and a spangling of snowy woodrush bask in the dappled light of late spring and early summer. (Beth Chatto Gardens, Colchester, Essex)

tend a spring and early summer meadow, alive with narcissi and tulips in spring, later spangled with dog daisies (*Leucanthemum vulgare*) and ragged robin (*Lychnis flos-cuculi*). This is cut and carted as early in summer as possible, as soon as the daisies look dog tired, which allows a later flush of geraniums that otherwise would be lost in the standing grasses. Cutting and carting away, which keeps the soil in a state of diminished fertility, is hard work, especially if you do it by hand. By all means be entranced by the romance, but take full account of the labour and time that meadows demand.

◀ The meadow at Great Dixter is as near to an Arcadian idyll as one might wish. Subjected to a consistent regime over many years—no fertilizer, no scarifying and always with cuttings collected and composted—ongoing meadow management at Great Dixter comprises 2–3 cuts annually depending on the vigour of growth, and occupies labour between August and November.

Horizontals and Tiers

A plant that lends a linear, horizontal line has several functions in a garden composition. The stable and placid horizontal line draws the eye along its length, balances vertical and diagonal lines, supports mounded forms and anchors the curves of arching or weeping lines. Think of it as a pictorial foreground or baseline.

Such plants need not have a horizontal habit, although flat-liners such as creeping thymes obviously do. Low-level horizontals may simply be closely set masses of plants of diminutive stature—ground-huggers to about knee high, depending on the scale of the scheme—that blur the junction between earth and planting.

Where plants lend a horizontal line at some height, with flat-topped flowerheads on tall stems, for instance, they will interrupt a flow of mounded curves, embroider a gauze of transparent plants or create a secondary line that makes towering verticals more emphatic.

Plants that form tiers lend a rhythmic and repetitious horizontal line. Often shrubs or trees, these can be plants of considerable mass or stature. They make bold statements if grown as specimens, or when sited to echo horizontal lines in hard landscaping. They're also invaluable for highlighting a simple vertical, in the form of a beautiful-barked bole rising above them, for instance.

What I look for is a horizontally tiered branch framework, often reinforced by the poise of leaves and disposition of flowers above or below the branches; some *Styrax* and many *Viburnum* species give the desired effect. Often I see more subtly etched lines, as when foliage creates a series of cloud-like strata in many of the Japanese maples. And while

▲ *Acer campestre* 'Silver Celebration'

I use relatively few variegated plants, in several a faintly tiered habit is rendered obvious by their leaf patterning; even the humble field maple, *Acer campestre*, is clearly tiered in its variegated forms.

Acer

Aceraceae • maple

The field maple, *Acer campestre*, is a common hedgerow tree in Britain, although in hedges it never achieves the domed outline with tiered, spreading branches that develops in open ground. In hedgerows it proves very tolerant of clipping, and the species or its golden-leaved variant 'Postelense' are good for structural hedges and barriers.

The dark green leaves are small and neatly lobed, and turn clear golden yellow in autumn. By the second year, the branchlets often develop corky wings, which emphasizes the line.

The horizontally disposed branch framework is clearest in variegated-leaved forms, such as *Acer campestre* 'Silver Celebration', with white margined leaves, or 'Carnival', with leaves margined creamy white, flushed pink as they unfold in spring. Both are slow growing and never reach the dimensions of the species; both make pretty specimens for small gardens, especially in contrast to the white canes of *Rubus thibetanus*.

◀ *Acer shirasawanum* 'Aureum'

Achillea

Asteraceae • yarrow

Although traditionally used in the herbaceous or mixed border, achilleas also look good in dry and gravel gardens, and especially in drifts among ornamental grasses—most of the taller species are native to grasslands of northern temperate zones. The flowerheads provide distinctly horizontal lines at knee to navel height; the flattened or slightly domed corymbs of many tightly packed florets are borne on erect stems well above the mounded basal clumps of fine textured foliage.

In those with *Achillea clypeolata* in their breeding, the feathery foliage mounds are silver-grey derived from the beautiful silvery jade leaves of that parent. Hybrids of *A. filipendulina* and *A. millefolium* have foliage in dark green or grey-green. *Achillea* 'Coronation Gold' and *A. filipendulina* 'Gold Plate' possess flowers of an unforgiving yellow that is too brash for more subtle schemes. Softer yellows, easier to place, are found at about knee to navel height,

Acer shirasawanum 'Aureum' has a broadly vase-shaped outline, but each ascending branch bears tiers of crisply layered foliage, looking naturally almost as if cloud-pruned in ranks of stratocumulus forms. The neatly lobed leaves are clear gold on emergence, then fresh golden green, returning to golden luminosity before becoming red in autumn. A small tree, and a beautiful specimen in gardens, in courtyards, even in large containers with careful attention to watering; like most Japanese maples, its shallow, compact root system adapts readily to pot cultivation. Close up, you can appreciate the tiny upright corymbs of red-purple flowers in spring, and the horizontally winged, late summer fruits. The Korean maple, *A. pseudosieboldianum*, with lustrous green leaves but more vibrant fall colour, is smaller but similar in habit.

Grows slowly to four to five times head height. Fully hardy, z4–8, *A. campestre*; z5/6–8, *A. pseudosieboldianum*, *A. shirasawanum*. Any moist but well-drained soil, in sun or dappled shade; protect from cold dry winds. Prune and shape when dormant to avoid sap bleeding. The judicious removal of tiers of branches emphasizes the horizontal lines of *A. campestre*. Mulch Japanese species before winter where frosts are hard or prolonged. Pruning is seldom necessary.

▲ *Achillea* 'Walther Funcke'

in *A.* 'Moonshine', *A.* 'Schwefelblüte', *A.* 'Taygetea' *A.* 'Forncett Citrus' and in *A.* ANTHEA 'Anblo', the last with sturdy heads of soft primrose above luminous blue-grey foliage,

◀ *Achillea* 'Summerwine'
with *Olea europaea*

▶ *Adiantum aleuticum*,
with *Hosta undulata* var.
undulata in front

which glows at twilight. The rich reds and burgundies, such as late-flowering, wine-red 'Summerwine' and blackcurranty 'Cassis', tone beautifully with the plummy sedums, astrantias and pink-tinted grasses, such as *Pennisetum* 'Karley Rose'. Several undergo a chameleon-like colour change with age: 'Lachsschönheit' (salmon to creamy buff); 'Wesersandstein' (pink to creamy buff); and 'Walther Funcke' (orange-red to creamy yellow). All bloom over long periods in summer, especially if deadheaded.

Fully hardy, z4–8. Any well-drained soil in sun.

Adiantum

Adiantaceae · maidenhair fern

In most adiantums the fronds give an arching line, and all are valued for their particularly delicate texture, the best known being the tender maidenhairs such as *Adiantum raddianum*, a florists' favourite. Yet some are remarkably hardy despite their fragile appearance, growing in the wild as far north as the Aleutian Islands, Nova Scotia and Alaska, in damp leafy forest soils. In *A. aleuticum*, *A. pedatum* and their variants, the emerald green pinnae and pinnules assume a flattened line at knee height as the fan-like fronds unfurl to lie parallel to the ground, the line emphasized by the dark, glossy and wiry stalks. In some, the fronds are tinted as they emerge; pink in *A. aleuticum*, bronze-pink in *A. a.* 'Japonicum', yellow in *A.a.* 'Subpumilum'. The Himalayan maidenhair, *A. venustum*, is equally hardy, at about mid-calf, and will give a lower line with triangular fronds.

They are perfect in horizontal swathes with the erect actaeas, or arching dicentras, and if you can induce carpeting mosses to grow with adiantums, their two forms make a perfect composition of elegant simplicity. Adiantums are deciduous in cooler zones, which adds another aspect to their beauty: the fascination of watching them uncoil from their dark shiny crosiers in spring.

Fully hardy, z4–9. Where conditions suit, the adiantums spread rhizomatously though seldom rampantly. Reliably moist, humus-rich, leafy, open-textured soil in partial or dappled shade. *Adiantum aleuticum* 'Subpumilum' is more wind tolerant.

Akebia

Lardizabalaceae • chocolate vine

Akebias are vigorous climbers; if left untrained they give swooping swags of foliage against a support, which may not give you the firm line you want. They twine unaided, frequently looping back upon themselves to become a bit of a jumble. I grow both *A. trifoliata* and *A. quinata* on substantial stone columns, and push the questing stems to the horizontal, so that they spiral slowly upwards instead of rocketing to the top. It is a technique I use with many climbers. In this way, I get a vertical column garlanded with a series of horizontal tiers, marked by the deep chocolate-maroon flowers in spring, which, though not showy, in *A. quinata* smell wonderfully of vanilla—very pervasive in a sheltered spot. Where springs are warm and summers hot, the long, ovoid-oblong purple fruit dramatically enhance the effect of the swags of leaves, dark green in *A. quinata*, and in *A. triphylla* golden bronze then emerald green.

Akebias are self-sterile, and two plants of different clones are needed to set fruit. If you are short of space, set them in the same planting hole.

To five times head height. Fully hardy, z5–10. Any moist but well-drained soil in sun or dappled shade.

Anemone

Ranunculaceae • windflower

One of the joys of spring when seen in the wild carpeting the woodland floor, this European native is also found in more open grassy habitats. *Anemone nemorosa*, wood anemone, is usually white flowered, but further west across its range, pink, mauve and blue variants are increasingly frequent, and it is from these wildlings that coloured forms, such as the ethereally blue 'Robinsoniana', have been selected and brought into gardens.

The plants are indisputably lovely when grown as ground flora beneath trees in a woodland garden, giving a perfectly simple, if transient, composition of vertical and horizontal lines. They're equally beautiful beneath single specimen trees—perhaps a white-barked birch—in short turf, or in a pebble mulch, where they take over as the foliage of *Cyclamen neapolitanum* fades.

Rhizomes may be slow to establish, but once settled they spread naturally to form an increasingly dense carpet. *Anemone nemorosa* prefers to have a relationship with microscopic soil fungi (mycorrhiza) which help it to absorb soil nutrients; it's a common need in many woodland plants. The fungi occur naturally in undisturbed woodland soils that are rich in leaf mould—I usually add some to the planting hole.

Ankle high. Fully hardy, z5–9. Moist, leafy, well-drained soil in dappled or partial shade.

Anemonella

Ranunculaceae • rue anemone

This slender and diminutive cousin of *Anemone nemorosa* fills similar niches in the open woodlands of eastern North America, from Florida to Ontario and west to Arkansas and Oklahoma. It can be used in much the same way—a horizontal mass beneath a vertical stem or trunk—but on a smaller scale; even when established it does not spread so widely as the European wood anemone. The fragile, cupped, white flowers (sometimes blushed pale pink) turn their faces upwards above delicate foliage from late spring to early summer, the poise of the flowers enhancing the line. It is especially good beneath tiered *Cornus alternifolia* or *C. controversa*, or beneath a snake bark maple such as *Acer capillipes*, with striped green and grey-white bark.

Ankle high. Fully hardy, z4–8. Leafy, open, well-drained soil in dappled shade.

Anthemis

Asteraceae • dog fennel

A silver-leaved, mat-forming perennial, *Anthemis punctata* subsp. *cupaniana* is a Sicilian native of open, sunny and well-drained habitats. It forms a long, low mound, three times as wide as high, giving a good horizontal line in a gravel garden, or at the front of a border. The pure white daisies, produced abundantly over long periods in early summer, are so slender stemmed as not to disrupt the line, and can be induced to give a later repeat if deadheaded before they fade. Use the non-flowering *Stachys byzantina* 'Silver Carpet', or the low-growing *S. candida*, both with silky silver leaves in the same tonal range, to reinforce the line with an emphatic contrast in texture. Since the finely divided foliage can become rather open by midsummer, clip over lightly when deadheading to maintain dense cover; it becomes impossibly lax and floppy in over-rich soils. Don't clip later than midsummer, as the soft late growth that results is more susceptible to frost.

Ankle to mid-calf high. Fully hardy, z7–9. Full sun in a freely draining, not-too-fertile soil.

Aralia

Araliaceae

From montane and submontane woodlands of eastern Asia, *Aralia elata* is a suckering species with thick, spiny stems sporting tiers of enormous pinnate leaves of a rich bright green. It is spectacular in bloom, with huge rounded umbels of greenish white flowers in late summer, followed by swags of small black fruits. The tiered habit is most defined in the variegated forms: *A. elata* 'Aureovariegata', irregularly margined in golden yellow, and *A. elata* 'Variegata', with margins of creamy white. In continental climates, where summers are long and hot and the soft pithy stems ripen fully, aralia makes a moderate-sized tree of 10 m (30 ft.) or so in height. Where the growing season is short and summer warmth scarce, aralias are more shrub-like (soft, unripened tip growth is

effectively pinch-pruned by frost)—so if you garden in a maritime climate, or provide very fertile soil with the aim of larger and more lush foliage, the aralia may not reach its full height. In either case, an aralia makes a beautiful architectural specimen when freestanding, in a lawn or sheltered courtyard.

To five times head height. Fully hardy, z4–9. Leafy, humus-rich soil, in sun for best flowering, or in dappled or part-day shade. Shelter from strong winds, which tatter the leaves.

Artemisia

Asteraceae/Compositae

In *The English Rock Garden* (1930), Reginald Farrer called the montane artemisias "a most lovely race of quite dwarf, silvery tuffets of aromatic foliage most ferny and beautiful". Some species are useful for low horizontal lines in finely and intricately textured hues of grey and silver, most of which are found in alpine habitats. A covering of fine, silky, light-reflective hair, or down, is common in high-altitude plants; it protects them from desiccation by strong winds, and from burning by intense

◀ *Artemisia schmidtiana* 'Nana'

sun and high levels of ultraviolet light. All are perfectly adapted to gritty, low-fertility soils and full sun; indeed they develop best colour in sun, and the most compact habits in poor dry soils. The rock garden, gravel garden and dry garden approximate their natural homes, and they do well in paving crevices on a hot dry

▶ *Aster* 'Ringdove'

terrace or when allowed to fan out over a stone mowing strip, or a gravel path next the border. They become impossibly lax and leggy in rich soil. Their immediate companions should be short(ish) and not too eager to jostle—smaller *Dianthus* are perfect.

Artemisias have flowerheads that in infancy are promisingly white-stemmed with silvery bobbles, but later open to a dirty yellow-brown. Time cutting back to induce bushier growth carefully; too early and they give up the ghost, too late and the soft new growth won't overwinter. It's about right when they're in full growth in early summer, and this also helps deter them from flowering.

In *Artemisia schmidtiana* 'Nana' the texture is silky, the colour a faintly green-washed silver, and the leaf lobes fine and narrowly linear. At ankle-high and three times as wide, it is a dwarf form of *A. schmidtiana,* which has similar attributes but is taller and broader. In *A. stelleriana* 'Boughton Silver' the texture is felted, the colour is white faintly washed grey, and the leaves neatly lobed; 'Prostrata' is similar but ground-hugging. In *A. caucasica* (which now

includes *A. assoana, A. lanata,* and *A. pedemontana*), the texture is woolly-downy, the colour is silvery white, and foliage is fern-like.

Ankle high. Fully hardy, z3–9. Poor, gritty, well-drained soil in full sun. See also pages 83 (Verticals and Diagonals), 183 (Clumps and Mounds) and 240 (Clouds and Transparents).

Aster
Asteraceae

My grandfather grew asters for my granny to cut, and for those of us most familiar with the legion highly bred, upright cultivars of *Aster novi-belgii* and *A. novae-angliae*, the wild ones are a revelation. Whether to treat them as transparents is a hard call, for their effect is of fine crosshatching in a line drawing; while most plants described in this section give a horizontal line, this line is an airy and light-filled one. They provide a good late nectar source for bees and butterflies, flowering from midsummer into autumn.

Aster ericoides occurs in dry, open places and in thickets in eastern and central North America. It is relatively early to begin flowering (from

▼ *Aster lateriflorus* 'Horizontalis'

midsummer), and among the most drought-tolerant of asters. It produces lax panicles at navel height, the branchlets bending to the horizontal under the weight of the tiny white-petalled, golden-centred daisies that wreathe them. *A. ericoides* 'Rosy Veil' has grey-toned, soft pink flowers, an interestingly impure hue that associates well with the pink-tinged buff of *Pennisetum alopecuroides* 'Hameln' and the metallic blue-grey of *Panicum virgatum* 'Heavy Metal'.

Taller than *Aster ericoides*, *A. lateriflorus* grows wild in fields, clearings and thickets, and on shorelines all over North America. With *A. lateriflorus* 'Horizontalis', you know exactly what to expect in terms of line; it has white petals that blush pink as they age, the effect enhanced by the deeper brown-pink at the centre. One of the finest cultivars is 'Lady in Black', with raspberry-pink-centred flowers on dark horizontal branchlets and deep plummy leaves—fabulous with the silvery red-bronze plumes of *Miscanthus sinensis* 'Morning Light'.

Navel to chest high. Fully hardy, z4–9. Any well-drained soil in sun or dappled part-day shade; *A. lateriflorus* needs more moisture retentive soils. See also page 241 (Clouds and Transparents).

Blechnum

Blechnaceae ▪ hard ferns

Creeping by means of slender runners to form decumbent colonies where conditions suit, *Blechnum penna-marina*, alpine water fern, is a hardy member of a mostly tropical and subtropical genus. The specific epithet means sea feather or sea pen, referring to its resemblance to that deep-sea soft coral that looks rather like a quill pen. It's a good description of its long, narrow fronds with slender pinnae—even the habit of growth is suggestive of fronds in swirling water when it spreads to form a colony, especially so in the crested cultivar 'Cristatum'. *Blechnum penna-marina* subsp. *alpinum* Paradise form has coloured new fronds in bright bronze-pink.

In damp woodland sites, or in shady places on moist acid, leafy soils, it spreads readily, a natural companion to arching ferns, or for simple compositions with moss and stone. *Blechnum penna-marina* occurs to high altitudes, with sphagnum mosses in boggy ground in temperate and sub-Antarctic South America and Australasia. It is also effective in swathes beneath *Enkianthus* and the feathered texture contrasts particularly well with glossy leaves of *Cornus canadensis*, or *Francoa*.

Ankle high. Fully hardy, z5–8. Reliably moist, humus-rich, acid soil in shade or dappled shade. Fronds burn in full sun, but are fairly resistant to wind, and more tolerant than most of dry atmospheres. Since the rhizomes are near the surface, it is essential not to plant too deeply, and it mustn't dry out during establishment. See also page 147 (Arcs and Fountains).

Campanula

Campanulaceae ▪ bellflower

The tinier bellflowers flower almost continuously through summer with slender-stemmed, bell- or star-shaped flowers in a range of blue, slate- and violet-blues, of almost universally delicate appearance, but with a tenacity that belies their apparent fragility. They self-seed into the tightest of niches, between paving slabs, into crevices in walls and rockwork, and weave themselves through other plants at the front of borders. *Campanula cochleariifolia*, at ankle high, produces tiny bell-shaped flowers in white, lavender blue and slate blue, all three shades present in self-sown populations.

▲ *Blechnum penna-marina*

◀ *Campanula carpatica,*
close up of flowers

◀ *Campanula
portenschlagiana*

Campanula carpatica is found among the rocks
of the Carpathian Mountains; the small leaves
form long low mounds covered by masses of
solitary, upturned, open bells in white, blue, or
violet-blue. In *C. portenschlagiana*, with tubular bells in intense violet-blue, and the more
refined *C. poscharskyana*, with starry lavender-blue blooms, the long flowering panicles
willingly tangle through neighbours. These last
three are alpine species, prone to losing their
natural delicacy on too rich a diet. In gravel,
and in poor gritty soils, they're rendered
diminutive by a size-zero diet, and are all the
more charming for that. If allowed to become

fat through overfeeding, they can become nuisance invasives.

Fully hardy, z3/4–9. Moist but well-drained
soil in sun, or light, dappled shade.

Cerastium

Caryophyllacea ▪ snow-in-summer, white rock

Rampant is the descriptor most frequently
applied to once-common *Cerastium tomentosum*, and it is deserved if planted in rich soils
in the wrong place. Its virtues lie in its dense
mat-forming habit, its silvery grey leaves which
become whiter in poor soils in brilliant light in
hot, dry places, and in its sheer abundance of
late spring and summer bloom in the cleanest,
crispest white. It is indestructible. I use it to
give a low horizontal line in the gravel garden,
in the interstices of a stone mowing strip at
the front of a border, and allow it to distribute
itself through crevices on a hot sunny terrace,
where it delineates the random patternwork of
the pavers. Shear back brutally as soon as the
flowers begin to look grubby to control invasive tendencies, and to renew a clean silver
carpet of foliage for the remainder of summer
and into autumn, often with a second flush of
flowers. If you can't bear the common touch,
there are more refined variants, among them
C. alpinum var. *lanatum*, more compact with
white woolly leaves.

Ankle height. Fully hardy, z4–9. Any poor,
dry soil in full sun.

▼ *Cerastium
tomentosum*

Chionodoxa

Hyacinthaceae

Chionodoxa luciliae and *C. forbesii* are often confused in the trade, and to the disinterested observer there isn't much to tell them apart. For solidity of colour in the low blue line that the starry flowers give in spring, *C. forbesii* is preferable; each raceme has four to twelve flowers instead of the three on each raceme of *C. luciliae.* Diminutive bulbs like those of *Chionodoxa* (and *Puschkinia,* and *Muscari*) are useful fillers for starting the season with herbaceous plants, in borders, or beneath tree and shrubs. Although they self-sow, and in open ground form a blue carpet in time, they are not so greedy as to materially affect their companions. The willingness to self-sow also makes them useful for crevice plantings.

Ankle height. Fully hardy, z4–7. Any well-drained soil in sun or dappled shade.

▲ *Convolvulus sabatius* with *Erigeron karvinskianus* and artemisia

◀ *Chionodoxa forbesii*

Convolvulus

Convolvulaceae ▪ bindweed

Convolvulus sabatius, Mauritian bindweed, is a carpeting, woody-based perennial that usually proves hardier than expected if grown with perfect drainage on a sunny slope in poor, dry, gritty or sandy soil, emulating the conditions in its native habitat of northwestern Italy, Sicily and northwestern Africa. It colonizes rocks and walls there, and I grow it on a hot sunny terrace, where its roots infiltrate beneath the stones, giving them protection from the worst of winter frost and rain; even if the top growth suffers, there are usually enough undamaged buds from which it will resprout in spring. Desired on account of its upturned, glistening, blue, funnel-shaped flowers, which appear throughout the summer and into autumn, this plant is a scrambler; it forms an almost perfectly flat carpet if unimpeded, but will weave through neighbours if given the chance, and looks especially lovely with the airy daisies of *Erigeron karvinskianus* and the more delicate artemisas such as *A. pontica.*

Ankle height. Hardy, z8–10. Poor or not-too-fertile, well-drained, gritty soils in sun.

Cornus

Cornaceae ▪ dogwood

Nearly all of the cultivated cornus are known for their elegant habit and beautiful flowers, but some have a distinctive mode of growth that gives well-defined horizontal lines.

Cornus alternifolia, pagoda dogwood, from

thickets, woodland margins and damp streamsides in eastern North America, is a small deciduous tree (to three times head height) that holds its branches horizontally, giving a markedly tiered line. It is beautiful in winter outline, and in spring, the tiers are emphasized by conspicuously veined, bright green leaves, which emerge with neat poise on the upper sides of the branches. Among the most distinctive of specimen trees, often naturally multistemmed, it also produces flattened clusters of tiny, creamy white flowers in early summer, and colours in shades purple and red in autumn.

In *C. alternifolia* 'Argentea', the greyish green leaves are margined with creamy white, which provides another delicate dimension to the beauty of its form; the paler leaf colour, dappled by shade from successive tiers, defines them more clearly than in the species. At only half the size of the species and of more refined appearance, it is a better choice for smaller spaces. Both cast relatively light shade, allowing underplantings of low, linear lines to reinforce the effect, and are best planted with a clear, uncluttered foreground that won't distract.

Cornus controversa 'Variegata' is larger and more vigorous, and with more conspicuous heads of tiny flowers, which emerge with the leaves in early summer in flat-topped cymes on the upper branch surfaces. It otherwise has very similar virtues, including good autumn colour and is much easier to grow.

Cornus canadensis is the odd one out in the genus, being a creeping, evergreen or semi-evergreen perennial. Seldom growing to more than ankle height, with veined leaves neatly arranged in whorls, it makes a dense low carpet of dark green foliage, studded in late spring and early summer by the typical white-bracted flowers.

Fully hardy, z4–7. Sun or dappled shade, in open, well-drained, leafy, humus-rich, near-neutral or slightly acid soil. They seldom need pruning, but branches can be selectively thinned during winter dormancy to space out

▲▲ *Cornus alternifolia* 'Argentea'

▲ *Cornus controversa* 'Variegata'

◀ *Cornus canadensis*

49

the tiers; cut them off when small at the point of origin. *Cornus canadensis* is shade tolerant and prefers leafy acid soils.

Cyclamen

Primulaceae

When first I saw *Cyclamen hederifolium* it was forming a low horizontal mass in the driest, most inhospitable situation: in desiccated conifer litter in deep shade beneath a row of *Chamaecyparis lawsoniana*. And there it flowered from late summer/early autumn through to late winter, above an increasing volume of grey and silver marbled foliage. *Cyclamen hederifolium* is preceded by *C. purpurascens* from mid to late summer, and the floral baton is taken up again in late winter by *C. coum*, with similarly long-lived flowers and rounder leaves, beautifully marked in shades of silver, or pewter in *C. coum* Pewter Group.

These species of *Cyclamen* and their variants are the hardiest. I grow them beneath trees both deciduous and evergreen, and have several colonies established in turf that is roughly mown throughout summer. They also—more formally—grace a swathe of large-pebble mulch beneath a pair of fastigiate trees, as well as bare soil beneath specimen trees. They self-seed particularly freely in these last two sites (though seedlings seldom survive the hoes of careless gardeners).

Cyclamen tubers need good drainage, and do best with a vegetative umbrella, such as a canopy of trees or shrubs, to protect them from excessive summer rainfall. Growth will rot before it reaches the light if you bury the tubers; plant the top of the tuber at or just above soil level.

I have made a number of rules for myself to ensure continued success with *Cyclamen*. Where naturalistic plantings are beneath trees, their bases are cleared of grass and other foliage in early August well before the first cyclamen flowers emerge, by hand pulling or strimming *very* low. Where I plant in rough grass, this is

◀ *Cyclamen coum*

▼ *Cyclamen hederifolium*

cut very short at the same time. In the pebble mulch, I burn off any unwanted vegetation with a flame gun. Timing is everything; even though I know when they will emerge and give them three weeks of grace, I look very closely before going in with guns blazing. These techniques make a difference to the growth of individual tubers, which get fatter and more productive each year.

Ankle height. Fully hardy, z6–9. Moderately fertile, humus-rich soil in dappled or partial shade.

Enkianthus

Ericaceae

The genus *Enkianthus* includes some of the most enchanting of woodlanders from the mountains of Honshu and other other islands of Japan, with some from similar habitats in the Himalayas and central and western China. Most species display a tiered branch architecture in that the leaves are arranged in whorls, and the clusters of flowers of early summer depend gracefully beneath them for emphasis. I noticed the tiered habit first in *E. campanulatus*, in which the tiny pale creamy pink bells are faintly rimmed in a toning rusty pink, so evocative of that delicate Japanese painting technique using a wet brush barely tipped with colour. In *E. perulatus* the habit is more open and the branches tinted in darker tones of deep red; the flowers are crystalline white. *Enkianthus cernuus* var. *rubens*, perhaps the best known, produces flowers of a rich, slightly rusty red. All produce brilliant autumn colour, turning gold through to scarlet and red-purple. *Enkianthus* species need little more than a mossy carpet to be seen at their best, but thrive in similar conditions to cercidiphyllums, which make beautiful companions.

These plants are flawless in every respect but for their insistence on acid soils—very frustrating for gardeners on chalk. Being shallow-rooted, they do well in containers in a lime-free ericaceous mix, and make graceful specimens for a cool sheltered courtyard.

Head height and above. Fully hardy, z5/6–9. Sun, with protection from hot midday sun, or dappled shade in moist, humus-rich, lime-free soil, with shelter from cold, drying winds.

Eranthis

Ranunculaceae • winter aconite

Any tuber so cheerily amenable as to form flat, low rivers of sunny golden colour in early spring is welcome, especially when it colonizes in almost any situation in which it finds itself.

◀ *Enkianthus campanulatus*

Eranthis hyemalis, the winter aconite, is one such, loved for its glossy yellow flowers and for the green ruffs they sit upon. You can fall out of love, though. The ruffs look rough by late spring, and can irritate the skin if you try to pull them out barehanded; the seed is scattered and germinates far and wide, and the rhizomes are no respecters of personal space either; this one shows all the family traits of the buttercups. *Eranthis* ×*tubergenii* is a more choice and thankfully sterile alternative with bronzed ruffs, and in its cultivar 'Guinea Gold' the flowers are fragrant too.

◀ *Eranthis hyemalis*

Ankle height. Fully hardy, z5–8. Reliably moist humus-rich soil in sun or dappled shade. Plant tubers as soon as they arrive; once you allow them to dry out, they become hard to establish.

Erodium

Geraniaceae • heron's bill, stork's bill

Found in sunny and rocky mountain habitats, usually on limestone formations, the erodiums include a number of very amenable plants that will give a low horizontal line when planted in multiples. Those described here are actually very low mound-formers with a useful density of very pretty foliage; they are seldom without flower throughout most of summer and into autumn. In order of height, the lowest is *E. chrysanthum*, with a spreading evergreen array of fern-like, finely divided, silver-green leaves and the palest sulphur-yellow flowers with the texture of crumpled silk. Similar in tolerances and virtues is the soft pink *E.* 'County Park'. *Erodium pelargoniiflorum* is taller, with rounded, slightly lobed entire leaves in soft grey-green; when I first saw it, it was forming ribbon-like drifts at a wind-blasted nursery on the chalk Wolds in Yorkshire, where it had self-seeded into gravel, paving niches, crevices at the base of walls…. Not only admirable

for toughness (z6), it bears white flowers, the upper petals marked maroon-purple, through summer until the frosts, with scarcely a break for winter.

Ankle height or a little more. Fully hardy, z7–10. Well-drained soil in full sun.

Euonymus

Celastraceae • spindle

For gardeners on chalky soils, *E. alatus*, winged spindle, offers the satisfaction of colouring as well if not better in autumn than it does on acid soils—one of the few exceptions to a general rule. It is a stiff, open shrub with tiers of branches outlined in the corky wings from which it gets its specific epithet (*alatus* meaning winged), and it assumes a distinctly flat-topped habit with age. It is not the most freely fruiting species, even when grown in a crowd to encourage cross-pollination; the flowers are infinitely tiny, only one to three to a cyme, and if you get a single fruit from a cluster you're lucky—they're red-purple capsules that open to expose a seed inside enclosed in a bright orange aril. In any case, I grow it for the habit and for the autumn colour, which is a glowing red-pink, leaning to the magenta.

Chest to head height. Fully hardy, z3–9. Well-drained but moisture-retentive soil in sun or

◀ *Erodium chrysanthum,*
close up of flower

▶ *Euonymus alatus*

dappled shade. A site sheltered from wind is best to prolong the autumn show.

Galanthus

Amaryllidaceae · snowdrop

It seems curious to include such upright little bulbs here, but en masse they are unsurpassed in giving a low horizontal swathe at ground level. Unless you have galanthophile tendencies, a snowdrop is a snowdrop, and the plain *G. nivalis* is a beautiful wildling that serves the purpose. If you want mass plantings of something more distinctive that will also persist and spread, and which is more strongly fragrant than the original, there are legion cultivars and species available. Some are collector's items, which are faintingly expensive and slow to bulk up under their own steam. Some of the strongest growers, available at more modest outlay, include *G.* 'Atkinsii', 'Magnet' and 'S. Arnott'. Plant a selection of these and the season is extended from winter through to early spring; all are tough enough to establish in turf. If planted on the top of a bank or slope, they will self-seed to form naturalistic drifts in time. *Galanthus elwesii*, with broader leaves of a more glaucous blue-green, is very vigorous and spreads freely; it's just best planted with room to spread harmlessly.

That you must transplant 'in the green' after flowering before the leaves die back is an oft-repeated myth; you can do so if you like. We have an annual robbing of established colonies to spread them about (in May), but when overtaken by other jobs, the bulbs are stored in open baskets in the cool and dark and bunged in when there's time. The important thing is to avoid letting them get desiccated. The commoner sorts of snowdrops are cool-temperate bulbs that don't like hot summers, which explains why the spring vision of a woodland floor absolutely carpeted in them is such a British thing.

Fully hardy, z6–9. Dappled shade in humus-rich soil that remains just moist in summer.

▶ *Galanthus elwesii* with winter aconite

▶ *Galanthus* 'S. Arnott'

▶ *Galanthus* 'Magnet'

Galium

Rubiaceae · bedstraw

Where snowdrops thrive, so does *Galium odoratum* (sweet woodruff). It grows wild in woods and hedgebanks, sometimes with sweet cicely, *Myrrhis odorata*, on wooded riverbanks; both share a good clear white in the flowers and a characteristic freshness of green in the young leaves. Although the most obvious place to grow sweet woodruff is as a carpet in the wild or woodland garden, I like it so much that I've planted it in almost every shady border I've designed; it forms a low carpet beneath perennials and never becomes so invasive as to compromise the vigour of its companions. (If it looks threatening, pull it up by the handful and dry it—it has a wonderful coumarin scent when dried.) Not only do the close mat of whorled foliage and delicate flowers give a beautiful texture in their own right, but they also make a gentle counterpoint to larger-leaved plants, such as veratrums and hostas. I also grow it with snowdrops beneath *Osmaronia nuttalii*, the oso-berry, with emerald green leaves and pendent clusters of tiny almond-scented flowers in early spring; woodruff takes over where the snowdrops leave off.

 Ankle height. Fully hardy, z3–9. Any damp, humus-rich soil in dappled shade or in sun where soils remain reliably moist.

Hepatica
Ranunculaceae

Hepatica species are found on the cool, damp and mossy floor of northern temperate woodlands—*H. nobilis* in Europe; *H. transsilvanica* from Romania; *H. acutiloba* and *H. americana* from eastern north America. The hepaticas offer two hits at the horizontal line; in flower—before or as the leaves develop—and after flowering, when the lobed leaves, which are sometimes marbled grey or silver and often purple beneath, expand fully. The leaves often persist through to the following winter, by which time you'll be sick of the sight of them—snip them away before the new season's flowers emerge.

Some selected colour forms change hands at vast expense, and even the less exalted forms aren't cheap; they don't establish quickly or spread rapidly either, are slow from seed and you need multiples to create a worthwhile swathe. But en masse, the upturned little bowls

◀ *Galium odoratum* with *Ajuga reptans*

▼ *Hepatica nobilis*

of flower in spring in shades of luminous blues are to live for.

Unless you garden on the scale that I do, with easy access to the wholesalers, I suggest that you join forces with others of like mind to make up to the bulb wholesalers' minimum order. That's good, but treacherous, advice: it won't just be hepaticas that you'll end up buying.

Ankle height. Fully hardy, z4–9. Cool, moist, humus-rich soil in partial or dappled shade. Mulch with leaf mould in autumn.

Houttuynia

Saururaceae

Houttuynia cordata is a denizen of damp, marshy and often shady habitats in China and Japan, and is most common in gardens in its variegated, tricolour form 'Chameleon', an epithet that assures a lurid exuberance of colour that is difficult to place. The species and the double-flowered form *H. c.* 'Flore Pleno' are quieter

▼ *Houttuynia cordata*

and more vigorous, even invasive in wet soils. They're not heartwrenchingly exciting, but useful and functional; both form low, lush carpets of overlapping, heart-shaped, lustrous green leaves, red-rimmed on emergence, which make dense cover in moist soils. They are effective as marginals, where they will float out from banks across the water's surface giving shelter to fish fry and baby amphibians. This is a good horizontal line as a foil to, for instance, the upright and arching water irises, or the more finely divided textures of astilbes and their upright plumes of flower. Hooligan tendencies are to be expected in most water plants; if it bothers you, confine them to a basket.

Ankle to calf high. Fully hardy, z5–10. In wet soils in regions without snow cover, mulch crowns in winter. Any moist, humus-rich soil in sun or dappled shade.

Hydrangea

Hydrangeaceae

It is easy to underrate hydrangeas if we consider only the mopheads (hortensias) that are the essence of coastal gardens on the English Riviera. Lovely as they can be, they give that intense electric blue only on acid soils; on limy soils, the blues turn to pinks that are often rather muddy. White flowers are unaffected by soil pH, however, and it is here that the 'lacecap' hydrangeas come to the fore. They give a horizontal line in a similar way to the lacecap viburnums (see page 66).

Hydrangea macrophylla boasts a number of lacecap cultivars that flower in late summer: 'Veitchii', 'Lanarth White' and 'Mariesii Grandiflora', all with white sterile flowers around a central boss of blue/lavender/pink fertile flowers (depending on pH).

Many species hydrangeas also bear flattened or slightly domed lacecaps in late summer and autumn; these include *H. aspera* and *H. sargentiana*, with white fertile florets and blue/lavender/pink centres. *Hydrangea serrata* also has several lacecap cultivars, often with exceptional

▲ *Hydrangea serrata*
'Bluebird'

◀ *Hydrangea macrophylla*
'Veitchii'

▶ *Hydrangea anomala*
subsp. *petiolaris*

autumn foliage colour, including the rich blue 'Bluebird' and 'Tiara'.

The summer-flowering climbing hydrangea, *H. anomala* subsp. *petiolaris*, has all-white lacecaps; it's self-clinging once established, and I grow it into trees, leading

it into the bark on a netting ladder. As it weaves its way up, it extrudes horizontal flowering laterals from bottom to top.

Most of the species hydrangeas are natives of shady woodlands and montane forest, and in the cool, dappled shade of the woodland garden those with white flowers are especially effective, blooming much later in the season than most woodlanders do.

Chest to head high. Fully hardy, z7–10, *H. aspera*, *H. sargentiana*; z4–9, *H. anomala* subsp. *petiolaris*; z6–10, *H. serrata*. Any moisture-retentive, humus-rich soil in sun or dappled shade, with shelter from cold drying winds. See also *H. paniculata* and *H. arborescens*, page 161 (Arcs and Fountains).

Jeffersonia

Berberidaceae ▪ twin leaf

Related to the woody barberries (*Berberis*) and the herbaceous epimediums, both jeffersonias are relentlessly vertical in growth, but form low-growing clumps that form a horizontal carpet when close-planted or when established enough to colonize. In *J. diphylla*, found in rich woodlands from Ontario to Tennessee, the delicate, cupped and upturned flowers are pure white and short-lived. They are longer lasting and an ethereal pale lavender-blue in *J. dubia*, which hails from Manchurian and Siberian forests. The blooms emerge in mid to late spring before and with the leaves, but I could almost grow them for their foliage alone. The twin lobes of each single leaf are folded tightly together on emergence, revealing pale, glaucous, veined undersides, opening like a blessing as they mature. In *J. diphylla* they are pale grey-green; in *J. dubia*, blue-green suffused with violet. Unlike many woodlanders, the leaves are not ephemeral; they persist well into autumn, when they are ornamented with leathery, pear-shaped seed capsules. Site them on a gentle slope and the seedpods scatter their seed generously downhill; they germinate freely when fresh, and infant plants then grow on unen-

▲ *Jeffersonia diphylla*

◀ *Jeffersonia dubia*

cumbered by parental competition. The species hybridize if grown together and offspring may not show the distinction of their parents.

Ankle to mid-calf high. Fully hardy, z5–9. Moist, leafy, humus-rich soils in dappled shade.

Oenothera

Onagraceae ▪ evening primrose

There are tall evening primroses that I might include in the verticals category if they weren't so untidy, but the genus includes some useful and very pretty, low carpeters that flower for

◀ *Oenothera speciosa*
'Rosea'

▼ *Oenothera macrocarpa*

Those with short-stalked, cupped, upturned flowers that hug the ground include *O. macrocarpa*, the Missouri evening primrose, and the day-blooming *O. speciosa*, the Mexican evening primrose; both are fragrant, with the fragile texture of crumpled silk, the former with bright yellow flowers, the latter satiny white ageing to soft pink. In *O. speciosa* 'Siskiyou', flowers are a soft mauve-pink, while in *O. s.* 'Rosea' they have darker pink veins; in *O. macrocarpa* 'Greencourt Lemon', they're sulphur yellow above silvery grey-green foliage. Individual flowers are short lived, needing a quota of sunshine before opening, surviving the night to be spangled with morning dew before fading—but they do keep coming and will self-sow.

Oenothera macrocarpa occurs on limestone bluffs and in rocky prairies, and *O. speciosa* on sandier soils. Like most oenotheras, they are drought tolerant—the poorer, hotter and drier the soil and site, the lower they grow. *O. speciosa* is invasive where conditions suit.

Ankle to knee high. Fully hardy, z3–9; from z5, *O. speciosa*. Any sunny site in poor, freely draining soil; alkaline soil for *O. macrocarpa*.

Omphalodes
Boraginaceae

For close, trouble-free cover I use the creeping forget-me-not, *O. verna*, in any place in the garden that approximates its damp mountain woodland home: at the margins of woodland glades, in forgotten corners and shady borders. Where I want a low spring tapestry of pointed fresh green leaves spangled with pure blue, I plant it among sweet woodruff, *Galium odoratum*; primroses and cowslips, *Primula vulgaris* and *P. veris*; violets, *Viola odorata*; and pulmonarias. *Omphalodes verna* spreads freely enough by runners to be considered rampant, but is not substantial enough to swamp neighbours.

O. cappadocica and its variants give a taller horizontal line of borage blue when massplanted; the most intense blue flowers of *O. c.* 'Cherry Ingram' are matchless, and although

inordinately long periods from early summer to early autumn, attracting various beneficial insects in the moth-bee-butterfly line. The prolific seed often attracts small finches and other seed-eating birds.

▶ *Origanum vulgare* 'Aureum'

◀ *Omphalodes cappadocica* 'Cherry Ingram'

◀ *Omphalodes cappadocica* 'Starry Eyes'

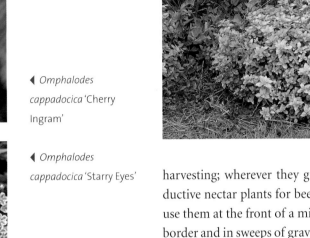

harvesting; wherever they grow, they are productive nectar plants for bees and butterflies. I use them at the front of a mixed or herbaceous border and in sweeps of gravel, but best of all in a hot, paved terrace where they spill out of the crevices and release their scent when brushed by passing feet. There I use golden *O. vulgare* 'Aureum' with the green, yellow-tipped *O. v.* 'Gold Tip' and the very low, creeping *O. vulgare* subsp. *hirtum* 'Humile' (the one to include in a herb lawn).

Ankle height. Fully hardy, z4–9. Well-drained, preferably alkaline, poor or not-too-fertile soil in sun.

Osteospermum

Asteraceae

I differentiate between the almost-hardy oste-ospermums and the legion colourful hybrids that are primarily treated as annuals and used in summer bedding and containers, even though the tender ones include those with whirligig flowers that I love. For creating a low-mounding, evergreen line that flowers all through summer, and which I don't have to lift and discard at the first sign of frost, I choose the South African *O. jucundum* and hybrids derived from it. I grow it on gravel banks, sunny slopes and wall tops, and at the front of borders in gritty soils.

Osteospermum jucundum occurs on in sandy soils on mountain slopes, among quartzite rocks, and in mountain grassland, and in the

those of *O. c.* 'Starry Eyes' are sky blue sweetly rimmed with white, it's much less vigorous.

Ankle high. Fully hardy, z6–9. Cool dappled shade in leafy, moist but well-drained soil.

Origanum

Lamiaceae ▪ oregano

Of all the oreganos, it is cultivars of common or wild marjoram, *Origanum vulgare*, that are most useful in giving low, frontline horizontals. The species is variable in height, and in the wild grows really low only in calcareous sheep-grazed turf. I don't restrict them to the herb garden, although they make fine edging there, and are kept tight by frequent culinary

Drakensberg grows at altitudes of up to 3,200 metres (10,500 feet). Its needs correspond with those of many other alpines in the respect that lean soils and excellent winter drainage are key to success—the combination of standing winter wet and low temperatures won't do. The species spreads by creeping rhizomes, forming dense mats of narrow grey-green leaves, and turn on their full charm as they begin to flower. From late spring to autumn, they produce neat and perfect long-stemmed daisies, with deep blue-purple disc florets at the centre, and ray florets in shades of magenta, pink and white—all with a contrasting reverse that is displayed daily since the petals close up in the evening and open in the morning sun. *Osteospermum jucundum* and *O. jucundum* var. *compactum* have soft mauve-pink to magenta flowers with a bronzed reverse. The hardiest *O. jucundum* hybrids include: 'Blackthorn Seedling', rich magenta; 'Langtrees', deep pink-purple; 'Hopleys', magenta, the blue disc rimmed

white; 'Lady Leitrim', white, fading pink, with a bronzed pink-purple reverse; 'Weetwood', white, flushed purple at the base, with a yellow reverse striped silvery green; and 'White Pim', pure white with a purple-flushed centre and a dusky pink reverse striped grey-purple.

To knee high. Hardy, z8–10. Sharply drained, light, open-textured, not-too-fertile soils in full sun.

Pachyphragma
Brassicaceae

There is more to the cabbage family than just winter greens, *Pachyphragma macrophyllum* being a case in point. In Turkey and the Caucasus it forms carpets on the floor of beech woodland, and it makes perfect low-line cover beneath shrubs and trees in cultivation. It produces broad corymbs of sparkling white flowers in spring, the earliest of which coincide with the snowdrops; it is very satisfactory to have such clean white flowers shining in dappled spring sunlight, I find. The glossy, rounded, dark green leaves unfurl and overlap to create dense cover by late spring; thereafter, they remain in good order until the first really cold weather. In milder climates, it is almost evergreen.

Ankle to calf high. Fully hardy, z7–9. Humus-rich, moisture-retentive soil in dappled shade or shade.

◀ *Osteospermum* hybrid (front) with *Perovskia atriplicifolia*

◀ *Pachyphragma macrophyllum*

Phlox

Polemoniaceae

Low lines in the genus *Phlox* are to be had from those that inhabit dry, rocky places, such as *P. bifida* (sand phlox), *P. douglasii*, and *P. subulata* (mountain phlox), as well as from woodland denizens like the stem-rooting *P. divaricata* and *P. stolonifera*. The first group generally have denser habits than the latter. Those from rocky habitats have enormous tolerance for hot, dry, sunny conditions—gravel gardens, sunny banks, hot borders, containers, terraces—while those from the woods will put up with more shade and enjoy moister soils.

Breeders who understand the charm of the massed small starry flowers, which are borne over long periods in spring and early summer, are increasingly hybridizing species to produce sturdy garden plants that tolerate both dry sun and damp shade; the stalwart, bright purple *P. ×procumbens* (*P. stolonifera* × *P. subulata*) was one of the earliest. The resultant forms of *Phlox* range in colour from pure white or pale lavender in *P. bifida*, through to soft pinks and lavenders in *P. subulata* and *P. douglasii* 'Rosea'; both *P. divaricata* 'Dirigo Ice' and *P. stolonifera* 'Blue Ridge' have flowers of that clear pale blue that gleams in twilight and moonlight. Cultivars also come in a spectrum of stronger colours: crimson, *P. douglasii* 'Red Admiral' and *P. subulata* 'Late Red'; violet-pink in *P. douglasii* 'Boothman's Variety'; and deep violet-purple in *P. douglasii* 'Violet Queen'. Some are honey-scented and all are attractive to bees, moths and butterflies. Long beloved by rock gardeners, they also make good ground cover elsewhere in the garden; clip after blooming to keep the evergreen foliage tight.

Barely ankle high. Fully hardy, z6–10, *P. bifida*; z2–9, *P. douglasii*; z3–9, *P. subulata*; z4–9, *P. divaricata*, *P. ×procumbens* and *P. stolonifera*. Well-drained, moderately fertile soil in sun; moist but well-drained soil in light shade for the woodlanders. See also pages 126 (Verticals and Diagonals) and 222 (Clumps and Mounds).

▶ *Phlox douglasii* 'Rosea'

▶ *Phlox stolonifera* 'Blue Ridge'

Ptelea

Rutaceae ▪ hop tree

Ptelea trifoliata, wafer ash, is a low, wide-spreading, rather shrubby tree that occurs as an understorey in damp and rocky limestone woods from eastern and central North America into Mexico. It has a natural tendency to be multi-stemmed, and left to its own devices is a rather picturesque species for native and naturalistic plantings; its flowers provide nectar for beneficial insects and its fruit food for birds and small mammals. But with early training to a short single trunk, it develops sinuous tiers of trifoliate, lustrous dark green leaves, delineated in early summer by corymbs of tiny starry, yellow-green flowers, and in autumn by clusters of wafer-like fruits, similar to those of elm. It has a quiet rather than extravagant beauty, but given a sheltered spot, in a small garden or in a container in a courtyard for instance, its fragrance is extraordinary, a compound of musk, orange blossom and vanilla, strongest in the flowers but present also in the leaves and bark.

◀ *Pulmonaria* OPAL
'Ocupol'

◀ *Ptelea trifoliata*

▶ *Pulmonaria angustifolia*
'Azurea'

▶ *Pulmonaria officinalis*
'Sissinghurst White'

Fully hardy, z3–9. Any moderately fertile, well-drained soil in sun, dappled, or part-day shade. Tolerant of hard pruning and shaping, in late winter-early spring.

Pulmonaria

Boraginaceae • lungwort

Found in a range of damp, wooded and often montane habitats from Europe to western Asia, the most useful, rhizomatously spreading pulmonarias form low carpets of evergreen or briefly deciduous foliage. Of moderate vigour—seldom rampant—they're perfect ground cover for wild and woodland gardens, grassy banks, between shrubs, at the margins of tree canopies, and shady borders. The foliage of evergreens is renewed after flowering, and if the old is clipped away as the new emerges, those with marked or spotted leaves give useful if low-key interest for much of the year.

The flowers are a valuable nectar source for bees emerging from dormancy and most bloom over a prolonged spring period. The earliest are red-flowered *P. rubra*, and *P. rubra* 'Redstart', though I find the reds rather muddy. The genus does, however, provide some of the most intense blue flowers, often emerging pink then turning deep blue or violet-blue at maturity. Particularly strong blues are found in *P. angustifolia* 'Azurea', *P. angustifolia* 'Blue Ensign', *P. a.* 'Cotton Cool' with glistening silver leaves, *P.* 'Lewis Palmer' with silver-spotted leaves and *P. longifolia* 'Bertram Anderson' with very narrow silver-spotted leaves. *Pulmonaria longifolia* subsp. *cevennensis* is late flowering, with good drought and sun tolerance. Choose the paler-flowered sorts for a more telling glow in the gloaming: *P.* OPAL 'Ocupol', *P. officinalis* 'Sissinghurst White' and *P. officinalis* 'White Wings', with pink-eyed white flowers.

Ankle high plus. Fully hardy, z4–8. Light or dappled shade and leafy, moderately fertile, moisture-retentive soil.

Puschkinia

Hyacinthaceae/Liliaceae

In the wild the charming tiny bulbs of *Puschkinia scilloides* range through montane meadows and stony places from Turkey to the Lebanon, flowering there at snowmelt. Planted en masse in the garden, they make pale blue rivulets of early colour in spring, an anchoring line beneath shrubs and trees, in borders, and outlining paving slabs where they naturalize by self-sowing into the interstices of sunny terraces. Like many of the small bulbs from their neck of the woods, they flower best after a dry summer rest, and their tolerance of light shade fits them well to plantings beneath shrubs where they are protected from summer rains.

Ankle high. Fully hardy, z4–6. Humusy, well-drained soil in sun or light shade.

Sanguinaria

Papaveraceae ▪ bloodroot, red puccoon

From rich wooded habitats east of the North American Rockies, in similar conditions to those of *Jeffersonia*, bloodroot is from the same maker's mould in terms of low lines in the garden. *Jeffersonia* and *Sanguinaria canadensis* also share a particular beauty in the way the folded, glaucous, blue-grey leaves emerge in spring, in *Sanguinaria* unwrapping to reveal the glistening, bowl-shaped, pristine white flowers. It will naturalize and form colonies, where suited, spreading by means of fleshy rhizomes, although the leaves will disappear by late summer. Plant in a naturalistic wild or woodland planting, or in a shady border

Sanguinaria looks especially good cohabiting with hepaticas, the woodland phlox, *Phlox divaricata*, and with the arching, upright stems of Solomon's seal, *Polygonatum biflorum*. In

◀ *Puschkinia scilloides*

▶ *Sanguinaria canadensis* f. *multiplex* 'Plena'

the double-flowered variants, *S. canadensis* f. *multiplex* or its cultivar 'Plena', what you lose in simple grace you gain in a longer blooming period. Although long in the pharmacopoeia of natural and native medicines, the juicy latex of the root is caustic, toxic and totally unsuitable for self-medication.

Ankle high. Fully hardy, z2–8. Humus-rich, leafy, moist but well-drained soil in dappled shade or shade.

Stachys

Lamiaceae

Few plants are so pleasurably tactile as the woolly species of *Stachys*. They have thick leaves of substantial texture and are more or less clothed throughout—leaves, flower stems and flowerheads—in soft, dense white hair. *Stachys byzantina*, lambs' ears, is a stalwart of the traditional border front for good reason; more than simply an excellent dense edger, its neutral grey-green-silver hues and fine textures offset and enhance plants of more brilliant colour. It is in leaf throughout the season and it hums with bees in summer when in bloom. Most woolly *Stachys* species occur in open, dry, rocky, scrubby and montane habitats and are equally adaptable to sunny banks and gravel and coastal gardens.

Stachys byzantina and most of its cultivars form low, ground-hugging mats of foliage with determinedly vertical, knee-high spikes of pink-purple flowers; *S. byzantina* 'Big Ears' is among the most satisfactory for its large leaves and silky texture. Non-flowering forms, such as *S. b.* 'Silver Carpet', and *S. b.* 'Cotton Boll', which hides 'bolls' of white-woolly flowers amid the foliage, give a more linear effect, as do *S. candida*, with purple-marked white flowers, which is altogether smaller and lower, and *S. citrina* with velvety leaves in soft lime green.

Ankle to knee high. Fully hardy, z4–10; z5–10 for *S. candida*, and *S. citrina* given excellent drainage. Well-drained soil in full sun; the higher the light levels the whiter the leaves. Keep

▶ *Stachys byzantina* 'Big Ears'

▶ *Stachys byzantina*

foliage compact, neat and clean by cutting back hard once growth is underway in spring.

Styrax

Styracaceae ▪ snowbell, storax

The Asian species of snowbell include some of the most singularly elegant and graceful deciduous small trees, with a distinctively tiered branch structure from which, in late spring or early summer, depend the sweetly scented clusters of delicate, bell-shaped white flowers that give rise to the common name. In *S. japonicus* the slender

◀ *Styrax japonicus*

◀ *Thymus ×citriodorus* 'Aureus'

▼ *Thymus pulegioides* 'Bertram Anderson'

branches spread widely from a short trunk to form open, almost fan-shaped tiers; *S. hemsleyanum* and *S. obassia*, the big-leaved storax, are more substantial species with bigger leaves and larger flowers; their scent is redolent of hyacinths, and they often have good autumn colour. (Although equally beautiful, the tiered habit is less marked in *S. americanus*, because it tends to be multi-stemmed.) These species of *Styrax* are woodlanders by nature; beautiful specimens for woodland gardens, they positively thrive in the company of other trees that provide the necessary side shelter from dry cold winds.

Grows slowly to five or six times head height. Fully hardy, z5–9; z6–10, *S. obassia*. Deep, leafy, humus-rich, moisture-retentive and lime-free soil in light dappled shade.

Thymus

Lamiaceae ▪ thyme

Almost without exception the thymes are low-growing, aromatic, small-leaved and fine-textured evergreens, with subshrubby species from dry, rocky habitats, and creeping ones from high altitudes and fine, frequently grazed grassland, often on limy substrates. All are drought-tolerant sun lovers, with nectar-rich flowers, in white and shades of pink and purple. They are exceptionally attractive to bees of all sorts—I've counted as many as two dozen bees per square metre. Thymes can be induced to flower repeatedly throughout summer by sequential clipping or brusque deadheading, and this also ensures a dense tapestry of new foliage in colours ranging from deep green (*T. herba-barona*, *T. polytrichus*) to gold (*T. ×citriodorus* 'Aureus' and 'Golden King', *T. pulegioides* 'Bertram Anderson') and silvery grey-greens (*T.* 'Fragrantissimus', *T. vulgaris* 'Silver Posie'). All of the sunny spots in my garden—dry slopes, sunny banks, paving crevices, rock walls, herb garden and border fronts—abound with them.

The subshrubs, such as *T. ×citriodorus* (lemon thyme), *T. vulgaris* (garden thyme) and their many cultivars, are really mound-formers,

but they are of such short stature that they give effective horizontals when mass-planted. The real flat-liners are the creeping species that seldom achieve a height greater than the sole of your shoe, and these I use wherever they may be trodden upon gently, so that they release clouds of fragrance as you pass. They include: *T. caespititius*, with dark green leaves and pale pink or white flowers; *T.* Coccineus Group, with dark green leaves and deep pink flowers; *T.* 'Doone Valley' with gold-spotted, olive green foliage and lavender flowers; *T. serpyllum* 'Pink Chintz', with grey-green leaves and pink flowers; *T. serpyllum* 'Snowdrift', with bright green leaves and prolific pure white flowers; and *T. serpyllum* 'Russetings', with bronzed leaves and clear pink blooms.

Thymus praecox, with dark green leaves and mauve flowers, and *T. serpyllum*, with purple flowers, are creeping species most often associated with grazed grassland; they will naturalize in fine turf in the garden. The silver-grey *T. pseudolanuginosus* (woolly thyme) needs good drainage, which can be achieved by planting it up to its neck in gravel and between paving stones.

Ground level to ankle high. Fully hardy, z4/5–9. Full sun, well-drained, neutral to slightly limy soil.

Viburnum
Caprifoliaceae

The genus *Viburnum* includes some one hundred and fifty species of fragrant-flowering, fruiting, autumn-colour shrubs, many of immense grace and beauty in habit. If life were tough enough to restrict me to a single genus, *Viburnum* would be it. And if I could only have one…it would probably be *Viburnum plicatum* f. *tomentosum*, the living epitome of the horizontal line. All cultivars of this form have a horizontally tiered branch habit that becomes more pronounced with maturity. This horizontal habit is strongly delineated during the plants' early summer blooming, when the flat, creamy

▲ *Viburnum plicatum* f. *tomentosum* 'Shasta'

▼ *Viburnum plicatum* f. *tomentosum* 'Mariesii'

white lacecap flowers are arranged in a double rank along the top of the branches. The leaves are bright green and neatly and deeply veined, turning rich maroon-red and purple in autumn; the fruits are red, then black—and readily consumed by birds. I concur with the often-heard recommendation to site specimens where they can be viewed from above, so that successive tiers appear to be clothed in cutwork lace, but I also love when they are sited to emphasize the horizontal lines of steps or terraces.

Among the older cultivars of *V. plicatum* f. *tomentosum*, 'Mariesii' is supreme; 'Lanarth' is more vigorous but less decidedly tiered; 'Rowallane' is less vigorous but fruits more freely.

One of the very best is *V. plicatum* f. *tomentosum* 'Shasta', bred at the United States National Arboretum in Washington, D.C. in 1970 by crossing well-formed *V. plicatum* f. *tomentosum* with 'Mariesii' to create a remarkably horizontal form; it is so free-flowering that the very leaves and branches are almost obscured by huge white blooms. *Viburnum plicatum* 'Shoshoni' is a 'Shasta' seedling suitable for smaller spaces, reaching only to chest high but flowering and fruiting equally profusely.

Head high or above. Fully hardy, z5–8. Any reasonably fertile, well-drained soil in sun or part-day shade.

▲ *Viola odorata*

Viola

Violaceae

I have never had a garden without violas. As a child I loved pansies, those legion hybrids with round, painted and whiskered faces that are grouped under *V.* ×*wittrockiana* and used mainly for seasonal bedding. I still love them, but in terms of permanence and versatility in cultivation, and in search of long low lines for my borders, I turn to the true violets, the violas and violettas.

While the Wittrockian pansies generally have a single-stemmed root system and a sprawling habit, and are essentially short-term plants, the violets, violas, and the dainty violettas have branching roots or creeping stolons below ground, with evergreen leaves, short-jointed stems and a neat compact habit above; this lends greater permanence and good cover… with a good tolerance of cutting back to keep them compact. In addition, they have smaller, more delicate flowers than pansies, and nearly all have a sweet heady fragrance—not only in bloom. On a sleepless night, go out into the cool dark and stand among them; the cloud of scent that emanates from the foliage of violets is heavenly. Planted beneath the Old Roses, with philadelphus and pinks, you'll wish you could bottle the perfume.

Species violas such as *V. odorata*, sweet violet, and its hybrids are nearly all spring flowering, although they retain their aromatic foliage through most of the year. *Viola cornuta* and its cultivars (with narrower petals and long-oval faces), the hybrid violas and violettas, bloom from early spring through summer and autumn. Some reliable and especially fragrant favourites among the hybrids of *Viola* include 'Ardross Gem', blue and gold; 'Columbine', white striped violet-blue; 'Etain' soft yellow flushed lavender; 'Eastgrove Blue Scented', rich lilac-blue, vigorous; 'Huntercombe Purple', deep purple; and 'Maggie Mott', silvery mauve-blue. Among the violettas are *Viola* 'Beatrice', pure white, dainty; 'Fabiola', lavender-blue, prolific; 'Little David', creamy white, slightly frilly petals; and 'Rebecca', cream and deep lavender blue. Finally, among the *Viola cornuta* cultivars are the white flowered Alba Group; 'Belmont Blue', pale sky blue, vigorous; 'Brimstone', cream and slate blue; and 'Kitten', pale blue with dark blue whiskers.

Ankle high. Fully hardy, z7–9. Moisture-retentive, humus-rich, well-drained soil in sun, dappled, or part day shade with a cool root run. Deadhead regularly to sustain blooming. Cut back in midsummer, or when foliage becomes straggly.

▲ *Viola cornuta* Alba Group with *Holcus mollis* 'Albovariegatus'

Verticals and Diagonals

◀ Rudbeckia maxima

The eye seizes upon the tension of a vertical line and exaggerates its dimensions. When the vertical is simple, as in a singular skyward thrust of cardiocrinums, hollyhocks, verbascums or the slender white stems of birches, it becomes an effective punctuation mark, arresting the eye as it moves through a scheme. The most elegantly minimalist compositions may be achieved by balancing and contrasting a vertical line with a horizontal one, satisfying the eye's desire for visual completeness, thus making a perfect focal point. Conversely, when used repetitively it's the simplest way of bringing a rhythmic backbone to a scheme—a rhythm that the eye happily follows.

But in a plant composition, where the aim is to create a tapestry of contrasting and complementary lines and forms, the vertical need not be stark and simple. A lightly etched series of verticals, as provided by the massed blooms of actaeas, or by wall-grown *Aconitum lycoctonum* where the flower spikes provide softer lines at greater height, may be what your picture needs.

The diagonal line gives a more dynamic effect; being less stable to the eye as it falls from the vertical, it lends a sense of motion. It also acts as a transitional line, linking the vertical and horizontal and makes a strong contrast to smoother, rounder forms. Those plants with stiff fans or ascending rosettes of firm, broadly sword-shaped leaves—the phormiums and yuccas, for instance—can make exceptional accent plants simply because their particularly strong diagonals offer great opportunity for telling contrasts. Here, the line is most effective when not jostled too closely by softer neighbours. Conversely, where more subtle and refined

▶ *Acanthus hungaricus*

◀ *Acanthus hirsutus*

◀ *Acanthus spinosus*
Spinosissimus Group
with *Hosta* 'Halcyon'

diagonals are needed to lend dynamism to softer, more blended contrasts, plants with sheaves of swords, such as crocosmias, agapanthus and hemerocallis, will give the effect you want.

Acanthus

Acanthaceae ▪ bear's breeches

Forming classically architectural mounds of large, sumptuously glossy, deeply cut, lobed and toothed leaves in darkest green, usually armed at the teeth with glassy spines, acanthus bear terminal flower spikes as straight and upright as soldiers. The two-lipped flowers, with spined, hooded, dusky maroon or purple bracts, are borne in close prickly ranks on the stem—ranked with military precision in *A. hungaricus*, which is scented of roses. The leaves of *A. spinosus* are cut to the midribs; in *A. spinosus* Spinosissimus Group, the more dissected, greyish green leaves have white marginal spines and gleaming white midribs. Both *A. hungaricus* and *A. spinosus* Spinosissimus Group are waist to chest high; *A. spinosus* is taller. They flower between early summer and midsummer, but seedheads persist into winter, which relieves you, for a while at least, of the pain of cutting them back (the Greek *akanthe* means thorn). They hold their own with shrubs and other substantial perennials, the dark mounds of foliage associating well with silver-leaved giants such as *Cynara cardunculus*.

From dry, rocky places around the Mediterranean, they are imperious colonizers if given a rich diet of fertile soils, but if well fed are less than obliging in their flowering. Tolerant of partial and dappled shade, and sometimes used as ground cover in woodland gardens, they flower best in full sun. This applies especially to the engagingly hirsute knee-high *A. hirsutus*, which has soft spines and lucent spires of creamy yellow flowers with large, downy, golden green bracts. It lacks stolons and stays put as an erect clump.

Knee to head high. Fully hardy, z6/7–10. Any deep, well-drained, moderately fertile soil in full sun.

Acer

Aceraceae ▪ maple

Where you want to use tree boles as a vertical line, the acers include several small deciduous trees that suit, with exquisite reinforcement of line in the exceptionally beautiful bark. For instance, *Acer griseum*, with peeling, russetty orange-brown bark, is wonderful as a backlit specimen and fabulous amid the glowing autumn colours of *Cercis* and *Cotinus*. All of the maples described here give gorgeous autumn colour.

The snake bark maples include *A. capillipes* with sinuous striations and patterning of small diamonds in tones of green, jade and silvery white; *A. davidii*, with silver striations on a more olivine green ground; and *A. grosseri* var. *hersii*, with marbled striations in grey, green and silver, which gleams when wet. There are also more compact forms: the upright and delicate *A. davidii* 'Cantonspark', with purplish green and silvery white striations; the erect *A. davidii* 'Madeline Spitta', with salmon pink young shoots; and *A. davidii* 'Serpentine', with red-purple young shoots, the same colour outlining the silver and green striations on older growth. In *A. pensylvanicum* 'Erythrocladum' young shoots are intensely red-pink, and older bark has silver-white striations on an orange-red ground.

For a good vertical line, train to a single leader with a clear stem to about head height,

◀ *Acer griseum*

◀ *Acer capillipes*

◀ *Acer pensylvanicum* 'Erythrocladum'

Verticals and Diagonals

◀ *Acer grosseri* var. *hersii*

◀ *Acer davidii* 'Serpentine'

A. davidii, A. davidii 'Serpentine' and A. grosseri var. hersii, and more ascending in A. davidii 'Cantonspark' and 'Madeline Spitta', A. griseum and A. pensylvanicum 'Erythrocladum'. Alternatively, grow snake barks as multi-stemmed trees—more bark for your buck.

Fully hardy, z4–8, A. griseum, A. pensylvanicum; z5–9, A. capillipes, A. davidii, A. grosseri var. hersii. Fertile, moist but well-drained soil in dappled light or sun.

Aconitum
Ranunculaceae • monkshood

Aconitums are erect herbaceous perennials with tall stems clothed in shallowly or palmately lobed dark green leaves that diminish in size towards the top of the stem, with vertical racemes or panicles of flower above them. Blooming takes place in early summer for Aconitum 'Ivorine', mid- to late summer for A. ×cammarum, A. lycoctonum and A. 'Spark's Variety', and late summer to autumn for A. carmichaelii and A. 'Stainless Steel'. The flowers have sepals like a hooded cowl, hence the common name of monkshood, with petals diminished to the status of nectaries that the bees don't have to see in order to find.

Aconitum 'Ivorine' at waist height, has dense racemes of ivory white that bleach in too much sun, but glow ethereally in semi-shade, looking splendid with corrugated hostas such as H. 'Lady Isobel Barnett', or the lime greens of Syrnium perfoliatum.

Aconitum lycoctonum subsp. vulparia, with pale yellow flowers, and A. l. subsp. lycoctonum, with creamier flowers, are inclined to sprawl, although flower spikes remain erect. They are most charming when supported in boho-chic style; grow on a fan of canes and string against a wall, for a semi-transparent screen of foliage etched in series of vertical spires.

Later-flowering aconitums come in range of blues; the erect branching panicles of A. ×cammarum 'Bicolor' are blue and white, and in A. 'Spark's Variety' intense violet-blue. Aconitum

gradually clearing the bole over four to five years. Take off laterals when they're about pencil thick, when fully dormant, to minimize scarring. Let the crown branch naturally from the desired stem height. The line of the crown is gently arching and spreading in A. capillipes,

◀ *Aconitum lycoctonum* subsp. *lycoctonum* with wall-trained rose

▶ *Aconitum carmichaelii* 'Arendsii'

◀ *Aconitum* 'Stainless Steel'

▶ *Aconitum xcammarum* 'Bicolor'

'Stainless Steel' has blue-grey foliage and spikes of pale glistening metallic blue flowers.

In *A. carmichaelii* 'Arendsii' the stems are sturdy and panicle branches ascending, giving a strong line in a most exquisite blue that is perfect with *Nepeta govaniana* and the paler yellow daisies of *Anthemis tinctoria*. The flowers are held closely and densely on the spike; it's the only one that I dare not to stake.

The rest need support. Twiggy pea sticks soon become invisible and it's worth the effort to maintain a good line. Alternatively, make an

issue of it, and create sculptural supports that are meant to be seen.

Waist to chest high. Fully hardy, z3–9. Humus-rich, retentive but well-drained soils in dappled shade or part-day sun, avoiding hot midday sun. A cool moist site suits them best.

Actaea
Ranunculaceae

The actaeas described here were formerly included in *Cimicifuga*, and if botanical classification had anything to do with ornamental

virtue, most would have remained there as they are more attractive than those that have always been actaeas. Although several have flower spikes that are sinuous or arching at the tip, their stems are strongly erect. The basal foliage forms mounds of long-stalked leaves divided into lobed and jaggedly cut leaflets, which make an elegant foil for other plantings early in the season. They wait until late summer and autumn before they send flowering stems rocketing upwards in spike-like racemes of tiny starry flowers, each with a prominent brush of pale stamens. Many have a honeyed scent.

Actaea japonica reaches waist high by late summer and early autumn, with erect bottle-brush wands of scented white flowers. *Actaea matsumerae* 'White Pearl' is taller and very free flowering, bearing dense bottlebrush spikes of white flowers that arch at the tip. They are luminous in shady places and are not dependent on good light to develop foliage colour—always green.

The chest-high *A. simplex*, white-flowered and green-leaved, has a slight purple flush that hints at latent possibilities. It has spawned the darkling race *A. simplex* Atropurpurea Group. Even those immune to the Gothic can be seduced by them. 'Brunette' was one of the earliest selections, with mahogany purple foliage, and deep purple stems bearing slightly sinuous racemes of purple-flushed white flowers. Two of the darkest include the fine 'James Compton' with bronzed, almost black leaves and dense, dark-stemmed racemes of highly scented white flowers. 'Hillside Black Beauty', so dark a purple as to be almost black, the effect enhanced by the matte surface of the leaves, has flowers of white, flushed pink. 'Black Negligee' is the sultriest of all, even if it won't win the feminist vote. The lacy foliage is green at first, gradually darkening to black, and with black-purple stems holding aloft purple-tinted white flowers.

Don't immediately think you've been sold a pup if the leaves emerge green. Several dark-leaved variants develop intense colour only

with maturity and in bright light. This makes them more versatile than the green-leaved forms, for they will associate with plants that are not committed shade lovers—they can look wonderful with red-flushed sedums such as *S.* 'Matrona', and *Angelica gigas*, and do well in conditions similar to those enjoyed by astilbes and *Athyrium niponicum* var. *pictum*.

Fully hardy, z3–8. Reliably moist but well-drained, humus-rich soils in light dappled shade or bright indirect light.

▲ *Agapanthus* 'Midnight Blue' with *Perovskia*

Agapanthus

Alliaceae

At one time, agapanthus aficionados who gardened in areas with proper winters were confined to the Headbourne Hybrids, whose original grace was long ago diluted by inferior seedlings. Otherwise we grew tender ones in urns, breaking our backs to scuttle them inside at the faintest hint of frost.

There has been a flood of introductions since then, the hardiest being deciduous perennials with strap-shaped, slightly bloomed green leaves and tall stems bearing open umbels of bell- or trumpet-shaped flowers in a colour range from pure white to deepest blue. Even the evergreens, held to be less hardy, overwinter with a mulch around the crown. Some are compact cultivars, such as *Agapanthus* 'Midnight Blue', in dark violet-blue, at about knee height. At mid thigh there is the violet-blue *A.* 'Ben Hope'; 'Black Pantha', deep violet-blue on very dark stems; 'Back in Black', almost black stems with black buds opening to deep blue-purple; and *A.* 'Timaru', vibrant caerulean blue. *Agapanthus* 'Loch Hope', violet-blue, and 'Underway', mid blue, are chest to head high.

They give a vertical or a diagonal line, for even when they fall from the upright they lean rather than arch. I grow them in mixed and herbaceous borders, with hostas, irises, and silver-leaved mound-formers such as santolina and lavender. Even when tall, their stems are so slender, and the umbels so open that agapanthus can be brought to the fore.

Fully hardy, Z7–11. Full sun, in moderately fertile, moisture-retentive but well-drained soil. Give a deep dry mulch in winter in their first year, annually thereafter in cold areas.

Agastache

Lamiaceae • giant hyssop

As denizens of dry habitats, on sunny slopes where natural drainage is unimpeded, agastaches are hardier than expected—as long as they are given excellent drainage in gardens. They're perfect for gravel gardens and sunny banks or borders, where from midsummer to autumn they buzz with bees, and in the right neighbourhood are animated by hummingbirds. All have spires of two-lipped flowers, in clear colours subtly shaded by darker calyces, and the etching of successive vertical lines, which rise above the foliage mounds, will draw the eye into and along the rhythm of a composition, especially when used in long narrow drifts.

Agastache foeniculum, anise hyssop, forms a leafy, aromatic basal mound of anise-scented foliage, the dense spikes of blue flowers with violet calyces rising to between waist and chest height; *A. foeniculum* 'Alabaster' and 'Alba'

▲ *Agapanthus* 'Back in Black'

▲ *Agapanthus* 'Timaru'

Agastache foeniculum at the front of a border

Agastache cana

Agastache 'Blue Fortune' with *Aster ×frikartii*

have white flowers. Candidates at mid thigh to waist high include grey-leaved *A. cana* with soft raspberry pink flowers, and *A. c.* 'Cinnabar Rose', pink with cinnamon undertones. *A.* 'Blue Fortune' is exceptionally long flowering, from late spring or early summer to late summer, with large blue-lavender spikes; spikes of

A. 'Black Adder' are dark stemmed, dense with dark buds, then a good violet-blue. *Perovskia atriplicifolia* will echo their line, a drift of airy *Verbena bonariensis* will emphasize it, and gauzy panicles of *Pennisetum alopecuroides* will provide an airy halo.

Fully hardy, z5–9. Perfectly well-drained, not-too-fertile soil in full sun. Incorporate coarse sand or grit to improve drainage, and site on a slope if you can.

Alcea

Malvaceae ▪ hollyhock

The tall spires of hollyhocks are cottage garden essentials. For me, they evoke the classic image of a white-painted hive surrounded by them—for, as William Robinson wrote in *The English Flower Garden* (1883), "Bee Keepers would do well to grow a few, for bees are fond of their flowers." The vertical lines are strongest in those with single flowers, with a lustre of silk-satin that isn't obscured by ruffles as in the peony-flowered doubles grown as biennials in order to subdue their inbred martyrdom to hollyhock rust. The species *A. ficifolia*, *A. rosea* and *A. rugosa* are less susceptible to rust; all self-sow, so there are always younger and stronger plants coming along, prolonging flowering to midsummer or later. They occur in rocky places on stony hills, and on the steppes of the Ukraine, southern Russia and Siberia, and some of the most successful plantings are in leaner soils in gravel gardens, on perfectly drained banks and in borders.

Alcea ficifolia has widely funnel-shaped yellow flowers, often soft primrose, sometimes with a wash of pink or maroon; *A. rosea* may have blooms in white, pink or purple, the deepest shade being the chocolate-maroon of *A. rosea* 'Nigra'. *Alcea rugosa* has satin flowers in deep yellow or pale orange. All have rough-textured, lobed and conspicuously veined, rather pale green leaves, and stout-stemmed terminal flower spikes, studded with button buds opening from bottom to top and easily reaching

Alcea ficifolia with verbascum

Alcea rosea 'Nigra'

head height or above. Grown hard, they're less towering but less likely to fall over. They're perfect companions for *Verbascum olympicum* and perovskia for repetition of the line, and with the arching mounds and spikes of cardoon, *Cynara cardunculus*, for contrast in form. Should any unattractive stubbly shins develop, disguise them—perhaps with *Nigella damascena* or *Coreopsis verticillata* 'Moonbeam'.

Head height and above. Fully hardy, z3–10. Full sun in well-drained soil.

Allium

Alliaceae

The ornamental members of the onion family are among the most useful of all hardy bulbs, without qualification. Unlike many bulbs, the leaves of alliums have usually withered by flowering time, the remnants easily disguised by companions. They seldom fade disgracefully; nearly all have ornamental seedheads.

The globe-flowered alliums are among the finest of punctuation marks: straight strong stems, with a sphere of starry flowers on top, which may be a hand span across (*A. aflatunense*, *A.* ×*hollandicum*), two hand spans (*A. cristophii*, *A.* 'Globemaster') or even four (*A. schubertii*). When planted in odd numbers throughout a composition, it's like threading a ribbon with points of colour to unify a scheme, to introduce a subsidiary rhythm, or to create a series of different incidents and associations. Interplanted with a hedge of lavender, for instance, they bring rhythm and repetition to an otherwise uninterrupted line. They reinforce the verticals of other plants, as when they rise to meet the cascading chains of laburnum, or echo the verticillasters of *Phlomis russeliana*. They are perfect counterpoints to the strongly mounded forms of blue fescues, *Festuca glauca* and its variants, and santolinas, or they can balance the horizontal platters of achilleas. They pierce and make more emphatic any transparency—of grasses, such as *Stipa tenuissima*, the lacework of the umbellifers, such as *Chaerophyllum*, or the translucency of love-in-a-mist, *Nigella damascena*. And they add detail to the erect or mounded clumps of silver and grey, as with *Artemisia ludoviciana* or *A*. 'Powys Castle'.

The nodding alliums, such as *A. cernuum* and *A. carinatum*, have straight stems that terminate in loose umbels, an array of many small nodding bells on pedicels of varying length—tiny cascades. They tend to clump up more rapidly than the globes, giving similar but more diffuse effects in more naturalistic and informal plantings. They are especially beautiful lending a little weight to transparent textures, or in creating strong textural contrasts when nodding above or through the fleshy leaves of sedums, for instance. Similar effects can be achieved with the globes with less dense inflorescences, such as *A. cristophii*, with heads of metallic purple stars, and the magnificent *A. schubertii*, which has each bloom on a stiff stalk of different length, making a huge metallic pink starburst.

Among the myriad selections available, certain alliums stand out. My choices include:

Allium aflatuenense: rounded umbels of bright pink-purple, waist high, in summer; *A. ×hollandicum* is similar

A. caeruleum: small rounded umbels of clear blue stars, mid thigh high, early summer

A. carinatum subsp. *pulchellum*: dusky purple bell-shaped flowers in nodding umbels, knee high, midsummer

A. cernuum: nodding umbels of deep pink bells, mid thigh high, summer

A. cristophii: large globes of starry, metallic pink-purple, long-stalked flowers, knee to mid thigh high, early summer

A. giganteum: rich lilac-pink globes, summer; lilac-purple *A.* 'Gladiator', waist to chest high, and deep purple *A.* 'Mars' slightly shorter, are similar

A. 'Globemaster': large orbs of deep violet stars, thigh high, summer; *A.* 'Purple Sensation' is similar.

A. schubertii: a huge starburst of metallic pink stars in summer, knee to mid thigh, fading to a stiff, sere, straw-coloured skeleton that persists through winter

A. sphaerocephalon: small, dense ovoid heads in deep pink or maroon, mid thigh, summer

Fully hardy, z4/5–9. Full sun, in any well-drained moderately fertile soil. Plant in autumn, a hand span deep, and give a protective mulch in cold winter zones.

◀ *Allium* 'Globemaster'

◀ *Allium caeruleum*

◀ *Allium carinatum* subsp. *pulchellum*

◀ *Allium cernuum*

▶ *Althaea cannabina*

◀ *Allium* 'Purple sensation'

▼ *Allium giganteum* with *Lilium regale*

Althaea

Malvaceae

Althaea cannabina, Siberian mallow, is strongly erect, tough but delicate-looking. Commonly reaching chest to head height, it seldom needs support. The stems, clothed in lobed, softly hairy, dark green leaves, produce long-stalked axillary clusters of button buds and small, satiny, dark-eyed, lavender-pink flowers over long periods from midsummer to autumn. So airy is it, with so many small flowers on so many wiry stems, that it's almost transparent—but it is determinedly vertical. Excellent in gravel and wild gardens, and in sunny borders, with *Phlomis fruticosa* or mounded artemisias.

Fully hardy, z4–9. Full sun in well-drained soil.

Amsonia

Apocynaceae • blue star

With several species of erect and willowy grace, as handsome in foliage as in flower, *Amsonia* has cymes or panicles of tiny funnel-shaped flowers with an open starry face of five-pointed petals. They come in a range of blues, both leaves and flowers with a faintly perceptible colour wash of grey, which is beautiful with the metallic blues of eryngiums, or the glaucous grey-greens of baptisia and thalictrum.

Amsonia orientalis, from grassy places in Greece and Turkey, produces a mass of wiry, pale stems to mid thigh, clothed in willowy leaves of rich grey green. Each stem terminates

◀ *Amsonia orientalis*

◀ *Amsonia tabernaemontana* var. *salicifolia*

leaves. *Amsonia hubrichtii* forms a billowing mass of waist-high stems set with thread-like leaves that give a sensuously soft texture. Clusters of powder blue flowers appear in spring and early summer, after which leafy stems ascend to their full height.

These amsonias assume golden autumn tints, but need plenty of summer sun and warmth for best colour, and the trigger of cooler nights to produce it; they don't colour well in shade and colour most intensely at more northerly latitudes. Both *A. orientalis* and *A. tabernaemontana* will grow in the dappled light of a woodland garden, but need several hours of sunlight to really thrive; *A. hubrichtii* is best in sun.

Fully hardy, z4–9. Tolerant of a wide range of soils, and surprisingly tolerant of dry soils, but best in a humus-rich, well-drained and moisture-retentive soil.

Anchusa

Boraginaceae

The stunning spire of deep, luminous blue-violet seen by roadsides around the Mediterranean belongs to *Anchusa azurea*, which ranges across Europe to Central Asia, on stony slopes and grassy steppes. It forms a clump of narrow basal leaves in mid green, and in early and midsummer produces upright stems with terminal and axillary clusters of small, open-faced tubular flowers. They open blue, intensifying as they mature, and repeat if cut back after the first flush.

The species can reach a towering head height, which is seldom self-supporting; *A. a.* 'Loddon Royalist' is sturdier and waist high, and rich deep blue. *Anchusa azurea* 'Opal' is also waist high, though paler—a favourite of Gertrude Jekyll. Pale yellows and oranges, whites, silvers and soft pinks make telling contrasts. Anchusas are hopelessly short-lived in heavy clay and in humid heat, and on rich soils they flop horribly.

Fully hardy, z3–8. Full sun, in poor to moderately fertile, deep, open-textured, well-drained soil.

in panicles of deep lavender-blue buds on dark pedicels, opening to a soft grey-blue, in early to midsummer. *Amsonia tabernaemontana* occurs in damp open woodland and on streambanks in eastern North America, and is very similar to *A. orientalis*, with handsome matt dark green leaves on purple stems, and cyme-like panicles of pale blue flowers; *A. tabernaemontana* var. *salicifolia* is more elegant, having narrower

◀ *Anchusa azurea* 'Loddon Royalist' with astrantias

▶ *Anemone ×hybrida* 'Honorine Jobert'

◀ *Anchusa azurea* 'Opal'

▶ *Anemone ×hybrida* 'Konigin Charlotte'

Anemone

Ranunculaceae

The hybrid Japanese anemone, A. ×*hybrida*, has spawned some truly lovely offspring. Their invasive tendencies are entirely forgivable; they tolerate dry soils and shade, never need staking, and are hearty, healthy and vigorous at chest to head height. On top of all this, they flower for up to three months.

Anemone ×*hybrida* forms a ground-covering clump of pointed, three-lobed, dark green leaves, from which emerge sturdy, upright, branching stems bearing umbels of tight, round, silky hairy buds—with the thrill of

▶ *Anemone ×hybrida* 'September Charm'

◀ *Anemone hupehensis* 'Hadspen Abundance'

▶ *Angelica archangelica* behind tarragon and pink-flowered *Geranium psilostemon*

anticipation, and redolent of months of pleasures to come. The open flowers are rounded, semi-double and soft pink, the glistening petals surrounding a tight dome of green carpels and a circlet of golden stamens. *Anemone ×hybrida* 'Honorine Jobert' is single and pure white, 'Luise Uhink' is semi-double and pure white, and 'Géant des Blanches' is a semi-double white with a green-tinted petal reverse. Pink shades range from the semi-double, soft pink of *A. ×hybrida* 'Königin Charlotte', the single pale pinks of 'Max Vogel' and 'September Charm', through to the rose pinks of 'Profusion' and the rich deep pink of 'Margarete'.

Anemone hupehensis 'Hadspen Abundance', which flowers slightly earlier, is intense deep pink with paler petal reverses. There are many more modern cultivars to know and love, but I'm an old-fashioned girl and faithful to first love(s).

Fully hardy, z4/5–8. Fertile, humus-rich, moisture-retentive soil in sun or dappled shade.

Angelica

Apiaceae

When I grew *Angelica archangelica* in the herb garden, I often thought about how statuesque it was and wondered why it wasn't grown as an architectural high point in borders, bog, or woodland gardens. Well, why not? Easily head high, it has wrist-thick stems, large, divided aromatic leaves, and huge domed umbels of tiny green flowers, in early and midsummer, that stand long after blooming. Even if it does die after seeding, there will be plenty of seedlings. It looks cool with big, blue-green hostas or interlaced with foxgloves, *Digitalis*, and complements ethereal blues.

Angelica gigas is chest high and lighter in weight. It has vitreous maroon stems, and huge leaf sheaths, as though of burnished metal (reminiscent of a Karl Blossfeldt photogravure), and each stem branch terminates in an almost spherical umbel of intense maroon-purple from midsummer onwards—splendid with echinaceas, or in a haze of golden grasses. It is a biennial or short-lived perennial; collect the seed, as it doesn't self-sow reliably.

Fully hardy, z4–9. Light dappled shade or part-day sun, in fertile moisture-retentive soil.

Anthericum

Anthericaceae

A grassy-leaved rhizomatous perennial with upright, waist-high spires of starry white flowers, *Anthericum liliago* (St. Bernard's lily) is a native of alpine meadows, blooming in late spring or early summer. Exquisitely delicate, but tough in constitution, it is perfect in the wild

◀ Anthericum liliago

▶ Artemisia ludoviciana
'Silver Queen'

meadow, resembling a white-flowered camassia, although it tolerates drier soils. It is lovely as a pale ethereal thread woven through borders, with dark-leaved companions rather than silver ones—the better to show off its pale beauty.

Fully hardy, z4–9. Fertile, well-drained soil in sun.

Artemisia

Asteraceae

There are three artemisias that I use for a vertical line in mixed plantings, sometimes all three in a unified silver theme. They make excellent textural contrasts with each other, and form a fine-textured, colour-neutral backdrop against which strong magentas, blues and purples are outstanding. *Artemisia ludoviciana* 'Silver Queen' at thigh high, shorter, less floppy, and mercifully less free-flowering than the species, has jagged leaves clothed in fine silver-white down; *A. pontica* has erect woody stems clothed in soft whorls of almost thread-fine, sage green leaves, from knee to thigh high; and the knee-high *A. alba* 'Canescens' has a fine filigree of curling silvery ash-white foliage. The first two are rhizomatous and vigorous, which I mind less in *A. pontica* because the offshoots mingle so well with neighbours. *Artemisia ludoviciana* spreads freely in open-textured soil, and is pulled out by the roots when it transgresses.

▶ Artemisia alba
'Canescens'

I cut it back hard before it flops or flowers; regrowth is fast, and coloured a much more luminous, creamier silver-white.

Fully hardy, z4–9. Full sun in well-drained or sharply drained, not-too-fertile soil. See also pages 44, 183 and 240.

Asclepias

Asclepiadaceae ▪ milkweed, silkweed

Many *Asclepias* species are irresistible to butterflies. The flowers produce copious nectar and, in their native ranges, have an amazing relationship with milkweed butterflies (including the monarch): the flowers manufacture cardiac glycosides, which the butterflies store, making them unpalatable or even toxic to predators.

Most asclepias are suitable for wild gardens.

◀ Asclepias tuberosa

◀ Asclepias incarnata 'Ice Ballet' with astrantias and tradescantias

▼ Baptisia australis

▶ seedpods

unbranched stems clothed in spirals of lanceolate leaves, and with terminal and axillary cymes of golden, hot orange or vermilion flowers. *Asclepias tuberosa* is a larval food source for the monarch butterfly in the United States.

Fully hardy, z3–7. Full sun in fertile, well-drained, open-textured soils. *A. tuberosa* is tolerant of drought and poor dry soils; *A. incarnata* prefers more moisture-retentive soils.

Baptisia

Papilionaceae ▪ false indigo

Indigo blue flowers, in combination with glaucous bluish green leaves on tall, glaucous, vertical stems, are enchanting. *Baptisia australis* is chest high and produces long, packed racemes of pea flowers in early summer. It retains the beauty of its foliage until it seeds, with inflated seedpods in a striking navy blue, later fading to dark grey. But after heavy summer rain you may find stems thrashed to the ground; this is a plant that I always support (with twiggy pea sticks). *Baptisia australis* 'Nelson's Navy' is shorter and with sturdier stems, the indigo flowers several shades darker than the species; *B. a.* 'Caspian Blue' has flowers of dusky blue-indigo, and more definitely blue-green foliage. The species is native to damp soils on riverbanks in the eastern United States.

For more structured plantings, *A. incarnata* has upright stems to chest height, the line enhanced by long narrowly ovate leaves and ascending branches bearing clustered flower cymes at the tip. The flowers are fascinating; pentagonal buds open to soft flesh pink or purple pink (white in 'Ice Ballet'), the petals reflexing to reveal a tiny crown of erect and fleshy appendages at the centre. The seedpods are erect and spindle shaped, splitting to release wind-borne seeds with long silky hairs. Although native to swamps and wet meadows of the eastern United States, it doesn't need, but does thrive in, wet soils, and is usefully late flowering (with astilbes and *Aruncus dioicus*) for a sunny spot in the bog garden or poolside. *Asclepias tuberosa* reaches waist height, with sturdily upright,

Baptisia alba bears white or creamy white flowers in erect spires on smoky grey stems. It's probably the tallest species, to head height, which is ideal when you choose to grow it—as in the wild—among prairie grasses.

Fully hardy, z3–9. Open-textured, deep, well-drained soil in full sun or light part-day shade; *B. australis* prefers more moisture-retentive soils.

Betula

Betulaceae

Most birches have beautiful spring and autumn colour, pretty catkins that emerge before the leaves, a light crown that permits underplanting, and a slender, elegant habit that suits relatively small gardens despite their final height. With their glorious bark they create a strong vertical or diagonal line—strongest when the bark is pale. They can be used as focal specimens when grown as single- or multi-stemmed trees. On the other hand, a series of single-stemmed trees creates rhythm, while an arcade lends perspective. The trees can frame a surprise view, or serve as a reinforcing echo for severely geometric modern architecture.

In *Betula ermanii* the bark is a warm creamy white, faintly pink-flushed like a porcelain complexion, cool and smooth to the touch.

◀ *Betula albosinensis* var. *septentrionalis*

▼ *Betula albosinensis*

▶ *Betula utilis* with *Papaver orientale* 'Patty's Plum', *Polemonium carneum* 'Apricot Delight' and *Digitalis purpurea* 'Sutton's Apricot'

The young bark of *B. albosinensis* shares that creamy colour, with a matt white bloom that later becomes warm, pale russet. In *A. albosinensis* var. *septentrionalis* the russet is suffused with pale red-pink and bloomed soft violet; it is one of the most outstanding of all ornamental barks. Brighter, startling whites are to be had from *B. utilis* var. *jacquemontii*, especially in selected clones, when unblemished whiteness extends even to younger branches. These include *B. utilis* var. *jacquemontii* 'Doorenbos', 'Grayswood Ghost', 'Jermyns' and the relatively compact 'Silver Shadow'.

To develop a clear stem that displays the bark to perfection, it's important that laterals or side-shoots be removed when they're no more than pencil thick, when trees are fully dormant. They bleed heavily if cut when in growth, scar badly if large branches are removed, and are susceptible to fungal infection when so wounded. I have been reprimanded by arborists for peeling back the bark to restore pristine colour to the birches. I do it nevertheless, but with discipline, removing only surface layers of loose old bark in spring. It's so addictive there is a danger of taking it too far; if you expose the cambial layers the tree is vulnerable to infection, and cambial damage in severe cold or drying winds.

Fully hardy, z2–8, *B. ermanii*, z3–8,

B. albosinensis; z4–8, *B. utilis*. Moist but well-drained, moderately fertile soil in sun or dappled shade.

Camassia

Hyacinthaceae • quamash

Occurring in the wild in damp, open meadows at forest margins and on riverbanks in western North America, camassias have narrowly strap-like upright leaves, and erect spires of starry flowers in late spring. They etch my meadows with drifts of blue verticals above spikes of pale yellow cowslips, *Primula veris*. White-flowered camassias, such as *C. leichtlinii* subsp. *leichtlinii*, stand out better in border and woodland plantings than in meadow. At thigh to waist high *C. l.* subsp. *leichtlinii* is the tallest, and in grassy places the blue-violet spires of *C. l.* subsp. *suksdorfii* are more visible. *C. cusickii* is shorter at knee to thigh high, with pale steel or china blue flowers; *C. c.* 'Zwanenburg' is an intense dark blue.

All thrive in dappled light in damp woodland, and in the upper reaches of the bog gar-

▲▲ *Camassia cusickii*

◀ *Camassia cusickii*

▲ *Camassia leichtlinii* subsp. *leichtlinii* with *C. leichtlinii* subsp. *suksdorfii*

den. I find prairie native *C. quamash* to be the toughest and most persistent in my own meadows, better in fine grasses than in rougher ones; it's more tolerant of soils that dry out in summer, and since it comes up in places I haven't planted, it's self-seeding freely.

Fully hardy, z4–8, *C. leichtlinii* subsp. *leichtlinii*, *C. cusickii*; z5–9, *C. quamash*. Full sun, or dappled shade in damp but not stagnant, free-draining, humus-rich soil.

Campanula

Campanulaceae

There is a distinct group within the campanulas that have a particularly erect habit, and I select from them those of some height, with leafless or sparsely leafy stems, and with spires rather than arching sprays of flowers to give a vertical line. *Campanula lactiflora*, at chest to head high, has strong stems that branch at the top,

◀ *Campanula lactiflora*

▶ *Campanula lactiflora*
'Prichard's Variety'
with *Leucanthemum*
×*superbum*

▼ *Campanula persicifolia*
with a drift of *Milium*
effusum 'Aureum'

◀ *Campanula latiloba*

bearing conical panicles of starry flowers in shades of white and blue throughout summer; *C. l.* 'Loddon Anna' is soft lavender pink, 'Prichard's Variety' a deep violet-blue. *Campanula latiloba* has mostly basal leaves, with stout stems to thigh high, topped by tightly studded racemes of stemless, starry lavender blue flowers in mid- to late summer (rich amethyst-pink in *C. latiloba* 'Hidcote Amethyst'). It is similar to the slightly shorter *C. persicifolia*, which flowers from early to midsummer, on wiry, sparsely leafy stems, bearing more open racemes of slightly nodding, open bells in shades of white or lavender blue (clear sky blue in *C. p.* 'Telham Beauty').

Campanula latifolia, the giant bellflower, reaches chest height, the stems bearing slender, spike-like racemes of tubular bells in shades of violet, lavender or white in mid- to late summer. Native to woods, mountain meadows, hedgerows and streambanks, it self-seeds freely and is perfect in more naturalistic plantings in places similar to those in habitat, where its prolific habits are welcome.

Fully hardy, z4/5–9. Moist but well-drained, fertile soils in sun or dappled shade.

Cardiocrinum
Liliaceae ▪ giant lily

The most majestic and covetable of lilies, reaching head height or twice that in ideal conditions, *C. giganteum* hails from moist forests and scrub at altitudes of 1,600 to 3,300 metres (5,250 to 10,825 feet) in the Himalayas to south-western China. The bulbs produce a basal

◀ *Cardiocrinum*
giganteum

▲ *Catananche caerulea*
'Bicolor'

rosette of large, leathery, shining dark green leaves and, at maturity, a dark thick stem bearing intensely fragrant, long-tubed trumpets of lucent creamy white in summer. They're followed by a candelabra of erect seedpods that darken before releasing myriad papery seeds in autumn. Mother bulbs die after flowering but produce offsets, which sustain a colony. Some of the most beautiful stands of cardiocrinums are seen in the lush gardens of Eire; they love cool humidity and near-constant moisture with the shelter of surrounding trees.

Fully hardy, z7–9. A sheltered coolly equable site in dappled shade, in deep, fertile humus-rich soil that is free draining but retentive.

Catananche

Asteraceae ▪ Cupid's dart

A short-lived but self-seeding perennial, *Catananche caerulea* bears silvery daisy flowers on upright, leafless, wiry stems, to thigh high, throughout summer into autumn. In the species, translucent papery bracts enclose pointed buds that open to reveal fringed ray florets in

soft blue or lavender; 'Bicolor' has purple centred white flowerheads. I used to grow them for cutting and drying, and found self-sown seedlings threading through perennials in nearby borders. They are too slender to make impact on their own, but wonderful for weaving through grasses and embroidering other transparents.

Fully hardy, z7–10. Any well-drained soil in sun.

Chelone

Scrophulariaceae ▪ shell flower, turtlehead

Both *C. glabra*, from the eastern and southern United States, and *C. obliqua*, from the central and southeastern States, are denizens of damp habitats like thickets, streambanks, swampy places and moist woods.

Waist-high herbaceous perennials with stout, stiffly upright stems, they bear dense terminal racemes of bearded two-lipped flowers opening from neatly ranked, pointed buds in late summer and autumn. In *C. glabra*, flowers are white or flushed pale lavender-pink, in *C. obliqua* deep pink or rose-purple, above dusky dark green leaves. Providing welcome late colour in the bog garden, in damp borders, or in reliably damp woodland soils, they bloom with actaeas and physostegias and are good contrasting forms against the late astilbes and eupatoriums. The generic name, from the

◀ *Chelone glabra*

▶ *Cortaderia selloana*

▶ *Cortaderia selloana*
'Sunningdale Silver'

▼ *Cortaderia selloana*
'Pumila' (left) with
Miscanthus sinensis
'Silberfeder'

Greek *chelone*, meaning tortoise, reflects the curiously turtlehead-like form of the flower.

Fully hardy, z3–8. Reliably moist, humus-rich soil, including heavy clays, in sun or light dappled shade.

Cortaderia

Poaceae • pampas grass

It wasn't until I saw an avenue planting of *Cortaderia selloana* 'Sunningdale Silver' that I realized how strongly vertical pampas grasses could be. No, it didn't look ghastly—it was magnificent. It was like seeing the grasses anew, their suburban image discarded. Despite being twice head height, and having great presence, it's a waste of good line and terrific texture to use them as lawn specimens. They look wonderful alongside other more arching grasses such as miscanthus, calamagrostis and the taller molinias, and with the open plumes of macleayas.

Cortaderia selloana forms a basal clump of arching, narrow dark green leaves, with margins like razors, and in late summer sprouts long, straight, stiffly erect stems terminating in a huge silky plume of silvery white that is mobile in breeze and lucent in autumn light. 'Rendatleri' has pale pink-purple plumes; 'Pumila' is just head height, with more golden plumes.

Fully hardy, z7–10. Well-drained fertile soil in full sun, with side shelter from strong winds. Wear stout gauntlets (heavy-duty gloves) to cut and comb out dead foliage before new growth resumes in spring. The 'fast burn' technique is dangerous; it risks destroying the growing points.

Crocosmia

Iridaceae • montbretia

While all of the cormous perennials of the genus *Crocosmia* sport diagonal shafts of sword-shaped leaves and beautifully poised, wiry-stemmed spikes of funnel-shaped flowers, there is only *Crocosmia* 'Lucifer' that bears such brazen, hot scarlet-vermilion flowers at chest height. It is often used in hot autumn borders amid ranks of brilliant yellow rudbeckias and heleniums—more of an assault than a colour theme. It associates well with close complementary blues of echinops, and with kniphofias. That 'Lucifer' and other crocosmias look so well among blonde and golden grasses should come as no surprise considering that the parents of the garden hybrids are native to grasslands in South Africa. Softer tones are found among the thigh-high options: *C. ×crocosmiiflora* 'Gerbe d'Or' with lemon yellow flowers, *C. ×c.* 'Lady Hamilton' with yellow and apricot blooms, and *C. ×c.* 'Star of the East' in clear soft apricot orange. *Crocosmia ×crocosmiiflora* 'Solfatare', with dusky olive bronze leaves and apricot flowers, is slightly less hardy, but one of the prettiest—so worth a warm, sunny and sheltered site.

Fully hardy, z5/6–9. Full sun or light dappled shade, in moisture-retentive but well-drained, moderately fertile soil, enriched with humus. Double depth planting, at 15+ cm (6+ inches)

◀ *Crocosmia ×crocosmiiflora* 'Solfatare'

▼ *Crocosmia* 'Lucifer' in a hot border

▶ *Crocosmia ×crocosmiiflora* 'Lady Hamilton' with *Aralia elata* 'Aureovariegata'

◀ *Crocosmia* ×*crocosmiiflora* 'Star of the East'

▶ *Cynara cardunculus*

▶ flowerhead

deep, produces stronger plants, and in cold areas it protects the roots from cold (as does a deep, dry leafy mulch, or a gravel mulch).

Cynara
Asterceae

The cardoon, *Cynara cardunculus*, is, as Graham Stuart Thomas put it in *Perennial Garden Plants* (1976), "one of the most magnificent of all herbaceous plants...the grandest of all silverlings". A vast sheaf of huge, deeply cut leaves ascend and recurve from a stout woody rootstock to form a wonderfully textured fountain mound of fine silvery grey. Between early summer and autumn, stoutly upright grey stems bear a succession of thistle heads, each brush of purple florets subtended by an almost globose involucre of spine-tipped bracts. It is the high point and focal point of the silver border, at head height in flower; its line can be echoed by acanthus, or echoed *and* overtopped by that other silver giant, *Onopordon acanthium*. It is the least difficult plant for which to find admirable associates; anything in blue, magenta, purple or dark red will look striking, providing it has sufficient heft. If you don't have room for the species, *C. cardunculus* 'Candy' is a narrower, chest-high mound, but equally architectural. The thistles are beloved by bumblebees, butterflies, finches and florists. The other *Cynara*, *C. scolymus*, is the globe artichoke, beloved by gourmet gardeners.

Fully hardy, z7–9. Full sun, in deep, moderately fertile well-drained soil, in a site sheltered from strong winds.

Dactylorhiza
Orchidaceae ▪ marsh orchid, spotted orchid

A measure of enchantment surrounds nearly every member of the huge orchid family, but I find none so heartstoppingly thrilling as hardy marsh orchids when I have stumbled upon them growing in habitat. From meadows, heaths and the damp banks of streams or ditches, *Dactylorhiza* species grow in low-fertility, moist but freely draining oils with plenty of humus, in symbiotic association with mycorrhizal soil fungi, which thrive in undisturbed

◀ *Dactylorhiza fuchsii*

◀ *Dactylorhiza elata* with *Matteuccia, Rodgersia* and *Iris sibirica*

◀ *Dactylorhiza foliosa*

natural soils untainted by agricultural fertilizer and fungicides.

At a close second to the thrill of discovering marsh orchids in habitat is the thrill of bringing them into cultivation, and finding them amenable to leafy soils that are reliably moist throughout the growing period, in light dappled shade or part day sun. If your soils are open textured, well aerated, rich in humus and innocent of garden chemicals, as they may be in undisturbed turf, woodland and organic gardens, then they will be rich in beneficial soil fungi, and marsh orchids will happily form colonies by natural multiplication of tubers and by self-seeding. The fungal relationship is not specific and *Dactylorhiza* associate with several species. Many in the trade are micro-propagated and inoculated with mycorrhiza before sale.

Dactylorhiza elata forms dense, knee- to thigh-high spikes of rich purple flowers between late spring and midsummer; *D. foliosa* is similarly robust, with flowers in shades of pink and purple; and *D. fuchsii*, one of the easiest to cultivate and establish in damp sunny meadows, forms shorter, more slender spikes of flowers in shades of pink to deep mauve in spring and early summer.

Fully hardy, z6–9. Do not cut meadow grass between early spring when the basal rosette forms, until after seed set and dispersal.

Darmera

Saxifragaceae ▪ umbrella plant

In the wild a colonizer of streambanks and damp woodland from northwestern California to southwestern Oregon, *Darmera peltata* is a great bank stabilizer for bog gardens and poolsides in cultivation. A slow-creeping perennial forming mats of thick rhizomes, it has two phases of growth. The erect flower stems, naked but for a covering of glistening hair, arise in spring from bare earth, with a single domed cyme of small pink flowers on top. They are followed by mounds of dramatic, almost circular,

deeply lobed, glossy green leaves, which remain handsome until autumn, when they turn red. Each leaf is borne on a stout stem to chest height or more, which is joined at the centre of the leaf; it forms a shallow cup that fills and then tips to shed rainwater. The foliage provides excellent contrast for the divided leaves of rodgersias and actaeas. Provided soils remain adequately moist, it can be grown in dappled woodland shade. The dwarf variant *D. p.* 'Nana' is hardier (z4/5) and, seldom reaching higher than mid thigh, better for small gardens.

Fully hardy, z6–9. Reliably moist humus-rich soil in part day sun or dappled shade.

Delphinium
Ranunculaceae

Unless you intend to grow delphiniums competitively, the most frequently grown Elatum Group hybrids are easygoing perennials that are unequalled in providing strong verticals in herbaceous and mixed borders, asking for little more than a sunny spot in good, fertile, well-drained but moisture-retentive soil, with plenty of organic matter. In relaxed circumstances, the thinning of shoots and fortnightly feeding is unnecessary; the flower spikes will be larger if you do, but almost inevitably the taller ones will then need some formal and obtrusive support. The plants should always be protected from slugs and snails. The Pacific Group, usually raised as annuals or biennials, behave as perennials in cool maritime climates; they look similar but are not as long lived or robust as the Elatums. Neither group thrives in extreme summer temperatures and humidity.

◀ ▲ *Darmera peltata* foliage and flower

▲ *Delphinium* 'Blue Dawn' with bronze fennel and alstroemerias

▶ *Delphinium* Black Knight Group with *Campanula lactiflora*

▼ *Delphinium* 'Butterball'

The long, narrowly conical racemes of cupped flowers, with an eye or 'bee' at the centre, come in several shades of white and all shades of blue from ethereally pale to intense dark-eyed deep purple (also in shades of red, pink and salmon; I don't know why). They are also categorized by size—small, medium, tall—which means head height, just below or above. Use them for an element of repetition, especially in a long border; using paler blues in the far distance grading to darker blues from your viewpoint gives the impression of greater length as the paler colours recede.

Fully hardy, z3–7. Cut back in autumn, when growth has withered.

Dictamnus
Rutaceae • burning bush, dittany

Dictamnus albus is a woody-stemmed perennial with aromatic, pinnately divided, leathery leaves and tall, upright wands of loosely packed, delicate white flowers with long protruding

◀◀ *Dictamnus albus*

◀ *Digitalis purpurea* f. *albiflora*

anthers, from early to midsummer. *Dictamnus albus* var. *purpureus* has dark-veined, mauve-pink flowers with dark stems and pedicels. The whole plant has an aroma redolent of citrus, produced by volatile oils in stems, flowers and especially the seedpods; on hot, still days the vapour can be ignited to a quick flash burn without harming the plant. These oils, as in the herb rue, *Ruta graveolens*, can cause blistering photosensitivity in contact with the skin. A deep-rooted native of dry rocky places and grassy steppes, it does well on sunny banks and in gravel plantings, but is equally amenable to border plantings, perhaps among the fans of sun-loving irises.

Waist high. Fully hardy, z3–9. Well drained or dry, poor to moderately fertile soil in full sun. Tolerates light dappled shade.

Digitalis

Scrophulariaceae ▪ foxglove

The genus *Digitalis* comprises some twenty-two species of biennials and short-lived perennials with clumps of basal foliage and delicate

or imposing spires of tubular bells. Where once we grew only *D. purpurea* in shades of pink or purple, and perhaps its white- flowered variant *D. p.* f. *albiflora* (a Jekyll favourite), there has been an explosion of interest in other species, greatly extending the colour range with much variation in the form of individual flowers.

Even in *D. purpurea* it is possible to select preferred colour forms, from the soft pale apricot of the graceful 'Sutton's Apricot'—an easy colour to place—through to the single-colour forms of the Camelot Series, in white, cream, soft lavender and rose pink. *Digitalis purpurea* f. *albiflora* comes true from seed only if you can control where the bees have been, but white-flowered seedlings have no pink staining on the base of young leaves; the rest can be weeded out. Several have spires in shades of yellow, borne from early to midsummer: *D. grandiflora*, with broad-mouthed creamy yellow flowers, in open waist-high spikes; its cultivar 'Carillon' has more slender bells, and 'Dwarf Carillon' is half the height. *D. lutea* is exceptionally graceful, having glossy, dark

▶ *Digitalis lutea*

▼ *Digitalis parviflora*

▶ *Digitalis purpurea*
'Sutton's Apricot'

▶ *Digitalis ferruginea*
with fennel

green leaves and slender, one-sided racemes of narrow pale yellow bells, to thigh high. The last weaves its way through many of my borders by self-sown seedlings, alongside *Polemonium pauciflorum*, creating threads of unifying colour that are especially lovely with blue and indigo flowers. Depending on when they germinate, they flower several weeks earlier or later than the main blooming period.

◀ *Disporum flavum* with *Galium odoratum*

Some of the most enticing foxgloves bring luscious shades of rusty gold, buff, milk-chocolate and mahogany, in slim spires that are pencil-straight and almost totally clothed in bloom. *Digitalis ferruginea*, at chest high, has pale golden brown flowers veined mahogany within, and with a hairy pouting lower lip, in mid- to late summer; *D. parviflora* has dense, cylindrical thigh-high racemes of chocolate flowers, veined violet with a mahogany lower lip, in early summer.

Fully hardy, z3–8/9; z5–9, *D. ferruginea*, *D. parviflora*. Any moderately fertile, preferably humus-rich, well-drained soil in sun or dappled shade; *D. ferruginea* and *D. parviflora* tolerate drier soils and more sun.

Disporum

Convalleriaceae ▪ fairy bells

Cool moist montane forests and lush damp scrub, often by streamsides, are characteristic habitats of both Asian and American species of *Disporum*. They have the luxuriant verdancy of committed woodlanders, spreading rhizomatously to form natural drifts and associating well with dodecatheons, trilliums, hostas and arching ferns. The tallest have sturdy, vertical stems clothed with deeply veined, more or less lance-shaped, shining leaves. Despite the strength of their stems, they often lean towards the light. They bear branching umbels of pendent, narrowly bell-shaped flowers in spring and early summer, sometimes with slightly reflexed tepals and long protruding anthers, which give rise to ornamental berries late in summer, before dying back in autumn.

Disporum flavens has pale yellow flowers in spring, on branching stalks from the upper leaf axils, and glossy black fruit. *D. hookeri* has umbels of creamy green or white flowers, and particularly elegant glossy leaves, long-pointed to form a drip tip; the orange-red fruits are also pointed like an inverted droplet. Slightly shorter *D. sessile* has matt dark green leaves, and tubular, creamy white flowers, the tips

of the tepals flushed green, the berries glossy black; *D. s.* 'Variegatum' is lovely in dappled shade, the leaves being very variably striped with white (broken stripes of green on white and vice versa).

Mid thigh to waist high. Fully hardy, z4–9. Constantly moist but well-drained, humus-rich soil in cool shade, dappled shade, or with a modicum of morning sun.

Dodecatheon

Primulaceae ▪ shooting stars

With exquisite natural grace, shooting stars are spring glories with erect and sturdy stems rising above a basal foliage rosette and then branching to form a slender, trembling candelabra of diminutive shuttlecocks (petals backswept

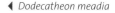
◀ *Dodecatheon meadia*

▼ *Dodecatheon meadia* f. *album*, the white-flowered variant

from long-pointed styles). They are scintillating with dewdrops in early morning light. The two most easily grown are *D. meadia*, from damp, rocky woodland glades, hill prairies and limestone bluffs in the eastern and central United States, and *D. pulchellum*, from western North America, occurring on mountain streambanks, alpine plains and montane meadows flushed with snowmelt. Being summer-dormant, they die back after flowering as conditions become warmer and drier. They're perfect in a lightly shaded border, on banks at woodland margins, and in fine turf for more naturalistic plantings.

Knee high or taller. Fully hardy, z3–8. Moist, humus-rich but well-drained soil in bright or dappled shade, or in more open areas where soils are reliably moist when in growth. They prefer slightly sloping sites, where drainage is good in winter.

Echinacea
Asteraceae ▪ coneflower

Without the widespread interest in prairie-style plantings, European gardens would still be using a couple of species and a handful of hybrids of *Echinacea*; currently there are some eighty listings under *Echinacea* in the Royal Horticultural Society Plantfinder. They have brought a rich and subtle colour range to the late summer and autumn garden—warm and vibrant, rather than red hot—and the flowers serve as last-chance saloons for bees and butterflies.

All have strong straight stems bearing daisy-like flowers with a prominent cone of dark central disc florets, surrounded by partially reflexed petals in *E. purpurea* and its variants, and by narrower, drooping petals in graduated shades of soft pink-purple in the elegant *E. pallida*. *Echinacea purpurea* cultivars range in colour from pale greens ('Jade', 'Green Jewel') and whites ('White Swan', 'White Lustre'), through dusky shades of earthy pink in 'Forncett Parasol', to clear pink in 'Magnus' and stronger pinks in 'Rubinglow' and 'Rubinstern'. *Echinacea*

▼ *Echinacea* 'Art's Pride'

◀ *Echinacea purpurea* 'Forncett Parasol"

▶ *Echinacea purpurea* 'White Swan'

◀ *Echinacea pallida*

◀ *Echinacea purpurea* 'Rubinglow' with *Festuca mairei*

▶ *Echinacea* 'Sunrise'

'Art's Pride' in red-flushed creamy orange, and *E.* 'Sunrise', cream-flushed apricot yellow, are particularly stunning among glistening golden grasses.

Echinacea species are native to the dry hills and prairies in eastern and central North America. Although these echinaceas all associate most naturally with prairie grasses, they're equally useful in late summer borders of the more traditional sort.

Waist to head high. Fully hardy, z3–10. Full sun, in deep, well-drained, humus-rich and moderately fertile soil.

Echinops

Asteraceae · globe thistle

With prickly, perfect spheres with the glint of steel, borne on pale sturdy stems in mid- to late summer, above mounds of spiny, jaggedly cut foliage, all of the echinops are architectural plants—outstanding on gravel banks and in gravel gardens. In *E. sphaerocephalus*, with a narrowly upright habit, to head height, the flowerheads are metallic silvery grey above grey-green leaves. Stronger colours on white-hairy stems are found in *E. bannaticus*, at waist to chest high; the deep blue *E. b.* 'Blue Globe' and the brighter blue, vigorous *E. b.* 'Taplow Blue' both repeat if deadheaded. One of the finest blues is found in the waist-high, repeat-flowering *E. ritro* 'Veitch's Blue' with mounds of cobwebbed, dark green leaves.

Fully hardy, z3–8. Any well-drained, poor to moderately fertile soil.

Echium

Boraginaceae

The Madeiran and Canary Island echiums tolerate little to no frost. They are, however, hardier than may be supposed if grown in sheltered hot spots in lean, stony soils with perfect drainage that approximate conditions in habitat. They are easily seed-raised; you're bound to have spares, so experiment. *Echium pininana* is the hardiest, forming basal rosettes of silver-hairy lanceolate leaves, each rosette producing a

◀ *Echinops ritro* 'Veitch's Blue'

▲ *Echium pininana*

spectacular spire of rich blue flowers in mid- to late summer; they can reach head high or twice that. I've grown *E. pininana* in open ground, and in large containers, on a sunny terrace but brought under frost-free glass for the winter. In open ground, *E. pininana* needs the protection of fleece at the immediate crown; the first year's leaves wither but growth resumes in spring if the growing point isn't frosted. It dies after flowering. If it wasn't so stunning, I wouldn't go to the trouble.

Fully hardy to frost-tender, z8–10 (*E. pininana*). Full sun in a sheltered spot; perfectly drained, poor to moderately fertile soil.

Eremurus

Asphodelaceae · foxtail lily

These tough, towering, fleshy rooted perennials could scarcely have been better designed as punctuation points, whether rhythmically woven through the gravel garden, among grasses, or in more traditional borders. Each basal crown of lance-shaped leaves produces a stout leafless stem adorned by a dense terminal of starry flowers, fuzzed with long protruding stamens.

Easily reaching head high, *E. himalaicus* has white flowers. In *E. stenophyllus* they're deep golden yellow; in *E. robustus*, they're peachy. The *E.* ×*isabellinus* hybrids tend towards warmer colours: coppery apricot-orange in 'Cleopatra', orange-red in 'Feuerfackel', earthy

◀ *Eremurus stenophyllus*

▶ *Eryngium alpinum*

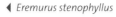

▶ *Eryngium ×zabelii*

◀ *Eremurus robustus*

▶ *Eryngium ×oliverianum*

pink in 'Oase', and salmon pink in 'Rexona' and 'Romance'.

Fully hardy, z5–8/9. Full sun, in fertile, open-textured well-drained soil. Dry mulch around the root zone in winter, avoiding the crown.

Eryngium

Apiaceae ▪ eryngo, sea holly

There is no single eryngo without charm. The signature of European and Asian species, denizens of dry, rocky and coastal places, is the intense metallic caste of the flowerheads, which comprise crowded cylindrical or hemispherical umbels of tiny flowers, subtended by conspicuous spiny bracts. They are borne on more or less branching stems above a tap-rooted basal rosette of foliage. Some are ascending but semitransparent, with freely branching stems and lots of small hemispherical umbels; one example is *E. tripartitum*, at thigh to waist high, with violet-tinted stems and a ruff of slender greyblue bracts beneath violet-blue flowers.

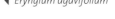

◀ *Eryngium agavifolium*

◀ *Eryngium eburneum*

▶ *Eryngium yuccifolium* with *Deschanpsisa cespitosa* 'Goldtau' in front and *Echinacea purpurea* behind

Those that are erect, with substantial bracts and larger, cylindrical umbels, make the strongest statement. At thigh high there is *E. alpinum*, in brilliant steely blue with long, softly spiny bracts, and *E. ×zabelii*, in intense metallic blue-violet. At waist high and a little taller, *E. ×oliverianum* has intense silver-blue stems, umbels and long, linear bracts, and at chest high *E. giganteum*, Miss Wilmott's Ghost, has long steel-blue umbels and broad, jagged silver bracts. They flower from midsummer to autumn, but inflorescences persist, making exquisite hoar-frosted winter sculpture. All are drought tolerant.

The South American species, from damper, grassy habitats, are very different but nonetheless strongly architectural, with rigid, almost bomb-proof flowering stems. *Eryngium agavifolium* forms a basal evergreen mound of viciously toothed, leathery, sword-shaped leaves, with stout, stiffly erect stems, branching only at waist to head height to bear fat cylindrical umbels of palest green that darken almost to black in winter. *E. yuccifolium*, at chest high, has similar but blue-green basal leaves and sparsely branched stems bearing many almost-white ovoid umbels. *E. eburneum* has spiny, linear basal leaves, and more freely branching stems bearing a constellation of ivory white ovoid satellites at head height and far above—a fabulous piece of botanical architecture, impervious to wind and weather.

Fully hardy, z5–8; z7–10, *E. eburneum*. Full sun, lean to moderately fertile, well-drained soil for European species and *E. yuccifolium* (from the southern and eastern United States). South American species prefer a well-drained but more moisture-retentive soil. Very attractive to bees.

Erythronium oregonum

Erythronium 'Pagoda'

Erythronium revolutum with *Matteuccia struthiopteris*

▲ *Erythronium hendersonii*

Erythronium

Liliaceae • trout lily

The trout lilies described here are knee-high woodlanders from the moist wooded foothills of western North America, from British Columbia and the coastal ranges of the Cascades and Siskiyou Mountains through to Oregon to California. With semi-erect, beautifully mottled and marbled leaves and erect, slender stems bearing exquisite pendent flowers in spring, they are summer-dormant bulbous perennials. Their natural grace reaches perfection in woodsy soils and dappled shade; they're at their most beautiful in the woodland garden. They need good drainage, but should never be allowed to dry out completely when dormant, nor before planting.

Erythronium californicum and *E. oregonum* are very similar; both with elliptic, glossy, mottled leaves and nodding white flowers with recurved petals. In *E. hendersonii*, the wavy-margined leaves are lightly marbled, the pale lilac tepals gracefully upswept. *E. revolutum* has more strongly coloured tepals in shades of lilac pink and beautifully marked leaves. *E.* 'Pagoda' is a vigorous hybrid with bronzed foliage and pale sulphur yellow flowers, the tepals recurving to reveal golden anthers.

Fully hardy, z3–9; z4–8, *E. revolutum*. Fertile, humus-rich, reliably moisture-retentive soil in dappled shade.

◀ Eucomis bicolor

Eucomis

Hyacinthaceae • pineapple lily

There are several beautiful pineapple lilies, all of which look tropical and exotic. Some, such as *E. bicolor* and *E. comosa*, are surprisingly hardy. They have an erect fleshy stem bearing a dense terminal raceme of starry flowers, with a tuft of bracts on top, resembling a pineapple. Flower stems arise from a basal rosette of glossy, wavy-margined leaves of smooth texture and great substance; they associate well with green-leaved hostas.

Flowering in late summer, *E. bicolor* has maroon flecks on its stems, with each bract and every tepal of its pale green florets rimmed in purple. In *E. comosa*, both stems and leaf undersides are adorned with purple spots,

and the starry white flowers have conspicuous purple ovaries at the centre. The vigorous *E. comosa* 'Sparkling Burgundy' is flushed wine red throughout, from its glossy red stems and burgundy leaves to the garnet ovaries at the centre of each flower.

Knee to mid thigh high. Fully hardy, z8–10. Full sun, in well-drained, open-textured, fertile humus-rich soil, moist in summer, and with a deep leafy mulch in winter.

◀ Eucomis comosa

Eupatorium

Asteraceae • Joe Pye weed

In terms of line, certain eupatoriums are dual-purpose. Both *E. purpureum* and *E. maculatum* are erect, the vertical line given resolution by the dark stems, and both have terminal corymbs of tiny, very nectar-rich flowers in white or shades of earthy pink, which give a horizontal line at about head height. They flower late in

◀ Eupatorium purpureum

the season, which is useful not only for butter-flies and bees, but also because they associate so well with the glistening late summer and autumn inflorescences of grasses. Natives of damp places, riverbanks, lakesides, woodland and meadows, they are also fine specimens for waterside and bog garden plantings.

Fully hardy, z3–9. Sun or dappled shade in any moist soil.

◀ *Francoa sonchifolia*

Francoa

Saxifragaceae ▪ bridal wreath

In effect, *Francoa sonchifolia* is very similar to *Heuchera cylindrica*, to which it is related. It forms an evergreen basal rosette of lobed, crumpled, broadly lance-shaped leaves, glossy or semi-glossy, and when close-planted it makes good cover in the woodland garden. The fuzzy-hairy, unbranched stems arise in midsummer, to about thigh high, with small pink flowers in dense terminal racemes, open-ing from deep pink buds, and with darker pink marks within. They last well in the vase. Vic-torian Head Gardeners used to support each stem individually in the cutting garden—oh,

the luxury of having labour to do jobs that don't need to be done. It was traditionally also used as border edging; no reason why not—the stems are all but transparent. I have it ramping away in a woodland garden, where it prolifer-ates faster than the pulmonarias and *Geranium phaeum* that accompany it.

Fully hardy, z7–9. Moisture-retentive but well-drained, humusy soil in dappled shade or sun.

Fritillaria

Liliaceae

Some of the least demanding of the fritillaries are strongly upright growers. Among them is the stout-stemmed *F. imperialis*, to waist high or more. It bears a terminal cluster of broadly bell-shaped flowers in gold, orange-red or mahogany red in late spring or early summer, each with a pineapple tuft of bracts on top, and with great beads of nectar within. The Persian name, *Ashk-e-Maryam*, translates as 'tears of Mary', fancying that it refused to bow its head at the Crucifixion, but has blushed with shame, bowed and 'wept' (hence the nectar beads) ever since. Despite their great elegance and sheer strength of line, the plants do have a bit of an odour of dog fox, so stand upwind to admire.

Fritillaria pallidiflora, with smaller, green-tinged, soft yellow bells, flowers at around the same time at *F. imperialis*. At knee height, it's at home in naturalistic plantings in the woodland garden or at its margins. Like several other fritil-laries including *F. meleagris*, it often shows faint chequering (tessellations) on its tepals which are sometimes compared to the chequered feathers of *Numida meleagris*, the guinea fowl.

Fritillaria pyrenaica, from montane mead-ows and rocky woods of southern France to northwestern Spain, flowers in spring and early summer. Distinctively coloured, with gold-tessellated, bronze-purple bells that are yellow within, it naturalizes easily in thin turf, and is fairly tolerant of summer moisture and light dappled shade, making it a good choice

◀◀ *Fritillaria pallidiflora*

◀ *Fritillaria pyrenaica*

◀◀ *Fritillaria thunbergii*

◀ *Fritillaria imperialis*

for open woodland glades. *F. thunbergii*, more graceful yet, is found in light woodland in China, and will colonize quite readily in cool dappled shade. Slender-stemmed with lax racemes of creamy bells cast with olive green, it reaches mid thigh.

Fully hardy, z5–8; z6–8, *F. thunbergii*. All fritillaries need deep planting, at four times the height of the bulb. Friable, well-drained soil in sun; *F. pallidiflora* and *F. thunbergii* prefer more humus-rich, retentive but well-drained soils.

Galega

Papilionaceae ▪ goat's rue

Lush herbaceous perennials occurring in substantial stands in damp meadows in the wild, galegas first attract attention for their handsome foliage: large, pinnate, bluish green leaves held horizontally on the vertical stems. How useful the head-high spires of white, blue, or mauve pea flowers are, going on from summer into autumn, scenting the air with an exotic waft of coconut. What a lovely backcloth for

◀ *Galega ×hartlandii* 'Lady Wilson'

▶ *Galtonia candicans*

mounding perennials, or for echoing spires of late-sown foxgloves.

All this I had in mind when I planted *G. orientalis*, with rich blue-violet spires; I didn't mind having to stake it, considering it a small price for a long performance. But in the fourth year since I removed it, I am *still* digging up self-sown seedlings and rhizomes, which invaded my well-worked soil with a vengeance. I now grow *G. ×hartlandii* 'Lady Wilson', with bicoloured, mauve-blue and white spires, and *G.* 'His Majesty', with spikes of darker lavender-blue and white. Both are less invasive, and although I've been assured that they're sterile, I still deadhead like mad—it soothes my anxieties and prolongs flowering.

Fully hardy, z4–9. Sun or light shade, preferably in moist soil. Fertile, open-textured soils encourage them to spread, and produce lush foliage at the expense of flowers.

Galtonia
Liliaceae

With broad, strap-shaped, glaucous, blue-green leaves and sturdy, leafless, waist-high stems of pendent, pristine, waxen white bells produced

in succession from mid- to late summer, *Galtonia candicans* ranks highly in the charm and elegance stakes. It is graciously accommodating in cultivation, provided soils are not too dry in the growing period nor too moist during winter dormancy. It occurs in damp grassland on mountain slopes at altitudes of 1,350 to 2,150 metres (4,430 to 7,055 feet) in the Drakensberg in South Africa. Lovely in a summer border, where its height and late flowering period are particularly gratifying, it looks wonderful among evergreen shrubs such as osmanthus and choisyas, and with big-leaved corrugated hostas.

Fully hardy, z6/7–9. Friable, well-drained, moderately fertile soil in sun. Leave undisturbed and treat to a dry mulch in cold winter areas. Protect from slugs.

Garrya
Garryaceae ▪ silk tassel

When not in flower, the swag-forming evergreen *Garrya elliptica* could easily give a tiered line to a backdrop planting against a wall, if trained espalier-style. But in winter and early spring it gives a tracery of strongly sketched vertical lines when festooned with pendent,

◀ *Garrya elliptica* 'James Roof'

▶ *Gentiana asclepiadea*

▶ *Gentiana lutea*

creamy silver-grey catkins, like a threaded chain of tiny inverted vases; the male cultivars *G. e.* 'Evie' and 'James Roof' have the longest catkins. Glossy, dark grey-green, oblong with undulate margins, and pale and downy beneath, the leaves have a wonderfully sculptural texture when well grown.

As many gardeners loathe *Garrya elliptica* as love it. The only reason I can imagine for such vehemence is that maybe gender preference was faulty (female catkins are not so showy), or the plants were sited in too-dry soils in the face of cold, dry, inland winds, when the foliage burns horribly. It doesn't seem to burn in maritime gardens, and it tolerates salt spray.

To twice head height. Fully hardy, z8–9. Well-drained, moderately fertile soil in sun (for best flowering), or in dappled or light shade; provide more moisture-retentive soil in inland gardens.

Gentiana
Gentianaceae

In a genus devoted to the small and perfectly formed, the height and poise of *G. asclepiadea* and *G. lutea* are upstandingly different. Wil-

low gentian, *G. asclepiadea*, is from mountain meadows and open montane woodland. In habitat, on natural unimproved soils in bright light at cool high altitudes, it is erect or slightly arching, but it's often more arching in the luxe soils of gardens, or if treated strictly as a shade plant. It has thigh-high wands arising from the rootstock, clothed in fresh green, lanceolate leaves with deeply impressed veins, and bears axillary and terminal clusters of intense, sapphire blue trumpets in late summer and early autumn. Lovely with ferns and golden grasses, if left undisturbed in open glades in a wood-

land garden it will colonize but slowly, making glorious stands in blues of an intensity so lacking among late-flowerers.

Gentiana lutea, great yellow gentian, is a deeply rooting species, with stout stems at chest to head height, bearing substantial, almost pleated, bluish green leaves, reminiscent of veratrum with which it associates well. It has dense axillary clusters of starry yellow flowers in midsummer, followed by handsome seedheads. A native of subalpine and alpine pastures, it is exceptionally long lived once established.

Fully hardy, z5–8/9, *G. asclepiadea*; z7–8, *G. lutea*. Provide a sheltered site with cool equable humidity, in good bright light, but shaded from hot sun. The ideal is a cool root run and well-lit top growth. In deep, moisture retentive, woodsy soil of open texture, both species tolerate slightly alkaline soils.

Helianthus

Asteraceae ▪ sunflower

I have little patience with most perennial sunflowers, finding them too coarse, roughly running, and brassy. But there are exceptions: the following choices are clumpers rather than runners, slender, upright and about head height, with simple daisy flowers from late summer until autumn frosts.

Helianthus 'Lemon Queen' has masses of lemon yellow daisy flowers from late summer to autumn. *H.* 'Bitter Chocolate', with chocolate-scented, pale yellow flowers on tall stems clothed with narrow leaves, is similar to but shorter than *H. salicifolius* which has willowy leaves that fountain down and outwards from towering stems (head high or twice that) topped by scented, dark-eyed, sunshine yellow flowers. It's native to prairies in the south-central United States. Some gardeners stake it to prevent it from toppling. *H.* 'Carine' has dark-stemmed creamy lemon yellow daisies, at chest high; *H. giganteus* 'Sheila's Sunshine' has dark-eyed, very pale yellow flowers. Fabulous inter-

woven with the blue wands of *Salvia uliginosa*, and with late grasses in wild and prairie-style plantings.

Fully hardy, z4/5–9. Full sun, in a warm site in poor to moderately fertile, moisture-retentive but well-drained soil. Subdue tendencies towards excessive height, and spread by growing in less nutritionally loaded soils.

Hemerocallis

Liliaceae ▪ daylily

The double-flowered daylilies are not part of my palette, their perfection too often mashed by rain, but I value increasingly the single-flowered, spidery or starry forms, or the more substantial rounded and triangular flower types with smooth or ruffled tepals. Evergreen, semi-evergreen or herbaceous, they have lush green sheaves of strap-shaped leaves, and a strong erect line in the flowering stems, which bear and drop flowers daily in long succession

▲ *Helianthus* 'Lemon Queen'

throughout summer. There are thousands of cultivars, from knee to waist high, ranging from self-coloured to those tipped, banded or zoned in two or three colours. Pure whites through pinks and lilacs such as *Hemerocallis* 'Catherine Woodbery' are best for cool pastel colour themes; gold and red, as in *H*. 'Stafford', and mahogany and plummy purple work well in hot themes that suit the late summer light; and

the darkest, velvety near-blacks, like *H*. 'American Revolution', lend high contrast to plantings at the warmer end of the colour palette. To my eye, the highly bred daylilies are at their best in more manicured plantings in mixed and herbaceous borders. *H. lilioasphodelus*, with slender lemon yellow flowers in early summer, is naturally graceful in elongated drifts in naturalistic plantings.

Fully hardy, z3/4/5–9/10. Moisture-retentive but well-drained, fertile soil in sun.

◀◀ Hemerocallis 'American Revolution'

◀ Hemerocallis lilioasphodelus

▼ *Hemerocallis* 'Stafford'

◀ *Hemerocallis* 'Catherine Woodbery'

Hibiscus

Malvaceae

In a genus of largely subtropical, tropical and warm-temperate beauties, the hardiness of *H. syraiacus* is all the more surprising. Long cultivated in China and Japan, it is a deciduous

◀ *Hibiscus syriacus* 'Oiseau Bleu'

◀ *Hibiscus syriacus* 'White Chiffon'

centres; 'Woodbridge' is a dark-centred rich pink, and 'Oiseau Bleu' a dusky lavender-blue with a deep maroon heart.

Fully hardy, z5–8/9. Full sun, in well-drained but moderately moisture-retentive, fertile, humus-rich soil.

Iris

Iridaceae

Most irises give a vertical and/or diagonal line, but not all make it strong and clear. Among those that do, the bearded (or Pogon) irises are the most familiar. The fan of sword-shaped, usually glaucous basal leaves presents a diagonal line long before and after flowering. They arise from a fat surface rhizome (which shouldn't be buried). In the soft-blue-flowered, thigh-high *I. pallida* 'Argentea Variegata' and 'Variegata', with leaves broadly striped silver-white and creamy yellow respectively, the line is outstanding. In spring to early summer, bearded irises produce vertical stems bearing heads of several showy flowers, each with three erect standard petals and three pendent petals, or 'falls', each fall having a conspicuous 'beard' at its centre. The colour range is huge, and the choice enormous, in every tone and hue from pristine white to intense, near-blackish purples. If you want impact, eschew all dwarfs and select from the taller intermediate bearded or the tall bearded irises at thigh high and above (the classification should be on the label).

The Sibirica irises are usually evergreen, tough but more delicate in appearance, and mostly from waist to chest high. They have a sheaf of narrow, more or less erect, rich green leaves, which arise from subterranean rhizomes and form substantial clumps with maturity. The stiff slender stems are strongly vertical and bear finely marked flowers in shades of blue, white, yellow or deep purple-red, in late spring.

The Laevigatae or water irises include the vigorous *I. pseudacorus*, to head high, in shades of yellow, and the robust but less vigorous

shrub of stiffly upright growth, blooming from late in summer until autumn, when most other shrubs are preparing for impending winter. Large and funnel-shaped, with satiny, slightly crumpled petals and a central column of anthers and stigma, flowers are carried with great freedom in the axils of the lobed, toothed, slightly downy dark green leaves. There are many cultivars of *H. syriacus*, but the finest include the pristine white 'Diana' and semi-double 'White Chiffon'; 'Lavender Chiffon' is equally beautiful with lavender flowers. 'Hamabo' and 'Red Heart' have white flowers with dark crimson

Iris 'Jane Phillips' (bearded)

Iris 'Benton Nigel' (bearded)

Iris 'Mallory Kaye' (bearded)

Iris 'Thornbird' (bearded)

Iris 'Jean Price' (bearded)

Iris 'Poem of Ecstasy' (bearded)

I. laevigata, at waist high, in shades of blue. These are the emphatic delineators of still or slow-moving water margins, providing invaluable contrasts for large moisture-loving mound-formers: rheums, rodgersias, and the finely textured aruncus and taller astilbes.

Pogon (bearded) irises: fully hardy, z3–8. Fertile, well-drained soil in sun.

Sibirica irises: fully hardy, z4–10. Fertile, moderately moisture-retentive, well-drained soil in sun, or light or dappled shade.

Laevigatae (water) irises: fully hardy, z4/5–9. Shallow water, or moist or wet, humus-rich, preferably acid soil in sun or dappled shade.

◀◀ *Iris pallida* 'Variegata'

◀ *Iris sibirica* 'Pirate Prince'

◀◀ *Iris sibirica* 'Alba' with *Angelica archangelica* and *Digitalis purpurea* f. *albiflora*

◀ *Iris laevigata* (left) and *Iris pseudacorus*

Kniphofia

Asphodelaceae

Having long disliked red hot pokers for their fearsomely brash colours, at the same time I've admired their uncompromising verticality and strength of form. Obviously I'm not the only one who quails at their manic combination of vermilion and yellow. The modern breeding trend is for softer colours, more pleasing and

easier to combine, without any loss of majestic habit and height. For luminous jades and soft yellows, at waist to chest high, the following complement all shades of blue: *Kniphofia* 'Green Jade', evergreen, with jade buds opening creamy lime; 'Ice Queen', deciduous, with rounded cylinders of creamy yellow; 'Percy's Pride', semi-evergreen, green in bud, creamy primrose when open; and 'Torch Bearer', in clear yellow. In warmer shades, at thigh to waist high, the following complement crimson and purple foliage, crocosmias, and tawny summer grasses: 'Alcazar', with dusky red buds opening luminous creamy orange; 'Strawberries and Cream' in coral and cream; 'Tawny King', with bronzed stems and tawny apricot buds opening

Kniphofia 'Green
Jade'

Kniphofia 'Percy's
Pride'

Kniphofia 'Tawny King'

cream; 'Timothy', with bronze stems and dark buds opening soft peachy salmon; and 'Toffee Nosed', with earthy apricot-brown buds opening cream.

Fully hardy, z6/7–11. Moisture-retentive but well-drained, deep, fertile soil in full sun. Give a deep dry mulch around the root zone in cold areas, avoiding the immediate crown.

Laburnum

Papilionaceae ▪ golden rain

The hybrid laburnum, *L.* ×*watereri* 'Vossii', has virtually replaced all other laburnums in gardens since its introduction in the nineteenth century, for although all possess the golden chains of yellow pea flowers, few produce them in such profusion or at such length. As a free-standing tree, it is the fountain of gold that once graced every suburban garden, with its inevitable companion the purple lilac. Hackneyed the association may be, but only because it's overly

Kniphofia 'Torch Bearer'

Kniphofia 'Alcazar'

familiar, and it surely brings joy to its owner as it marks the cusp of spring and summer.

Laburnum ×*watereri* 'Vossii' will reach three times head height as a freestanding specimen. Training to an arch is one of the most glorious ways to grow it, for it allows the chains to free-fall into space, unobscured by the palmate dark green leaves. If you have space for a tunnel, that's heaven; if you grow it on a tunnel with wisteria, that's divine. The effective line in this case is definitively vertical, especially when, as with Rosemary Verey's inspired planting, you team it with the rising verticals of alliums (see page 33).

Start with a two-year-old feathered maiden (a single-stemmed tree with few sidebranches, or laterals). Tie in the leading shoot vertically to the supporting framework as it grows, when the wood is still flexible. Tip back the laterals (sideshoots) to encourage branching and formation of flowering spurs low down. In the

▲ *Leucojum vernum*

▶ *Leucojum aestivum*

◀ *Laburnum ×watereri* 'Vossii' with *Wisteria sinensis*

second and subsequent years, continue training the leading stem up and over the arch, and tip back laterals and sublaterals. Do this between late summer and midwinter. Stop the leading shoot when it has topped the curve. Once established (at about four to five years), you are committed to annual tipping back of laterals when growth slows at the end of the season, along with removal of deadwood and badly placed shoots. Patience has its own reward.

All parts of the plant are poisonous, especially the seeds, so keep curious or omnivorous children and dumb pets away from them.

Fully hardy, z5–8. Full sun and any moderately fertile, moisture-retentive soil that is neither droughty nor waterlogged. Laburnums dislike hot, dry or humid summers.

Leucojum

Amaryllidaceae ▪ snowflake

Leucojum vernum, the spring snowflake, flowers in late winter and early spring with the last of the snowdrops (*Galanthus*), and *L. aestivum*,

summer snowflake, follows on from late spring to early summer. They both have nodding, waxy white bells with green-tipped tepals on upright stems arising from erect, strap-shaped, glossy green leaves; *L. vernum* seldom reaches knee high, while *L. aestivum* is mid thigh height. Both need reliably moist soils, and will naturalize in thin grass; *L. aestivum* tolerates boggy situations, often forming colonies in bog gardens and beside ponds. It flowers with the trilliums, and associates well with ferns such as *Matteuccia* and *Osmunda*, and the emerging new leaves of epimediums.

Fully hardy, z3/4–9. Damp, humus-rich soil in sun or light dappled shade.

Liatris

Asteraceae ▪ blazing star, gayfeather

A native of damp lowland meadows, savannahs and prairies in eastern and southern North America, *Liatris spicata* is robustly erect, the stems clothed in narrow leaves, and with long, dense, terminal spikes of clustered buttony buds that open from the top of the spikes downwards. They flower between late summer and autumn—pure white in *L. spicata* 'Alba' and 'Floristan White', to shades of mauve, magenta, deep pink and violet, which associate well with the echinaceas in prairie plantings and with grasses. The emphatic vertical is evident even when in bud; it can serve as an echo to chelones, or an echo and contrast to eupatoriums. Excellent also in more traditional herbaceous or mixed borders, and at the margins of a bog garden, they are very attractive to bees and butterflies.

◀ *Liatris spicata*

▼ *Liatris spicata* 'Alba'

Waist to head high. Fully hardy, z3–10. Moist but well-drained, moderately fertile, preferably open-textured soil in sun.

Libertia
Iridaceae

A native of New Zealand damp scrub and grassland, *Libertia grandiflora* is the tallest of the libertias, and carries its flowers well clear of the foliage. Flowering in late spring and early summer, it forms an ascending, fine-textured fan of linear, glossy, dark green leaves, with

erect, flexuous stems bearing airy and elegant panicles of pure white flowers at waist height. It's always beautiful in traditional borders and as edging; associating it with fine mobile grass such as *Stipa tenuissima* emphasizes its foliage colour and rigid form, especially in the gravel garden. It's a gently spreading rhizomatous perennial and will self-seed gently (into the interstices of terrace paving, with luck).

Hardy, z8–10/11. Full sun or light shade, in moist but well-drained or dry soil, poor to moderately fertile. Tolerant of drought and coastal conditions.

Ligularia
Asteraceae

Two of the ligularias give most definitive verticals in their towering spires of flower: *L. przewalskii* and the hybrid *L.* 'The Rocket'. Both have basal mounds of handsome foliage: deeply cut, jaggedly lobed and toothed in *L. przewalskii*, more rounded and markedly toothed in 'The Rocket'. Although they do need moist soil, I find them to be less susceptible to the unattractive swooning seen in those with rounded foliage platters, such as *L. dentata*, at the first suggestion of thirst. The dark yellows of their

◀ *Libertia grandiflora*

▶ *Lilium candidum*

◀ *Ligularia* 'The Rocket'

◀ *Ligularia przewalskii*

daisy-like flowers would be brash were they not offset by the depth of colour of the stems that bear them soaring to head height and above in mid- to late summer—deep purple in *L. przew-alskii*, ebony black in 'The Rocket'. The flowers are dramatically defined and outstanding even from a distance. They're best on streamsides, on poolsides and in bog gardens, with *Darmera peltata*, *Rheum palmatum* and *Lysichiton*.

Fully hardy, z4–8. Deep, humusy, fertile and reliably moist or wet soil, in sun or dappled shade, with shelter from wind. Provide after-noon shade in warm-summer climates.

Lilium

Liliaceae

Many highly bred hybrids of *Lilium* are so stun-ning, and in turn attract so much attention, that they're difficult to blend in to more subtle, relaxed or naturalistic plantings. The species, however, retain a grace that I find easier to place. *Lilium candidum* and *L. regale* are the clas-sic beauties of the sunny summer border. The turkscaps thrive in borders but are perfect in woodland gardens. All need well-drained, leafy, humus-rich soils, in sun or dappled shade.

It would be unfeasible for me to represent all nine divisions of the genus *Lilium* here, but it's perfectly within my grasp to mention some more amenable hardy species that give a vertical line (and illustrate a variety of flower forms):

Lilium candidum (Madonna lily): to head high, with racemes of sweetly scented, pure white trumpets in midsummer. For neutral to alkaline soil in sun, z3–7.

L. henryi: waist high to three times that, with racemes of scented black-spotted, fiery orange turkscap flowers in late summer. Thrives in neutral to alkaline soil, z4–9.

L. lancifolium (tiger lily): thigh to head high, with racemes of shining, purple-spotted, deep scarlet turkscap flowers in late summer to autumn. Lime tolerant, but best in damp acid soils, z3–9.

◀ *Lilium regale*

▶ *Lilium henryi*

◀ *Lilium lancifolium*

▶ *Lilium mackliniae*

◀ *Lilium martagon* var. *album*

▶ *Lilium ×testaceum*

L. mackliniae: to mid thigh, with racemes of nodding, ethereal pink, bowl-shaped flowers in early to midsummer. z5-9.

L. martagon: waist to head high, with racemes of shining, pendent, pink, red or in var. *album* white, sharply scented turkscap flowers in early and midsummer. Vigorous, for any well-drained soil, z3–10.

L. regale (regal lily): waist to head high, with umbels of highly scented, broadly trumpet-shaped, white flowers flushed purple without, in midsummer. Any except very alkaline soil in sun, z3-8.

L. ×testaceum (Nankeen lily): to head high, with racemes of fragrant, palest apricot turk-scap flowers in early to midsummer. Tolerates lime. z4-9.

▶ *Linaria purpurea* 'Canon Went'

Linaria

Scrophulariacae

With all the attributes of a cottage garden perennial, thriving on a total lack of attention, and in bloom from early summer till frosts, *Linaria purpurea* is perhaps tainted by over-familiarity. But its slender waist-high spires of grey-green leaves have a willowy grace and dense racemes of tiny violet snapdragon flowers give a line that is as useful in naturalistic and gravel plantings as it is in grey- and silver-themed herbaceous borders. It's a delicately etched vertical that is lovely interspersed with more sophisticated flower forms, such as those of *L. candidum* or *L. regale*. *Linaria purpurea* 'Canon Went' has flowers in a shade of pale earthy grey-pink, and more glaucous leaves than the species. Both attract bees, hoverflies, butterflies and moths, including the hummingbird hawk moth. They self-seed freely, delightfully so into wall and paving crevices or when forming natural drifts in poor stony soils.

Fully hardy, z5–8. Any poor to moderately fertile, well-drained soil in sun.

Lobelia

Campanulaceae

Lobelia ×speciosa and its parent species (cardinal flower *L. cardinalis*, and blue cardinal flower *L. siphilitica*) form a group of lobelias far removed from bedding and basket annuals, having tall spires of flowers from mid- to late summer or autumn. Although few reach above thigh to waist high, they make an imposing contribution in damp but sunny sites on account of the sheer intensity of colour in the racemes of two-lipped, tubular flowers. The reds appear to positively emit light: *L. cardinalis* 'Bee's Flame' in glowing crimson, *L. cardinalis* 'Queen Victoria' in blazing scarlet, and *L. ×speciosa* 'Tania' in shocking purple-magenta—all having dark, glossy stems and foliage in shades of beetroot and bronzed purple. Newer hybrids, such as *L.* 'Isabella's Blush', are nonetheless glowing but in soft mauve pink with magenta eyes. *Lobelia siphilitica* has leafy spires, up to chest height, of lucent bright blue flowers, and has brought purple tones to hybrids such as *L. ×speciosa* 'Vedrariensis' in dusky violet purple.

In habitat—swamps, meadows and streambanks—they are pollinated by hummingbirds. Ranging from Canada to Mexico, they are very

◀ *Lobelia* x*speciosa* 'Tania'

▼ *Lobelia cardinalis*
'Queen Victoria'

▲ *Lobelia siphilitica*　　▲ *Lobelia* 'Isabella's
　　　　　　　　　　　　　　　Blush'

cold hardy, but in damp maritime climates will not thrive in standing winter wet and are sometimes lured into premature growth by warm spring days, only to be dashed by later frosts. Provide a deep dry mulch for insulation where this is the case.

Fully hardy, z3–9/10. Deep, reliably moist, fertile and humus-rich soils in sun or dappled shade.

Lupinus

Papilionaceae

So well known are the vertical spires of the legion summer-flowering hybrid lupins that they scarcely need description. They are clump-forming herbaceous perennials that can be selected for height (thigh high, Gallery Series; waist high, Russell hybrids; chest high, Band of Nobles Series) and colour (selfs or bicolours, ranging from the creamy white of 'Polar Princess' through yellow, orange, pinks and reds, to the dusky violets of 'Masterpiece'). Lupins are enjoying a resurgence in modern schemes, mainly on account of the strong, elegant line they bring to a planting.

The Russell hybrids, raised in York, England by George Russell and introduced in 1937, were widely cultivated in the villages of Yorkshire, and are a frequent garden escapee there, lining the routes of railways, the explosively ejected seeds whisked along in the air streams

of passing trains. (Similarly, the annual Texas bluebonnets, *L. texensis* and *L. subcarnosus* line the highways of Texas.) Most have reverted to the blue-violets of one of the parent species, *L. polyphyllus*, native to damp meadows of western North America. This has inspired me to use the waist-high spires in more naturalistic plantings; they are stunningly beautiful with lacy *Anthriscus*, *Myrrhis odorata* and aquilegias in meadows and on grassy banks.

The tree lupin, *L. arboreus*, has a more permanent presence. An evergreen or semi-evergreen shrub to chest height, with typical lupine leaves: silky hairy, palmate, and greyish green, holding a bead of dew at the centre, with spires of white or pale yellow pea flowers in late spring and summer. It has the poise of a perennial and looks well in a herbaceous border, its light verticals associating perfectly with stronger uprights, such as *Phlomis russeliana*, and mounds of hostas, santolinas, and the soft yellow daisies of *Anthemis*. Although often

◀ *Lupinus arboreus*

\

short-lived, it self-seeds and seedlings can be transplanted when very young.

Fully hardy, z7–10, *L. arboreus*; z4–7 for hybrids. Full sun in well-drained, open-textured, moderately fertile soils.

Lysichiton

Araceae ▪ skunk cabbage

Lysichitons are the essential specimens for bog gardens and streamsides; what's more, if you can arrange to grow them beside a pool of still water, the reflection of the elegantly upright spathes more than doubles the line of beauty. Both species are marginal aquatics from swamps and wet woodlands, *L. camschatcensis* with ivory white spathes, *L. americanus*

◀ Lupins and cow parsley

▶ *Lysichiton camschatcensis*

in shining yellow. The inflorescences emerge from bare wet earth in late winter and early spring, followed by huge, glossy, leathery leaves, like huge bright green paddles, reaching waist height and taller, effectively smothering weeds beneath their canopy. Like *Darmera peltata*, with which it associates brilliantly, it should be planted with ample space for the foliage, which is disproportionately huge in comparison to the inflorescence but makes a wonderful backdrop to clouds of *Alisma plantago-aquatica* later in the season.

Fully hardy, z5–9, *L. camschatcensis*, z4–7, *L. americanus*. Deep, humus-rich, wet and fertile soils in sun or dappled shade.

◀ *Lupinus* Gallery Series

◀ *Lysimachia atropurpurea*

▶ *Lysimachia clethroides*

▼ *Lysimachia ephemerum* (top right) with *Kniphofia* 'Painted Lady', *Achillea* 'Moonshine', heleniums and hemerocallis

Lysimachia
Primulaceae

Several of the lysimachias are erect perennials, with stiffly upright stems bearing racemes of starry flowers. *Lysimachia atropurpurea* has wrinkled, wavy-margined leaves that are pale veined and silvery grey, and bears thigh-spikes of deep claret stars from early to late summer; *L. atropurpurea* 'Beaujolais' has darker flowers and more silvery foliage, and makes good foliage and colour contrasts with the domes of anaphalis; *L. ephemerum*, with narrow, leathery, grey leaves, has erect stems that terminate in tapering waist-high spires of grey-toned white stars, from mid- to late summer, giving

ethereally pale hues that seem to recede when used at the back of a border. In *L. clethroides*, the racemes of starry white flowers are sinuously curved, all in the clump snaking in the same direction, like a flock of farmyard geese on a mission. It reaches waist high, and can be invasive in loose, humusy, moist soils. It will form colonies in a bog garden, streambank, damp meadow or wild garden, but is more constrained if grown in drier or less fertile soils, in light shade.

Fully hardy, z3/4–8; z6–8, *L. ephemerum*. Humus-rich, reliably moisture-retentive but well-drained soil in sun or light shade.

Monarda
Lamiaceae ▪ bee balm, wild bergamot

It is often the case that taking a plant out of its usual context highlights its strength of form or line and suggests hosts of new associations. That is certainly true of the aromatic bee balm, *Monarda*; once most often seen in herb gardens, it has a new lease of life when used in modern prairie plantings. The plants are strongly erect, with an exclamatory tuft of asymmetrical, two-lipped tubular flowers and coloured bracts atop each leafy stem. Their primary drawback, susceptibility to powdery mildew, can be reduced by selecting newer, resistant selections and providing adequate moisture right through the season, especially late in summer when hot dry

◀◀ *Monarda didyma* with *Echinacea purpurea*

◀ *Monarda* 'Aquarius' with *M.* 'Cambridge Scarlet'

◀ *Monarda* 'Scorpion'

conditions stress the plants and contribute to the spread of the fungus. Other contributory factors are mass planting, which reduces air circulation, and the failure to clear away debris at the end of the season. Leaving seedheads to stand through the winter, though pretty when frost-rimed, contributes to a resource of spores for reinfection the following year. These plants associate so well with eryngiums, veronicastrums, echinaceas and grasses that there is seldom need to have them massed too closely and autumn clearance is an enjoyable task.

The Zodiac Series (pale violet 'Aquarius', magenta 'Capricorn' and violet 'Scorpion'), and Oudolf's Indian range (soft pink 'Cherokee', true scarlet 'Squaw' and deep mauve-lilac 'Mohawk') are held to be mildew resistant. *M.* 'Cambridge Scarlet' is a good clear red; *M. didyma* ranges from pink through scarlet. They are all balm to bees and butterflies, and manna for slugs.

Waist to chest high. Fully hardy, z4–8. Sun, in moderately fertile, humus-rich, moisture-retentive but well-drained soils.

Morina

Morinaceae ▪ Himalayan whorlflower

Having a basal evergreen rosette of very glossy, thistle-like, emerald green leaves, with a pleasantly musky scent and waist-high flowering spikes, *Morina longifolia* is one of the most elegant of plants. I have grown it in all my borders since first we met, and it's also a sweet piece of architecture for gravel gardens. The midsummer flowers, borne near the top of a stout stem in well-spaced whorls with spiny bracts, are long-tubed, waxy and white, blushing pink when fertilized (don't we all?). It later gives rise to attractive, long-persistent seedheads with glossy black seeds. The seeds germinate freely if sown as soon as ripe, so you can easily have

Morina longifolia, close up of flower

Nectaroscordum siculum subsp. *bulgaricum*

Morina longifolia

Nectaroscordum siculum subsp. *bulgaricum* seedheads

lots of whorlflowers for planting in long drifts in borders.

Fully hardy, z6–9. Moderately fertile, moisture-retentive but well-drained, open-textured soil. in sun.

Nectaroscordum
Alliaceae

Whether you choose the species, *N. siculum*, for its terminal umbels of pale-hued bells in shades of white, green and purplish pink, or *N. siculum* subsp. *bulgaricum*, with more purple-flushed flowers, these upright cousins of the alliums are wonderful for threading through other plantings, especially in the dappled light of a woodland garden where they will push their

way through lower foliage masses of brunneras, dicentras and pulmonarias (for instance). They thrive equally well in sunny sites. They do self-seed, scattering seed from upright, multi-pronged, triton-like seedheads, but seldom at the expense of their companions.

Fully hardy, z5–9. Sun or light dappled shade, in any moderately fertile, well-drained soil.

Onopordum
Asteraceae

Beginning its short life as an innocent-looking seedling with two furry leaves, *Onopordum acanthium* forms a basal rosette of spiny, deeply cut leaves clothed in dense, silvery hair. In its second year, it rockets upwards to head height

men as a companion to trilliums and arisaemas in the woodland garden.

Fully hardy, z5–9. Consistently moist, humus-rich, woodsy soil in dappled or partial shade.

Paris polyphylla

Perovskia

Lamiaceae • Russian sage

Perovskia atriplicifolia, from dry, rocky, open habitats in Afghanistan, is a deciduous sub-shrub with grey stems clothed in deeply cut, grey-green leaves terminating in long spires of tubular, two-lipped flowers in violet-blue. It is one of the probable parents of *P*. 'Blue Spire' and its offspring is a superior garden plant in every respect. The upright stems are almost chalk-white, the leaves silvery grey, and the branching panicles of rich violet flowers with white woolly calyces are produced in profusion from midsummer to autumn. Exceptionally

Onopordum giganteum

and above, its stout, winged, spiny stems cob-webbed in silver, branching to form a candelabra of globose, silver and green, densely hairy thistle heads, with tufts of rosy purple on top. Once with it, never without it—for it self-seeds freely. Seedlings are easily recognized and can be moved to their proper place (or culled). It is the architectural focal point to live for, and bees and butterflies love it.

Fully hardy, Z3–9. Full sun, in fertile, near-neutral or slightly alkaline, well-drained soil.

Paris

Trilliaceae

Each smooth stem of *Paris polyphylla* rises to thigh high from a rhizomatous rootstock, producing a whorl of shining, lanceolate green leaves at the tip, forming a platter to present the single, green-tepalled flower with spidery, pale yellow threads of inner tepals, many yellow anthers and a purple stigma at the centre. Weird...but a wonderfully architectural speci-

Perovskia 'BlueSpire'

graceful, it is perfect in the silver-themed border, or in dry and gravel gardens. It associates beautifully with golden grasses, such as *Stipa gigantea*, makes a great contrast in form with the tall and airy *Verbena bonariensis*, the mounded sedums and echinaceas, and is a wonderful closely toning colour with agapanthus.

It is wonderfully versatile, then. The only qualification I make is that to get perfection of form in 'Blue Spire', it needs to be pruned; otherwise, it can look disappointingly untidy. Simply cut it back to a low, woody framework as the lower stems buds begin to break in spring.

Fully hardy, z5–10. Full sun, any poor to moderately fertile soil, including chalky ones, with good drainage. Tolerates dry soils, and good in coastal gardens.

Persicaria

Polygonaceae

Long grown in herbaceous and cutting borders for its dense, cylindrical racemes of tiny, soft pink flowers, *P. bistorta* 'Superba' forms a semi-evergreen, ground-covering mound of long pointed, ovate leaves. Flowers are produced at waist height over very long periods from summer into autumn. It is easily grown, and undervalued for the erect line of its inflorescences, which make an imaginative contrast to the shuttlecocks of *Matteuccia*, for instance, or the foliage mounds of actaeas and rodgersias.

Persicaria amplexicaulis, also semi-evergreen and equally long flowering, brings a more finely etched line. Its very slender stems ascend to chest height, with delicate but strong racemes of tiny flowers, well above the puckered, pointed, narrowly ovate leaves. In *P. a.* 'Firetail' the wands are intense, glowing red, outstanding among the blondes of late summer grasses such as *Deschampsia cespitosa* or taller *Molinia* cultivars. With *P. amplexicaulis* 'Alba' and 'Rosea', which have white and pale pink flowers respectively, the effect among grasses, perhaps with gauras, is infinitely subtle, giving a warm,

almost monochrome tapestry in which textural difference is all—like embroidered gauze, especially when glistening with dew or rain.

Fully hardy, z5–9. Sun and any moist soil.

▲▲ *Persicaria bistorta* 'Superba' with *Matteuccia*

▲ *Persicaria amplexicaulis* 'Alba' with *Gaura lindheimeri* and *Molinia*

◀ *Persicaria amplexicaulis* 'Firetail'

125

Phlomis

Lamiaceae

Phlomis russeliana is an evergreen perennial forming a low ground-covering mound of long, heart-shaped leaves, of rough texture and in a soft deep sage green, slightly upturned at the margins to reveal paler undersides. In summer, pale stout stems bear hooded, creamy yellow flowers in architectural whorls to waist height; they stand sere into winter, a host to hibernating ladybirds, and wonderful when frosted. I use *P. russeliana* with *Baptisia* and *Lupinus arboreus*, fronted by fans of *Sisyrinchium striatum*. *Phlomis tuberosa* has darker green leaves, rugose and beautifully poised, the stems soaring to head height, adorned in whorls of soft mauve; 'Amazone' gives a particularly effective line, since stems and calyces are very dark, almost purple. *Phlomis tuberosa*, from dry steppes and stony hillsides from central Europe east to Siberia, is a committed lover of sun and excellent drainage—a perfect punctuation point in gravel gardens, but intolerably floppy in rich soils. *Phlomis russeliana* will grow almost anywhere, in anything from poor dirt to more fertile border soils.

Fully hardy, z4–8. Sun, poor to moderately fertile, freely drained soil. See also page 222.

Phlox

Polemoniaceae

It may seem a tad pedantic, but *Phlox maculata* seems to me to give a more clearly erect line than *P. paniculata*. It is more slender, with very upright stems, and its flower panicles are more cylindrical than pyramidal, the individual flowers being smaller—and the overall effect is lighter. *Phlox maculata* is also more resistant to powdery mildew, seldom needs staking and, though lovely in borders, has a natural grace that suits woodland and more naturalistic plantings. A native of damp meadows and lowland woods, the species is very highly scented in a clear soft mauve that is luminously beautiful in the dappled light of a woodland garden; the white flowered sorts, *P. m.* 'Alba', 'Reine du Jour' and 'Schneelawine',

◄ *Phlomis russeliana*

◄ *Phlomis tuberosa* 'Amazone'

◄ *Phlox maculata* 'Omega'

are also outstanding in semi-shade. 'Princess Sturdza' is vigorous, and generous with an abundance of deep mauve flowers.

All of the above are worth seeking out, especially if you prefer plain, self-coloured blooms. Alan Bloom's introductions, as always, have stood the test of time. They include *P. m.* 'Alpha' in a strong lilac mauve, 'Omega', white with a lilac-pink eye, and 'Delta', white with a soft violet eye.

Fully hardy, z3–8. Light dappled shade or sun, in fertile, humus-rich, moisture-retentive soils; an annual mulch of leaf mould or similar helps conserve moisture. See also pages 61 and 222.

Phormium

Phormiaceae

Phormium could have been custom-made as an architectural focal point, whether in a mixed border, standing proudly as a specimen in a sweep of gravel, or in containers on a terrace. The majestic *P. tenax* forms stiff basal fans of broadly linear, evergreen leaves, to head height—smooth-textured and greyish green in the species, dark bronze-purple and handsomely sheened in *P. t.* Purpureum Group and delineated with broad creamy stripes in *P. t.* 'Veitchianum'. When they flower in summer, they produce plummy grey, rigidly vertical stems, each with candelabra of dusky red flowers to twice head height. *Phormium cookianum* is similar but half the height, giving the same strong line but suiting smaller spaces. Both *P. tenax* and *P. cookianum* have been parents to a range of hybrids (several hundreds in a range of exotic colours, heights and habits). At waist high there is *P.* 'Jester', deep rose pink with bronze margins; and 'Maori Chief', bronze, red and pink; 'Maori Sunrise', bronze, gold, apricot and pink. *Phormium* 'Sundowner', at head height, has upright fans in bronze, salmon, cream and rosy pink. They are very tolerant of wind and coastal exposure, and of a wide range of soil types, associating equally well with traditional border perennials and ornamental

grasses, as with the strong forms of euphorbias, and the South American eryngiums. They have a reputation for slight tenderness, more so in the highly coloured cultivars, but it is the softest and youngest leaves produced late in the season that are most vulnerable; given a deep,

▲▲ *Phormium* 'Maori Sunrise'

▲ *Phormium tenax* Purpureum Group

◀ *Phormium* 'Jester'

dry, leafy mulch at the root zone, they usually resume growth the following spring.

Fully hardy, z7–11. Moderately fertile, moisture-retentive but well-drained soil in full sun.

Phyllostachys

Poaceae

Although they are rhizomatous and running in optimal conditions, in cool temperate climes *Phyllostachys* species behave as clumping bamboos, and despite their great potential height they have a relatively small footprint that suits them well to plantings in confined courtyards and borders, and in containers. Where they do spread, they are perfect for the creation of bamboo groves, in the woodland garden, or as screening for privacy.

The eventual height depends somewhat on soil fertility, but more so on climate. Those described reach twice head height in cooler

regions but in warm-temperate conditions are truly majestic, to ten times head height with wrist-thick culms and an indefinite spread.

The coloured cane variants offer strength of vertical line augmented by depth of colour, most clearly seen when the canes are thinned and the lower nodes cleared of branches, so that the tessellated, lanceolate leaves arise in a rustling, mobile cloud atop the stems. *Phyllostachys aureosulcata* and *P. a.* f. *aureocaulis* have rich golden yellow culms, while those of *P. nigra* become glossy black in their second or third year. The canes of *P. viridi-glaucescens* are a smooth glaucous green.

Fully hardy, z7–10/11. Deep, fertile, moisture-retentive, humus-rich and well-drained soil, in light dappled shade.

Physostegia

Lamiaceae • obedient plant

That the hinged flowers of physostegia can be twiddled about and will then stay put in the new position is well known—but why, how and by whom it was discovered remain among life's small mysteries. *Physostegia virginiana*, from damp prairies, riverbanks and thickets in eastern North America, is an erect herbaceous perennial, with terminal racemes of oh-so-neatly ranked, tubular, two-lipped pink flowers from midsummer to autumn. It reaches up to chest high; most of the named selections, including white-flowered 'Crown of Snow' and Summer Snow', are thigh to waist high and less likely to flop and spread widely on fertile soils. *P. virginiana* var. *speciosa* 'Variegata' has white-margined grey-green leaves, and magenta

▲▲ *Phyllostachys nigra*

▲ *Phyllostachys aureosulcata* f. *aureocaulis*

◀ *Phyllostachys viridi-glaucescens*

 *Primula beesiana*

◀ *Physostegia virginiana*
var. *speciosa* 'Variegata'

▶ *Primula japonica*

▶ *Primula sikkimensis*

▶ *Primula florindae*

▲ *Physostegia virginiana*

flowers. They associate well with plumy aruncus and astilbes on the banks of a pool or bog garden, and reinforce the verticals of monardas, echinaceas and eupatoriums in naturalistic meadow plantings or among prairie grasses. The flowers attract butterflies and hummingbirds whether in the wild garden or in more traditional herbaceous border plantings.

Fully hardy, z2/3–9/10. Sun or part-day shade, in any reliably moist, fertile, humusy soil.

Primula

Primulaceae

Within a huge genus of jewel-like beauties are two botanical sections that bear their floral gems aloft on erect stems above a basal rosette of foliage: the Candelabra (Proliferae) and Sikkimensis primulas. Both need consistently damp soils, and cool dappled shade or part shade, and are perfect in drifts in damp woodland, or in bog gardens and streamside plantings, among hostas, *Iris sibirica*, astilbes, rodgersias and rheums. They self-sow, and candelabras hybridize promiscuously; neither can bear hot, humid lowland summers.

The candelabra primulas bear more or less salverform flowers in whorls towards the top of the stems, to about mid thigh, in late spring and early summer. There are many named hybrids of complex parentage involving *P. beesiana*, *P. bulleyana*, *P. japonica*, *P. pulverulenta* and others. The hybrids come in a range of vivid colours including orange, gold, apricot, scarlet, magenta and mauve—they're not noted for their subtlety, especially not when grown in massed admixture. If the thought makes you shudder, choose the species: dark-eyed crimson, pink, or white in *P. japonica*; carmine pink in *P. beesiana*; red-purple in *P. pulverulenta*. *Primula bulleyana* is red in bud, clear golden orange when open.

The elegant Sikkimensis primulas, occurring in moist alpine meadows and mountain streambanks from the eastern Himalayas to western China, have umbels of nodding, sweetly fragrant, funnel-shaped flowers to about waist height, soft yellow in *P. florindae*, and *P. sikkimensis*, dusky rose-purple in *P. secundiflora*.

Fully hardy, z5–8/9. Deep, humus-rich, slightly acid to neutral reliably moist soil in cool, partial or dappled shade.

Romneya

Papaveraceae · Matilja poppy, California tree poppy

The ascending line is strong in *Romneya coulteri*, but made infinitely more effective by the very pale, grey-green stems and divided leaves, along with the sheer grace of its fragrant crystalline flowers. With tight globose buds opening to reveal glistening white petals, pleated and crumpled around a boss of golden stamens, it blooms throughout summer, becoming deciduous in autumn and looking alarmingly as though it has given up the ghost until re-emergence in spring. It occurs in gravelly

sands and red clays of chaparral and coastal sage scrub communities in southern California and New Mexico, and in climates and conditions approximating those in habitat it spreads fiercely and indefinitely by stone-breaking suckers. It is more subdued in cool temperate climates, where it appreciates the freest of drainage and a warm sheltered site. It associates well with artemisias, ballota, caryopteris and dictamnus, and is excellent in gravel gardens and sunny borders.

Fully hardy, z6/7–10. Deep, poor to moderately fertile, well-drained soil in sun. In areas with prolonged frost, give it a dry winter mulch at the root zone.

Roscoaea

Zingiberaceae

From mountain woods and meadows of Sichuan and Yunnan, *Roscoea cautleyoides* is an exotic but hardy member of the ginger family. Its exquisite orchid-like flowers are borne on stout fleshy stems from the upper axils of ascending, lush green, stem-clasping leaves in mid- to late summer. Flowers are a luminous pale yellow (sometimes white or purple) in the species, which reaches about knee high; *R. cautleyoides* 'Kew Beauty' is taller, with larger, soft yellow blooms; 'Purple Giant' is vigorous

◀◀ *Romneya coulteri*

◀ *Roscoea cautleyoides*

and later blooming, with purple flowers. Some vigorous forms of *R. purpurea* are slightly taller; they are late summer blooming and include 'Brown Peacock' with soft violet flowers, and purple-flowered 'Peacock Eye', both with dusky, red-flushed foliage that reinforces the ascending line. Those described emerge late enough to escape the last frosts and appreciate the added protection of deep planting and a deep leafy winter mulch. They need a cool, sheltered site in dappled or partial shade, and are perfect woodland companions for *Disporum*, *Paris* and *Uvularia*.

Fully hardy, z6–9. Deep, leafy, open-textured, moisture-retentive but well-drained soil.

Rubus

Rosaceae

Two of the Chinese brambles are invaluable for the winter presence of their strongly ascending stems. In *R. cockburnianus*, with pinnate dark green leaves that are white beneath, the stems are purple with a brilliant chalk-white bloom. In *R. thibetanus* leaves are ferny, more finely divided, and silvery green above and beneath; the purple stems are heavily bloomed blue-white. It's often sold as 'Silver Fern', a descriptive but invalid name.

If you are into 1970s retro style, grow them with heathers in an island bed. Otherwise, these brambles are a wonderful backdrop to dark evergreen shrubs, such as *Osmanthus*, and are themselves outstanding against a dark background of yews, for instance. The cleanest whites are produced on first-year stems, so cut all stems back to the base in early spring; they reach head height in a single season. (This also helps to control thicket-forming tendencies.) The flowers are fairly insignificant and, like the related raspberries, stems become brown and unattractive once flowered.

Fully hardy, z5–9. Sun, in any well-drained moderately fertile soil.

▲ *Rubus thibetanus* with *Pulmonaria officinalis* 'Sissinghurst White'

◀ *Rubus cockburnianus* with *Helleborus foetidus*

Rudbeckia

Asteraceae • coneflower

Quite different from the usual run of rudbeckias in exuberant reds, golds and oranges, the flowerheads of *Rudbeckia occidentalis* 'Green Wizard' and 'Black Beauty' are reduced to a central black cone with a ring of green bracts beneath, each on a sturdy, upright, waist-high stem well above the foliage. *Rudbeckia maxima*, great coneflower, is a native of prairies, plains and damp pine woods in the southeastern United States—*maxima* being the operative word. Reaching almost twice head height, it has drooping yellow ray florets and a very prominent central black cone, a handspan or more in length, on strong stems that rise well clear

◀ *Rudbeckia occidentalis* 'Green Wizard'

▶ *Salvia* ×*sylvestris* 'Mainacht'

of a rosette of huge glaucous blue-green leaves. They bloom from mid- to late summer and are perfect among gold and blonde prairie grasses.

Fully hardy, z3/4-9. Full sun, in well-drained, reliably moisture-retentive, moderately fertile soil. Tolerant of hot humid summers.

Salvia
Lamiaceae

To ensure a summer-long supply of erect spires in strong indigo-blues and blue-violets, employ a little cunning. The thigh-high, early to midsummer *Salvia* ×*sylvestris* 'Mainacht' begins the season; it has great line and colour but always seems be over far too quickly—so follow through with waist-high *S. verticillata* 'Purple Rain' for mid- to late summer, and

▲ *Salvia verticillata* 'Purple Rain'

▶ *Salvia sclarea* var. *sclarea*

with *S. nemorosa* 'Ostfriesland' and *S.* ×*superba* 'Superba' through midsummer into early autumn. That takes care of a continuous nectar source for bees, and a succession of associations that begins with the mound-forming santolinas and nepetas, continues with astrantias and artemisias and, for a finale, highlights the autumn echinaceas, gauras, grasses, monardas and sedums.

For single-handed summer-long flowering, *S. sclarea* var. *sclarea* is hard to beat. Biennial and freely self-seeding, the overwintering young plants begin to bloom in early summer; seedlings that germinate later flower until frosted in autumn. With large, wrinkled, hairy grey-green leaves and candelabra of two-lipped, earthy pink flowers that ascend

◀ *Salvia* ×*superba*
'Superba'

◀ *Salvia nemorosa*
'Ostfriesland'

▶ *Sanguisorba canadensis*
with *Molinia caerulea*
subsp. *arundinacea*
'Variegata'

to chest height, it is wonderfully aromatic, and versatile in a range of associations (all of those mentioned above); it has sufficient heft to hold its own with *Onopordum* and *Cynara cardunculus*. Take care that its hooligan offspring are where you want them; they rapidly overshadow less vigorous neighbours.

Fully hardy, z4/5–9. Full sun, moderately fertile, moisture-retentive but well-drained soil.

Sanguisorba

Rosaceae ▪ burnet

Increasing in popularity and availability along with the rising interest in ornamental grasses with which they associate so well, most of the now commonly grown sanguisorbas are damp meadow and grassland natives. All have

pinnate leaves, with very neatly toothed and veined leaflets, and bear erect, wiry-stemmed flowers well above the foliage over long periods in summer, sometimes well into autumn, followed by persistent seedheads in winter. The terminal flower spikes fall into two main types: bottlebrushes, with long prominent stamens, and tight, ovoid or cylindrical bobbles. *Sanguisorba menziesii* has tight bottle brushes in intense maroon purple, at about thigh high in early to midsummer. *S. tenuifolia*, at waist to chest high or above, is later flowering and very variable, but all have particularly slender leaflets of very fine texture and long catkin-like spikes that may be fat, erect and dark purple-maroon (*S. tenuifolia* 'Purpurea'); slender, pink and slightly nodding ('Pink Elephant'); or

◀ *Sanguisorba tenuifolia*

◀ *Sanguisorba menziesii*

◀ *Sanguisorba obtusa*

elegantly pendent and fluffy in some forms of the species. *Sanguisorba canadensis* has strong stems and upright bottlebrush spikes of creamy white flowers at head height or above from late summer into autumn. One of the prettiest is waist-high *S. obtusa* which has beautifully glaucous foliage and produces nodding, very fluffy, rose pink bottlebrush spikes in mid- to late summer, looking for all the world like a bobby-soxer's pony tail.

Fully hardy, z2/3–8, *S. menziesii*, *S. canadensis*; z4–9, *S. obtusa*, *S. tenuifolia*. Reliably moist but well-drained, fertile soil in sun or light dappled shade.

Sidalcea

Malvaceae ▪ prairie mallow

Long esteemed for the erect and graceful summer spikes of silk-satin flowers like ethereal hollyhocks, and grown in cottage gardens and herbaceous borders in Europe since Victorian times, these American beauties are native to high coastal meadows, montane and subalpine glades and streambanks of central and western North America. Most of the cultivars are about waist high, and are hybrids of *S. candida* and *S. malviflora*, ranging from the silvery pinks of *S.* 'Reverend Page Roberts', the soft shell pinks of 'Elsie Heugh' with fringed petals, to the deeper clear pinks of 'Rose Queen' and 'Sussex Beauty'.

◀ *Sidalcea* 'Rose Queen'

◀ *Sidalcea* 'Elsie Heugh'

▶ *Sisyrynchium striatum*

◀ *Sidalcea* 'Reverend Page Roberts' with *Galega* ×*hartlandii* 'Lady Wilson'

▶ *Sisyrynchium striatum* 'Aunt May'

Sidalcea candida 'Bianca' is pure white. They will always be lovely in the traditional border, but it's no surprise, given their native habitats, that they also look so well with echinaceas, gauras, *P. amplexicaulis* 'Alba' and 'Rosea' among deschampsias, stipas and other gauzy grasses. With reliable summer moisture they bloom from mid- to late summer.

Fully hardy, z4–8. Sun and moderately fertile, moisture-retentive soil.

Sisyrynchium

Iridaceae

Both waist-high *Sisyrinchium striatum* and its shorter variegated cultivar 'Aunt May' form a stiff fan of diagonally poised grey-green leaves, the form neatly delineated in 'Aunt May', with sword-shaped leaves broadly striped in rich

cream. The flower stems rise vertically in early and midsummer, bearing flexuous spikes of small creamy white flowers. They mark the front of a border with precision, and are well suited to gravel and terrace plantings, where they will self-sow.

Fully hardy, z7–9. Near-neutral to slightly alkaline, poor or not-too-fertile soil with good drainage in sun.

▲ *Tellima grandiflora*

Tellima

Saxifragaceae ▪ fringe cups

Denizen of damp forests and meadows of western North America, *Tellima grandiflora* is a plainer but more elegant relative of *Heuchera*, with rounded, scalloped, semi-evergreen leaves in basal rosettes, often red-flushed in autumn. In spring and early summer, it produces upright stems, to thigh high, with racemes of tiny cupped, pale creamy green flowers with fringed petals. They are sweetly fragrant, especially in 'Bob's Choice' and the Odorata Group. In *T. grandiflora* Rubra Group, the pale green flowers are rimmed in dusky red. They make good ground cover in wild and woodland gardens and in partly shaded borders, and despite their preference for moist soils they are remarkably drought tolerant once established.

Fully hardy, z4–8. Damp leafy soil in dappled shade or part-day sun.

Tricyrtis

Convallariaceae ▪ toad lily

Remarkably easy to grow and willing to spread, both *Tricyrtis formosana* and *T. hirta* produce exotically oriental, exquisitely formed autumn flowers, poised on firm, slender, flexuous stems to about thigh high. Although these herbaceous perennials look fragile, they are remarkably tough, the stems remaining erect throughout the long flowering period. *Tricyrtis formosana* has star-shaped flowers with rather fleshy petals, white but heavily spotted with deep pink or purple, sitting upright on branching stems; *T. hirta* has funnel-shaped flowers, white spotted purple, or pure white and very elegant in *T. hirta* var. *alba*. They flower at the same time as *Kirengeshoma palmata*, and the association is perfect in dappled woodland shade. The lance-shaped, prominently veined, lush green leaves of these late-flowering species emerge late enough to avoid frosts, but in cold winter areas the rootstock is probably best protected with a deep leafy mulch.

Fully hardy, z5/6–9. Moist but well-drained leafy soil in dappled shade

Uvularia

Convallariaceae ▪ merrybells

Uvularia species are late spring flowering herbaceous perennials of languid grace from damp, wooded, often limestone slopes in eastern

◀ *Tricyrtis formosana*

▼ *Uvularia grandiflora*
var. *pallida*

North America. *Uvularia grandiflora* has lush, lance-shaped leaves that drape like heavy silk from the vertical stems, which arch at their tips to bear long bell-shaped, yellow flowers with twisted tepals; *U. grandiflora* var. *pallida* bears pale creamy yellow later in spring. Reaching mid thigh, they associate well with the related disporums and polygonatums, and with epi-

▲ *Uvularia grandiflora*

mediums, trilliums, lacy dicentras and ferns in woodland gardens, beneath a canopy of deciduous trees, or in borders in dappled shade. Given woodsy soils that are moist and open-textured, they will form colonies; adequate moisture sustains luxuriant foliage until they become dormant later in summer.

Fully hardy, z3–8. Moist but well-drained humus-rich soil in dappled or fairly deep shade.

Veratrum

Melanthiaceae

From damp woods and meadows, all veratrums are imposing perennials when in flower. Their vertical, chest- to head-high spires of tiny star-shaped flowers are borne on ascending branches in summer, but their beauty begins early in the season, as the leaves begin to emerge from long, tightly folded buds, opening and unfolding pleated and glistening like the silk of a Fortuny dress. *Veratrum nigrum* has dark mahogany, almost black, flowers, while those of *V. viride* are emerald green; guess what colour those of *V. alba* are. They associate beautifully with corrugated hostas, *Euphorbia stygiana* and the

137

◀ *Veratrum viride*

▶ *Verbascum* 'Helen Johnson' with anthriscus and poppies

▼ *Verbascum bombyciferum* 'Polarsommer'

emergent foliage of *Paeonia mlokosewitschii*. All parts are toxic; don't eat them.

Fully hardy, z3–8. Dappled shade or part-day sun, in deep, open-textured, fertile soils that are reliably moisture retentive and humus rich.

Verbascum

Scrophulariaceae ▪ mullein

The taller mulleins bear flowers in spikes or racemes arising from a basal foliage rosette. Some, like *V. bombyciferum* and *V.* 'Helen Johnson', are unbranched or sparsely branched, which gives a clearer line, while *V. olympicum* branches freely and forms an erect candelabra of flower spikes. *Verbascum bombyciferum* forms a rosette of large, densely silky hairy basal leaves, with white woolly stems and felted buds that open to soft yellow flowers on spires to head height and above in summer; *V. b.* 'Polarsommer', 'Silver Lining' and 'Arctic Snow' are especially white-hairy. *Verbascum olympicum* is similarly tall and grey-white hirsute, with brighter yellow flowers from early to late summer. They usually die after flowering (being monocarpic) but self-seed freely, and spent flower stems are long standing. Although height usually confines them to back border placement, both *V. bombyciferum* and *V. olympicum* are invaluable in lending rhythm and repetition, placed at intervals to draw the eye through a scheme. All verbascums will thrive in freely draining, low-fertility soils, and the taller species especially are best treated mean and lean. They are perfect in wild and gravel gardens; they become lax and need support on rich soils.

▲ *Verbascum olympicum*

▲ *Verbascum chaixii*
'Album'

▲ *Verbena bonariensis*

Shorter verbascums include *V. chaixii* with greyish green leaves and slender spires in pale yellow at waist height—and in case you thought all verbascums were yellow, *V. chaixii* 'Album' has white flowers with a dark mauve-pink eye. *Verbascum* 'Helen Johnson' bears branched spires throughout summer, in earthy, dusky pink, at about waist height, a beautiful colour for associating with dark-leaved shrubs, bronze fennel or the dusty pinks of grasses such as *Pennisetum orientale* 'Karley Rose'.

Fully hardy, z4/5–9. Sun and poor to moderately fertile, well-drained, preferably alkaline soil.

Verbena

Verbenaceae

By the time a plant becomes as ubiquitous as *Verbena bonariensis*, several things have happened: it has become hackneyed by overuse, and sneered at by cognoscenti—and we have lost sight of why it is deservedly popular. Few other

◀ *Verbena hastata* f. *rosea*

139

plants carry such strong colour in flat heads at head height, on dark, slender, stiffly vertical and almost leafless stems, with a transparency that is exceptionally useful in bringing height to the front of a scheme, and for embroidering more gauzy textures of gauras, polygonatums and grasses. It flowers from midsummer well into autumn. The skill is to use its undoubted attributes well. A smattering is all that's needed, which means selectively controlling its profuse self-seeding, and probably allowing self-sown seedlings to create some of their own accidental incidents.

Verbena hastata exhibits a similar rigidity of line, but with a branched candelabra of blue-violet flower spikes at chest to head height; for more ethereal effects, try the white- flowered *V. hastata* 'Alba' or the pink *V. hastata* f. *rosea*.

Fully hardy, z3–8, *V. hastata*; z7-10, *V. bonariensis*. Sun and poor to moderately fertile, well-drained soil.

Veronicastrum

Scrophulariaceae ▪ culver's root

From thickets and rich woodland and prairie grasslands of eastern North America, *Veronicastrum virginicum* is a natural choice for bringing late summer and autumn colour and line to prairie plantings, and with ornamental grasses such as *Pennisetum orientale* and *Panicum virgatum*. It is tall and sufficiently graceful to bring strong lines to gravel gardens, or mixed and herbaceous borders, where it associates well with astrantias, echinaceas, *Helianthus giganteus* and *H. salicifolius*. Its erect stems, with whorls of lanceolate leaves, bear slender, elegantly tapering spires of tiny flowers with long stamens, at their tips and from the upper leaf axils, at chest to head height. The stiff seedheads are long standing. The species has white, pink or pale purple flowers; in *V. virginicum* 'Album' white flowers are borne on dark stems; in *V. virginicum* f. *roseum* and *V. v.* 'Erica' flowers are soft pink (in the latter the leaves are tinted red). Stronger colours are to

◀ *Veronicastrum virginicum*

▶ *Veronicastrum virginicum* f. *roseum*

▼ *Veronicastrum virginicum* 'Fascination'

be had in *V. v.* 'Fascination', clear lavender blue with red anthers; *V. v.* 'Temptation', soft rose-purple; and *V. v.* 'Lavendelturm' with lavender flowers.

Fully hardy, z4–9. Sun and moist, moderately fertile soil; drought tolerant once established.

Wisteria

Papilionaceae

The most obvious line presented by the wisterias is the descending vertical of the racemes of pea-like early summer flowers, although depending on how you choose to grow and train them, horizontal swags of foliage and bare winter branches formed by espalier training are equally valid categories. And with age they all develop a sinuous, twisting and increasingly characterful winter outline that might easily have inspired the children's illustrator Arthur Rackham.

The strong vertical line, if that is your choice, depends on careful selection among the species and cultivars, and fearless pruning. *Wisteria floribunda* generally produces more slender

▲ *Wisteria sinensis* 'Alba'

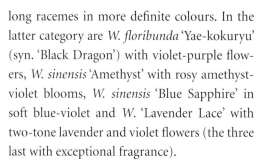

racemes than *W. sinensis*, but bears them *among* the young foliage. *W. sinensis* flowers precociously *before* the leaves emerge fully, so that plumper flower chains are more clearly visible. But selections, hybrids and cultivars are available that either have exceptionally long racemes, as in lilac-blue-flowered *W. floribunda* 'Multijuga' (syn. 'Macrobotrys'), or produce fairly long racemes in more definite colours. In the latter category are *W. floribunda* 'Yae-kokuryu' (syn. 'Black Dragon') with violet-purple flowers, *W. sinensis* 'Amethyst' with rosy amethyst-violet blooms, *W. sinensis* 'Blue Sapphire' in soft blue-violet and *W.* 'Lavender Lace' with two-tone lavender and violet flowers (the three last with exceptional fragrance).

▲▲ *Wisteria floribunda* with *Geranium* ×*magnificum*

▲ *Wisteria floribunda* 'Multijuga'

The flowers are borne on lateral spurs on mature wood, and to ensure good spur formation (and the control of rampant growth), you need to prune in midwinter during dormancy, and in summer about six to eight weeks after flowering. It's time consuming but easy and rather therapeutic. Spend the first three years forming a permanent framework: during summer, tie in a leading shoot to the vertical and select laterals (sideshoots) to form horizontal arms, and tie them in to wires. Remove excess laterals, and prune any sideshoots growing from the horizontal arms to three to four buds. In winter, shorten horizontal arms by about a third of their length, and cut back the vertical leader to where you want the second tier of horizontals to emerge. Do the same in summer and winter in years two and three, or until the framework is complete. Thereafter, summer pruning involves cutting back all sideshoots to within five to six buds of the main woody framework; in winter, shorten the summer-pruned sideshoots back to two or three buds of the main framework.

Fully hardy, z5–9. Sun or dappled shade, in moisture-retentive but well-drained, fertile soil.

Yucca

Agavaceae

Despite their succulence and exotic appearance, several of the yuccas are remarkably hardy—especially those that form a stemless rosette of more or less sword-shaped leaves which give a highly dynamic architectural accent with their broad evergreen fans of diagonal lines. The second (but by no means secondary) line is the boldly ascending vertical of the stems that bear stiffly erect panicles of pendent bell-shaped, creamy white flowers in mid- to late summer, to head height in *Y. filamentosa* and *Y. flaccida*, even more majestic in *Y. gloriosa*. They are excellent in dry and gravel gardens, where a clean foreground emphasizes the strong line.

Fully hardy, z4/5–11; z6-10, *Y. gloriosa*. Full sun in any well-drained soil.

◀ *Yucca gloriosa*

◀ *Yucca filamentosa* 'Variegata'

Arcs and Fountains

Arcs and Fountains are the plants that bring curving, arching, rising and falling lines to the garden composition. They may mimic the ascending arcs of mounded forms, echoing and reinforcing their subsidiary line as they rise above them. A dynamically rising line is more graceful than a vertical one, and when tall enough to overarch, the curves give a sense of comfortable enclosure and visual completion to a planting. In plants that form fountains, the stems ascend almost vertically, and then arch at the top—often, like weepers, bringing about a cascading effect that is dynamic and kinetic, nearly always responsive to the breeze and frequently bringing an element of soft, susurrating whispers to the scheme.

In practice, I often find that woody plants used for their arching line reveal the clearest curves when pruned specifically to enhance the effect; the deutzias, kolkwitzias and philadelphus are good examples. Not that I would be so shallow as to prune simply for good line: all of these flower on the previous season's wood, and cutting back to a low framework immediately after their early summer flowering induces strong new shoots that arc more graciously and bloom more bountifully the following year, provided of course that you feed and water well to help them overcome any shock.

The same principle applies to late-flowerers such as *Buddleja davidii* cultivars and *Sorbaria* species, except that late-flowering shrubs are pruned in spring since they usually flower on the current year's growth. With *Sorbaria*, *Neillia* and *Stephanandra* there are additional advantages: the winter stems are glossier on younger growth. Since such well-directed

▲ *Abelia ×grandiflora*

pruning also avoids congestion and buildup of dead wood in the long term, it's equally good for health and the line of beauty.

Abelia
Caprifoliaceae

Not all abelias have the arching habit of *A. ×grandiflora*, the toughest hybrid. An evergreen shrub with small glossy leaves, shimmering after rain, it bears fragrant clusters of pink-tinted white flowers from mid- to late summer or early autumn. Without pruning, *A. ×grandiflora* forms a basal mound of twiggy growth with longer, clearly arching canes rising above it, finally reaching way above head height; however, if grown in good fertile soil, once it is well-established and growth is vigorous, it can be cut to a low framework in early spring, and fed and watered to urge it on. The result is long arching canes of bloom—perhaps flowering a little later in summer, but going on well into

autumn. I grow it with mounded choisyas, and shrubby lilacs (see page 230) to form a series of sheltered coves for bulbs and lower perennials.

Hardy, z7–10. Deep, fertile, well-drained soil in full sun.

Amorpha
Papilionaceae

Multi-stemmed, deciduous *Amorpha fruticosa* forms a tall, ungainly shrub in the wild, and left to itself in the garden it gives similar results. It is aromatic, with graceful, dark green leaves divided into well-spaced leaflets, and in spring or summer it bears long racemes of deep purple flowers spouting orange anthers from between their lips; the colour is particularly rich in *A. fruticosa* 'Dark Lance'. It flowers on the current season's growth, and by cutting back to a low woody framework in spring you gain a handsome, head-high, arching specimen that flowers usefully late in the season. Found

◀ *Amorpha fruticosa*

▶ *Athyrium niponicum*
var. *pictum*

in the wild on riverbeds and in damp thickets, it's useful for streambanks and poolsides, yet remarkably tolerant of drier soils. It's a weed in some states (Connecticut, Washington), being toxic to livestock and potentially invasive.

Its subshrubby cousin *A. canescens*, to waist height, is entirely clothed in dense ash grey down—stems, flower buds and the almost mimosa-like leaves; in mid- to late summer, it produces slender spikes of violet-blue flowers. A native of savannas, plains and prairies of central North America, it associates well with prairie grasses, such as *Panicum* or *Stipa*. It makes a very attractive, arching mound when pruned as for lavender.

Fully hardy, z2–9. Full sun in any light, open, well-drained soil; *A. fruticosa* tolerates light dappled shade. Most species sprout from the rootstock if cut down by harsh winters. A good nectar and larval food source for beneficial insects.

Athyrium
Woodsiaceae

Only a couple of the hardy species of *Athyrium* are commonly seen in gardens. *Athyrium filix-femina*, lady fern, with soft light green fronds in the form of an arching shuttlecock at waist height, has many crested, congested and plumose sports which, though beautiful, muddle the clean arching line. They are totally deciduous, dying back in autumn. The species is graceful and lacy—wonderful in the dappled light of a woodland garden. Among the fancy sports, *A. filix-femina* 'Vernoniae', to mid thigh, is a feathery clear bright green, slightly crested but not so as to spoil the line, while 'Dre's Dagger' is shorter still, with exceptionally narrow, arching fronds, crested at the tip and clothed in narrow, cruciate pinnae that criss-cross to form an elegant lattice on either side of the stipe.

Athyrium niponicum is usually seen as *A. niponicum* var. *pictum*, with dark red-purple stalks and fronds of metallic silvery grey suffused with deep red and purple.

Both species occur in damp, sheltered, cool-humid habitats and are perfect for bog gardens, damp woodland and shady borders.

Fully hardy, z3–7. Fertile, moist, humus-rich, neutral to slightly acid soil in dappled light or shade.

Blechnum
Blechnaceae

Blechnum chilense is much hardier than usually credited, especially if protected at the crown with a winter mulch or a litter of its own dried fronds. It's an imposing fern of great substance, which when mature arches from a short trunk. Tightly coiled, tawny hairy crosiers expand late in spring (missing the worst frosts), finally unfurling to massive, arching fronds about a metre (three feet) in length, with broad, leathery, deep green pinnae with undulating margins. Although evergreen, the previous year's fronds are in a parlous state after the winter,

Blechnum chilense

Buddleja alternifolia

Buddleja davidii 'Black Knight'

and are best cut away; it creeps slowly to form an undulating sea of green if left unchecked. If you intend to give a free rein, grow in a woodland garden with plenty of room to expand. Otherwise, grow in a shady sheltered border.

Thigh high. Hardy, z8–10. Reliably moist, humus-rich acid soil in shade or dappled shade, with shelter from drying winds. See also page 46 (Horizontals and Tiers).

Buddleja

Buddlejaceae

Viewed from the train, it's a hard call whether *Buddleja davidii* is an alien invasive or a naturalized guest, for escapees from gardens have colonized most of Britain's railways—benefiting, one supposes, the butterfly and bee populations that drink its nectar. Even wildlings have long, arching stems tipped with long, arching racemes of tiny scented flowers, but to ensure a strong line, both *B. davidii* and *B.* ×*weyeriana* must be pruned. Cut back to healthy pairs of buds on a low woody framework in early spring—to knee high if you dare; they flower from midsummer onwards on the current season's growth. The former bears tiny fragrant flowers in long, dense, arching panicles, ranging in colour from white in *B. davidii* 'White Profusion' to the strong deep magenta of 'Royal Red', the clear violet-blue of 'Empire Blue' to the deep indigo of 'Black Knight', with all shades of pink and lavender in between. For smaller spaces, try *B. davidii* 'Nanho Blue' or 'Nanho Purple', with finer foliage and more slender racemes. *Buddleja* ×*weyeriana* has rounded flower clusters in arching, interrupted panicles, in warm shades of yellow, but in 'Moonlight' a mix of soft apricot and violet.

Buddleja alternifolia flowers early in summer on the previous season's wood, and is naturally arching, but when left unpruned it rapidly becomes a tangled, formless mass. It bears strongly fragrant, lilac-purple flowers in dense rounded clusters along the length of the previous year's growth. By far the best way to achieve arching elegance is to train it as a clear-stemmed standard and prune out flowered shoots immediately after flowering to upward- and outward-pointing buds or shoots.

For distinctive texture and outstanding

Buddleja davidii 'Nanho Blue'

Buddleja ×*weyeriana* 'Moonlight'

foliage, there is sweetly scented *B. fallowiana*, with panicles of pale lavender flowers, as well as *B. fallowiana* 'Alba', with orange-eyed white ones; more compact than *B. davidii*, the leaves are densely white-felted, and borne on white woolly stems. Best in a warm, sunny sheltered site, it should be pruned more gently than *B. davidii*. Perhaps the loveliest buddleja is *B.* 'Morning Mist', an evergreen with the whitest foliage of all, and short dense panicles of fragrant, orange-eyed white flowers. A sterile hybrid (so no seedlings), it's at least as hardy as *B. fallowiana* in the same conditions. Against a warm sunny wall, it flowers from early summer till Christmas.

Head high and above, even if pruned. Fully hardy, z4/5–9; z8–9, *B. fallowiana*. Any moderately fertile, well-drained soil in full sun.

Carex

Cyperaceae • sedge

Although most sedges occur in damp and wet habitats like bogs, moors, damp woodland and riverbanks, many of those commonly used in gardens are easily pleased. Some, such as *C. pendula*, tolerate dry shade. All provide a more or less arching line, but for this to be effective in a composition they need to be knee high or taller, and with some strength of colour to recommend them. *Carex buchananii* makes a knee- to thigh-high, neatly symmetrical, fine-textured clump of very slender, arching leaves in tawny brown that associates particularly well with dusky pinks, apricots and darker reds in a border, although its symmetry also lends itself to plantings in tall containers. *Carex flagellifera* and *C. f.* 'Auburn Cascade' are similarly symmetrical and foxy in colour, but taller. The three last colour best in sun and tolerate most soils unless they're very dry or wet.

Carex elata 'Aurea', Bowles's golden sedge, is deciduous but each spring pushes up slender, lime green then golden yellow, arching leaves, narrowly outlined in green, making a dense clump to mid thigh height. It grows in moist or

▲ *Carex elata* 'Aurea'

▶ *Carex oshimensis* 'Evergold'

wet soils, and is shade tolerant—lovely in dappled light and for illuminating shady places. *Carex oshimensis* 'Evergold' is evergreen, below knee high, and excellent for contrasts of colour and form throughout the year. The leaves have a central stripe of bright yellow, fading to creamy yellow margined with dark green, and although it thrives in sun or partial shade, it colours best in light shade.

Carex pendula, to chest high, is as graceful in its sheaves of broad, leathery, dark green leaves as it is in flower in early summer, when long, pendent dusky catkins hang from arching stems. In *C. pendula* 'Moonraker' the new cream leaves pass through yellow and lime green before becoming dark green in late summer. It comes true from seed. These are robust sedges that will grow in sun or shade in dry, moist or wet soils—very effective when arching over open water, and a good anchor among other grasses of lighter texture.

The coloured sedges, used in borders, as edging and for their potential contrasts with other non-grassy plants, are effective in massed plantings, creating drifts or sinuous forms in the landscape.

Fully hardy, z5–9, *C. pendula*; z6/7–9 *C. buchananii*, *C. elata*; z7–11, *C. flagellifera*.

Cercidiphyllum

Cercidiphyllaceae • katsura

I know a woodland glade with a grove of *C. japonicum*, all seed-raised. The natural variation is astonishing. There are tall trees with tiered skirts of arching, downswept branches wreathed in heart-shaped leaves that are golden bronze when young and a stunning array of gold, russet, apricot and crimson at leaf fall. Others are vase-shaped fountains, a few are twisted and gnarled. I know they've never been pruned or shaped, so...am I on a bit of a sticky wicket in claiming they are arching? *Cercidiphyllum japonicum* f. *pendulum* is truly a weeper, but I suspect there is more than one form in cultivation. The tree I first admired, which inspired me to buy one, was gracefully arching; the one I now have has firmly downward-pointing branches and wouldn't be out of place in a Victorian cemetery.

Cercidiphyllum japonicum 'Amazing Grace' forms a series of long, arching, leafy cascades from sinuously arching branches; 'Tidal Wave' is similar, and both make specimens that are wider than tall (five times head height in ten years). *C. j.* 'Morioka Weeping' also cascades, but is a narrower form; it grows vertically

▶ *Cercidiphyllum japonicum*

when young, adopting an increasingly weeping habit with age. So it pays to buy a named cultivar, and give it pride of place as a specimen in an open glade. If your tree develops multiple stems, allow it the privilege—and may your cascades multiply. The trees need shelter from dry winds and adequate summer moisture to prevent burning of the leaf margins. In a sheltered place, you should detect a sweet aroma of caramel as the leaves take on their stunning autumn colours and begin to fall.

Fully hardy, z4–8. Deep, moisture-retentive, humus-rich soil, preferably neutral to acid, in light dappled shade or sun.

Cercis

Caesalpiniaceae

It is easy to forgive a gawky adolescence and an ungainly vase-shaped youth, for as *Cercis canadensis* matures the arching line of the slender branches becomes evident. When tall enough to develop a clear stem and an open canopy of thin-textured, heart-shaped leaves, the leaves filter sunlight in shades of green and

◀ Cercis canadensis
'Forest Pansy', autumn
colour

▶ Cercis canadensis
'Forest Pansy'

gold—equalled if not surpassed in beauty by the rich red-purple leaves of *C. canadensis* 'Forest Pansy', which filters graduated shades of red-gold and crimson. It's a performance that's repeated in both, as leaves take on hues of gold and crimson before falling. The canopy is light enough to plant beneath—the roots go deep and offer little competition to companions.

The flowering habit of *Cercis* species is endearingly described by botanists as cauliflorous. From bare branches sprout stalkless clusters of pink, crimson, or purple pea flowers, bursting out before the leaves. The western redbud, *C. occidentalis*, is a multi-stemmed shrub or small tree, denser in habit, forming an ascending starburst in every shade of pink that is stunning when in full bloom in the wild, on dry, brushy slopes of the western foothills of California. *Cercis canadensis* reaches five to six times head height in optimal conditions, but very slowly, and only half that in cool-maritime gardens; *C. canadensis* 'Forest Pansy' is shorter and slower still. *Cercis occidentalis* reaches twice head height, by as much across.

Fully hardy, z5–9. Full sun in deep, fertile, moist but well-drained, acid or alkaline soil, preferably loamy-sandy soils, but tolerant of heavier clays. Drought tolerant when established. *Cercis* dislike transplanting.

Cerinthe

Boraginaceae • honeywort

I first introduced *Cerinthe major* 'Purpurascens' to my borders as an annual filler, admiring the bloomed, deep grey-green leaves and the arching line of the nodding cymes of deep purple flowers enclosed in large bloomy bracts tinted with grey, blue and purple. It is wonderful with grey- and silver-leaved plants, and bees love it. Although grown as an annual, it will behave as a biennial, self-sown seedlings germinating during summer and flowering the following year. The densest and most beautifully coloured clumps develop in paving niches or gravel, and in other hot, dry sites in poor soils and full sun. Those that scatter themselves in more fertile soils become floppy, and very frost sensitive. They smother neighbours, and

◀ *Cerinthe major* 'Purpurascens'

▶ *Cerinthe major* 'Purpurascens', inflorescence

as flowered stems die back, they smear their soggy selves all over their companions.

Knee high. Hardy, z7–10. Full sun, in poor, gritty, well-drained soils.

Chusquea

Poaceae

I have had bamboos foisted upon me. While I admire their arching line, their often handsomely coloured culms, and their graceful wind-rippling movement, many bamboos look best when you thin out the culms and strip the lower leaves to expose their full colour and beauty. This is hard and time-consuming work when faced with extensive stands.

On the other hand, I have *Chusquea culeou*, from high altitudes in temperate montane forests in the Andes, which I resolutely refuse to touch with secateurs or loppers. It is one of the most naturally graceful of arching fountains, a clumping bamboo with thick, glossy, olive green culms, marked with white wax at the nodes, punctuated by papery white leaf sheaths, and with lightly chequered, linear green leaves arising in alternate branched sprays from the nodes. My favourite specimen, three times my height by as much across at twenty-five years old, was heartbreakingly beautiful in flower, when each culm sported a shimmering, honey-gold plume, glistening in dappled light. Then, of course, it died. Nevertheless, the seeds germinated like grass and I anticipate a long love affair with the offspring—the perfect specimens in dappled light in a woodland garden.

▼ *Chusquea culeou*

Fully hardy, z7/8–10. Moist but well-drained, open-textured humus-rich soil in dappled shade or sun, with shelter from strong and dry winds.

Cotinus

Anacardiaceae · smoke bush

I first saw *Cotinus coggygria* as a mounded ground layer beneath mature maples and red oaks forming an amphitheatre of breath-taking autumn colour. For years I used cotinus in all its forms as large, mound-forming specimens, loving the smoky haze of flowers that haloed them in mid- to late summer. They flower on two- to three-year-old wood, and are pruned minimally for best flowering, when they will reach two to three times head height. But there are good reasons for pruning: to create a fountain of foliage for great colour contrasts in sum-

mer and blazing arcs of scarlet and crimson in autumn, and to induce larger-than-average, translucent, light-filtering leaves in summer. I've planted stands of *C. coggygria*, *C. coggygria* 'Royal Purple', *C.* 'Flame' and *C.* 'Grace' which grew so fast in their first summer that they split out at the branch junctions in their first winter. I pruned them back to a low framework in early spring, only to find I had on my hands a group of shrubs with long, arching branches. I liked the effect so much that I now cut a couple in each group back every year to within a couple of good strong buds of the framework; the wands get to head height in a season. Working

▼ *Cotinus coggygria* 'Royal Purple'

154

on a three-year cycle, I leave the others to grow on to flowering haze stage.

Fully hardy, z4/5–10. Any moderately fertile, moist but well-drained soil in sun or dappled shade.

Deutzia

Hydrangeaceae

Deutzias are mostly deciduous shrubs, from montane scrub and forest in the Himalayas and eastern Asia; among them are several that flower on young shoots arising from arching canes formed the previous season. They bow naturally, and if you don't enjoy pruning they can be left to form mounds of arching branches, each arc delineated by terminal and axillary clusters of starry flowers in late spring and early summer. In truth, though, once the plants are well-established, the clearest lines are had by cutting back flowered shoots to strong pairs of buds low down on the same shoot immediately after flowering. I think it's absolutely necessary, the counsel of perfection that they deserve.

There are no harsh or vivid colours in deutzia flowers; their clean whites, soft pinks and lavender pinks, in late spring and early to midsummer, are lovely where a darker backdrop can be arranged. I use them with philadelphus and viburnums, *Dipelta* and *Kolkwitzia*, on the sunny side of woodland just beyond the shade canopy of trees; my forester friends call it a light-demanding edge mix. They serve as a transitional zone between formal and wilder parts of the garden.

At waist to chest height: *D. gracilis* is fine-textured, with small bright green leaves and open, upright racemes of fragrant, glistening white flowers; *D. monbeigii* has darker green leaves with pale undersides and corymbs of starry white flowers.

At head height: *D. ×elegantissima* 'Rosealind' has starry corymbs in soft carmine pink; *D. ×hybrida* 'Magicien' has panicles of open bell-shaped flowers in soft mauve-pink, edged white and with a darker reverse; quietly aristocratic

D. longifolia 'Veitchii' has long, greyish green, lance-shaped leaves and dark young shoots, with panicles of starry, pale-lavender-pink flowers. *Deutzia setchuenensis* var. *corymbiflora* must be one of the most elegant of the genus, with slender, gracefully disposed branches, long-pointed grey-green leaves, and airy, open corymbs of pearly white buds that burst to wide-open stars of glistening white.

Fully hardy, z4/5–9; z6–9, *D. longifolia*, *D. setchuenensis* var. *corymbiflora*. Most types of moderately fertile, moist but well-drained soil in sun, or light, dappled, part-day shade. Tough: pollution and drought tolerant.

Dicentra

Papaveraceae ▪ bleeding heart, lyre flower

From deep shady valleys and woods of Siberia, northern China and Korea, in all cultural respects, *Dicentra spectabilis* has the same requirements as the clump-forming dicentras (see page 194), but its pendent heart-shaped flowers are strung out along such definitely arching stems, above arching mounds of

▶ *Deutzia setchuenensis* var. *corymbiflora*

◀ *Cotinus* 'Grace'

◀ *Cotinus* 'Flame'

◀ *Dicentra spectabilis*

◀ *Dicentra spectabilis*
'Alba', with trilliums and
epimediums

▶ *Dipelta floribunda*

Dipelta

Caprifoliaceae

Of the dipeltas most frequently seen in gardens, *D. floribunda* is the more common, and *D. yunnanensis* the shorter, more arching, more elegant and with glossier foliage. Although tall, they are narrow at ground level, the sturdy stems shooting upwards, then branching in graceful arcs clothed with drooping lance-shaped leaves, then bowing to present fragrant corymbs of tubular, bell-shaped flowers in late spring and early summer. In *D. floribunda* they're palest pink, while *D. yunnanensis* has

divided pale green leaves. The species has rose-pink hearts enclosing white inner petals and flowers in late spring and early summer.

Dicentra spectabilis 'Alba' is a much better plant, for not only are its pure white flowers and paler foliage more outstanding in shade, but it also blooms for a much longer period, going on until midsummer. I use it with dark-flowered hellebores and blue pulmonarias; it outlasts them both, then takes up with drifts of dame's rocket, *Hesperis matronalis*, *Lamium orvala* and *Myrrhis odorata*.

Knee high. Fully hardy, z4–9. Fertile, humus-rich, moisture-retentive soil in partial or dappled shade. See also page 194 (Clumps and Mounds).

orange-marked, creamy white flowers; both produce clusters of fruits with papery wings, which persist into winter.

The tall canes of *D. floribunda* are extremely handsome when of an age for the golden brown bark to flake and peel. Once established, canes produce further extension growth from the top, and another taller layer of arcs. As the shrubs mature, these often shade out the layers beneath, which spoils the line and obscures the bark. Strong new growth is usually produced from the base, however, so that the oldest flowered canes can be cut out at the base immediately after flowering. Both *D. floribunda* and *D. yunnanensis* are beautiful specimens in a shrub border, and your first instinct may be to site them at the rear, denying the pleasure of looking into their faces. Next to a door or path is better, and if you have terracing or steps, better still—site a dipelta alongside, so that flowers greet you as you reach the top.

Twice head height. Fully hardy, z6–9. Moderately fertile, moist but well-drained, preferably alkaline soil in sun, or light, dappled, part-day shade.

Dryopteris

Dryopteridaceae • buckler fern, shield fern

Mostly northern-temperate ferns from woodlands, streambanks and other damp places, the bucklers are mostly deciduous, with long, pinnate, or more finely divided fronds. The species that take the shuttlecock formation, with fronds arching from an erect central rhizome, have the clearest of lines. Several are valued for the translucent tinting of the fronds in spring, and for the shades of gold, bronze and glistening burnt sienna lent by the dense covering of scales on the emerging crosiers and midribs. They are at their most impressive in low, glancing, dappled light rather than in unadulterated shade.

The fronds of *D. affinis* and *D. affinis* subsp. *borreri* are soft pale golden green on emergence, in startling contrast to the golden brown scales on the midrib; they later turn deep lustrous green. *Dryopteris affinis* 'Cristata' is tightly crested at the frond tip and on the pinnae, but nevertheless retains a clearly arching outline, and at waist high, is as tall and stately as the species. *D. wallichiana*, from Japan, China and the Himalayas, is the most handsome; waist high is a conservative estimate, for it reaches twice that in optimal conditions. The huge fronds are spectacular on emergence: olive-tinted, buttery green, with dark, shaggy, rufus scales outlining the crosiers and the broad tapering midrib—a beautiful contrast to the coppery reds of new rodgersia leaves.

Dryopteris erythrosora has a slow-creeping rhizome and sheaves of arching fronds, to

about mid thigh height. They have red stems and strong tints of coppery red as they unfurl, later becoming a deep, semi-glossy green.

All appreciate a leaf mould mulch to help conserve moisture, and must be adequately watered during establishment. The instinctive response to give ferns the damp, shaded conditions they experience in habitat is a good one, but can be qualified; many ferns, including *Dryopteris*, are surprisingly drought tolerant once established and more useful in drier shade than

▲▲ *Dryopteris erythrosora*

▲ *Dryopteris affinis* subsp. *borreri*

157

▶ *Elaeagnus umbellata*

▲ *Dryopteris wallichiana*

◀ *Elaeagnus commutata*
with *Lupinus* 'Polar
Princess'

might be imagined. An adult fern—the fern we are most familiar with —is perfectly adapted to life as a perennial land plant. It's only when it comes to reproduction, when the process of fertilization is dependent on free moisture, that they *need* damp habitats.

Fully hardy, z6–9. Fertile, moist, humus-rich soil in dappled light or shade.

Elaeagnus
Elaeagnaceae

Elaeagnus species glisten. Minute, mica-like scales clothe stems, leaves, buds, flowers and fruit in silver, bronze or gold depending on the species. They give the arching, silver-leaved species a shimmering quality on days of sunshine, breeze and scudding clouds. Nobody ever says how fabulous the flowers of elaeagnus are, but there is something wonderfully cryptic about them. Invariably tiny, they make little visual impact, but their scent carries and is disproportionately wonderful—your guests may sniff like pointers, but will seldom be able to pinpoint the source.

The three silver archers I use most are deciduous: *E. commutata* and *E.* 'Quicksilver', which are silvery throughout the season, and *E. umbellata*, with leaves that emerge silver, then turn green but remain silvery beneath—especially effective when upturned by wind. All three have tiny silver-scaly, pale yellow flowers with delicious scent in late spring and early summer, later producing small scintillating fruit. They are large billowing shrubs, to twice head height and more, but accept quite hard pruning (after flowering) if you want to grow them in more confined spaces—with arching *Miscanthus*, the verticals of lupins and digitalis, or the feathery plumes of fennel (*Foeniculum*). They are useful for foliage contrasts, especially with red and purple variants of *Cercis* or *Cotinus*.

Fully hardy, z3–9. Any fertile well-drained soil in sun. Beware of suckers.

Exochorda
Rosaceae ▪ pearl bush

When the skill of propagating was new to me, I took soft tip cuttings of *Exochorda racemosa*. One took off like Topsy, growing as a single stem, and I trained it as a standard. It was one of the most beautiful small trees I had ever seen. With a head of arching branches wreathed in

◀ *Exochorda ×macrantha* 'The Bride'

its potential in the garden, looking worryingly weedy in the interim. But as it matures it develops a fountain-like array of airy, light-filled cascades of slender green shoots, like pendent

▶ *Genista aetnensis*

oval, emerald green leaves and smothered in racemes of cupped, pure paper-white flowers in early summer, it was luminous. It's so seldom grown like that, but a clear stem clears the way for underplanting, in this case with *Iris* 'Florentina', a white-flowered *germanica* iris, and *Hosta* 'Krossa Regal'.

All exochordas have an arching habit of growth in a pristine combination of emerald and white and all are exceptionally free-flowering. *Exochorda ×macrantha* 'The Bride' is the most compact, eventually to chest high. Both *E. racemosa* and *E. giraldii* var. *wilsonii* are taller, the first with racemes of slightly larger white flowers, the second having white flowers almost twice the size of those of *E. ×macrantha*. They establish easily and grow rapidly, and I prune them in much the same way and for the same reason as I do the deutzias (see page 155).

Chest to head high. Fully hardy, z5–9. Fertile, moist but well-drained soil in sun.

Genista

Papilionaceae ▪ Mount Etna broom

From the dry, sun-baked hills of Sardinia and Sicily, *G. aetnensis* takes several years to achieve

sprays of rushes, from every branch. The length of the current year's growth is studded in late summer with yellow pea flowers, exuding a coconut-vanilla scent. It is virtually leafless— even the tiny juvenile leaves soon fall, but the green shoots give it every appearance of being an evergreen. Given its origins, it's no surprise that it is drought tolerant, and does well on hot dry banks and in sunny gravel gardens. It may reach five times head height in more fertile soils, or half that in poor ones, but since it casts virtually no shade, its sparse, elegant height is no bar to its use at the back of borders. Mounds of *Phlomis fruticosa* will echo its line, and verticals, perhaps *Verbascum olympicum*, will emphasize it. With all that yellow, there needs to be some blue—*Perovskia atriplicifolia*, perhaps.

Hardy, z7/8–10. Well-drained, poor to moderately fertile soils in full sun.

Hakonechloa

Poaceae

A deciduous grass from damp cliffs and montane woodland in Japan, *Hakonechloa macra* is usually cultivated in its variegated forms: 'Aureola', striped bright yellow and green, and a taller, slightly paler form, 'Alboaurea', with leaves striped white, bright yellow and rich green; both take on pink and red tints as temperatures fall in autumn.

While superficially similar to *Carex oshimensis* 'Evergold', the habit of *H. macra* is unmistakable. The arching, linear leaf blades have long stalks, and grow upright before arching over; the effect is of a cascade—or a beautifully layered haircut by very skilled hands. It provides very interesting textural effects when mass-planted as ground cover beneath a canopy of dappled shade with trees or shrubs, and is an elegant container specimen. Excellent for contrasts with blue- or gold-leaved hostas and crocosmias, and dramatic with dark-leaved heucheras.

Knee high. Fully hardy, z5/6–9. Humus-rich, moist but well-drained soil in light or dappled shade for best foliage colour, in deeper shade for lime green tints, or in part-day sun for stronger yellows; the plants bleach in hot sun.

Halesia
Styraceae • silver bell, snowdrop tree

Halesias make me yearn for acid soil. In spring the arching branches of these large shrubs or small, multi-stemmed trees are festooned with pendent, pristine white bells, hanging in small clusters from the leaf axils; *H. carolina* blooms on dark branches, before the emergence of the fresh bright green young leaves; *H. diptera* blooms with the leaves, *H. monticola* before and after. They are perfect specimens for the woodland garden or semi-shaded shrub border.

Halesia carolina and *H. diptera* were introduced to the UK in the 1750s and are found here in any woodland garden worthy of the name—along with the much taller *H. monticola* in larger gardens. While the two former seldom reach more than two or three times head height, *H. monticola* will make a tree to twelve metres (thirty-six feet). Although they are native to the southeastern United States,

◀ *Hakonechloa macra* 'Aureola'

▶ *Halesia monticola*

◀ *Halesia carolina*

▶ *Hydrangea paniculata*

in woodland, as understorey and occasionally as pure stands—how glorious—they are less frequently grown as garden specimens there, which is no surprise considering they get to twice the size in a continental climate as in a cool maritime one. In Britain, they don't get sufficient sun and warmth to fully ripen the wood, resulting in twig kill in winter. Trees recover, but it's a check to growth that ensures restricted size, and a shrubby and multi-stemmed habit.

Fully hardy, z4/5–9. Moist but well-drained, humus-rich lime-free soil in light dappled shade or sun. Halesias flower on the previous year's wood; if you need to restrict their size, prune them back after flowering.

Hydrangea

Hydrangeaceae

A long way from the mounds of mophead hortensias, *H. paniculata* saves its best for the last weeks of summer, going gracefully into autumn with long shoots arching inexorably earthwards under the weight of the foot-long, conical panicles of flowers. They bloom with the astilbes and Japanese anemones, *A. ×hybrida* 'Honorine Jobert' for a cool green and white theme, or *A. hupehensis* 'Hadspen Abundance' to pick up pink tones as flowers mature.

Hold back with secateurs and *H. paniculata* makes a substantial wide-spreading specimen

to twice head height, truly wonderful in the dappled light of a large woodland garden. But it reaches half that and, moreover, really give its all with a little simple pruning, both in flower size and grace of line.

I classify cultivars of *H. paniculata* according to whether I want full power, or need a more delicate effect. Some have really dense panicles of mainly sterile flowers that overlap to obscure the smaller fertile ones: creamy white ageing to pink in 'Grandiflora'; unfading creamy white in the huge-flowered 'Phantom'; very broadly conical in the creamy-flowered 'Unique'. There are two green-flowered cultivars, both with mainly sterile flowers: 'Limelight' has lime-green florets that fade creamy white; 'Green-spire' is a softer green. Others have lighter and

▶ *Hydrangea paniculata*
'Limelight'

airier flowerheads with an open admixture of creamy white fertile and sterile flowers: 'Brussels Lace', 'Chantilly Lace' and 'Kyushu'.

To keep the size of the shrub within suitable bounds for modest-sized gardens, and to gain larger, more spectacular flowers, prune back in spring to within a few buds of a permanent woody framework, knee high or thigh high depending on the flowering height you desire.

Fully hardy, z3–9. Any moisture-retentive, humus-rich soil in sun or dappled shade, with shelter from cold drying winds. See also page 55 (Horizontals and Tiers).

Indigofera

Papilionaceae

I have great empathy for gardeners in cold continental zones. We suffer the same sort of zonal debility in northern Britain, when plants are reckoned to be too tender for any but 'favoured locations' in 'our warmer counties'. I hate it so when it applies to plants I love, ones that flower continuously through summer and autumn, with elegant spikes of pea flowers and beautiful foliage. The indigoferas are a case in point.

They have an interesting pattern of flower production, with spikes appearing continuously from each new leaf axil of the growing shoots, and they have a strong will to live, usually resprouting from the base, or from low down on a branch framework if cut by winter cold. It is not necessary, nor even an advantage, that they grow into large shrubs. Use it as a die-back shrub—treat it as a perennial. Whether top growth is cut down by miserable winters or by hand, the result is a fountain of strong new shoots clothed in bee-laden bloom that is eminently welcome in shrub, mixed or herbaceous borders, where they will reach from waist to chest high in a season.

Indigofera amblyantha has leaves divided finely into greyish green leaflets, and upstanding racemes of pale pink, rosy salmon or deep rose pink; *I. heterantha* has even more finely pinnate leaves of a greyer green, and erect

racemes of rosy purple flowers; and the glory that is *I. pendula* produces long, pendent racemes of downy rose-purple pea flowers like a miniature, spaced-out wisteria chain. Wonderful with the blue spires of perovskia, the deep blues of *Caryopteris* ×*clandonensis*, the silky mounds of *Convolvulus cneorum* or the tall, late pinks of echinaceas.

Hardy, z6–9. Full sun, in any moderately fertile, very well-drained soil, including dry and chalky ones.

Kolkwitzia

Caprifoliaceae • beauty bush

When my trainee and I pruned *K. amabilis* 'Pink Cloud', thinning out the oldest flowered wood before it wasted energy on setting seed, we noticed how attractive the peeling, honey-coloured bark is, how exceptionally free-flowering the beauty bush was this year, and how generously it produces sturdy, strongly arching new shoots that will bear next year's flowers in abundance. *Kolkwitzia amabilis* has long, ovate, dark green leaves and twinned, bell-

◀ *Indigofera amblyantha*

▲ *Indigofera heterantha*

◀ *Kolkwitzia amabilis* 'Pink Cloud'

▶ *Lavatera* cultivar at the back of a pink border

▲ *Kolkwitzia amabilis*

shaped flowers in corymbs at the tips of each lateral shoot. In the species they vary from pale to deep pink, suffused with yellow at the throat. 'Pink Cloud' has flowers of a brighter, deeper pink, with yellow throats freckled red pink, and is the most reliably abundant clone. It was raised at RHS Wisley from seeds sent by the Morton Arboretum in Lisle, Illinois.

Twice head height. Fully hardy, z4–9 Any good fertile, well-drained soil, including chalky ones, in full sun.

Lavatera

Malvaceae ▪ mallow

It is misleading to refer to lavateras as tree mallows or tree lavateras, for most are, strictly speaking, woody-based, semi-evergreen, shrubby perennials. No matter—they're valued for the strong arcs that the wands of summer-long bloom bring to sunny banks, mixed borders, cottage-, coastal- and gravel gardens. Most belong to a group classified under *L. olbia*, *L. thuringiaca* and the hybrids between them, *L. ×clementii*. All produce wide-open funnels of satin-textured petals, in short, packed racemes along arching stems amid palmately lobed, velvety, sage- or grey-green leaves. They range from pure white in *L. thuringiaca* 'Ice Cool' and 'White Satin', through soft pale pinks of *L. ×clementii* hybrids such as 'Bressingham Pink', to intense clear pinks in *L. ×clementii* 'Kew Rose' and 'Bredon Springs'. One of the strongest colours is in the dark-stemmed *L. ×clementii* 'Burgundy Wine' with glossy, dark-veined, purple-pink blooms. Several have dark-eyed flowers: *L. ×clementii* 'Barnsley', with red-eyed white flowers is the best known. *Lavatera* 'Grey Beauty' is less familiar, with similar flowers, and this and *L. ×clementii* 'Lavender Lady' have pale, very silvery-hairy foliage, which is useful for contrasts of texture and colour. The latter also has pretty, satiny pale lavender flowers.

New stems are produced annually with great vigour, and if you cut them back to the base in spring, they reach head height by the time they finish flowering in autumn. It's the best way to treat them in cold areas, and even in warmer zones, they can be pruned annually or every other year to keep them looking fresh.

Head high and above. Fully hardy, z7–9/10; z5 if treated as a perennial with a dry winter mulch. Grow in a warm, sunny site in full sun, in light, open soil, preferably poor to moderately fertile, with excellent drainage. On rich soils they produce too much soft foliage at the expense of flowering.

◀ *Ligustrum quihoui* (left), with *Morus alba* 'Pendula' and *Phormium cookianum* subsp. *hookeri* 'Tricolor'

Ligustrum

Oleaceae • privet

Far—*very* far—from the immediate image of privet (those dull, dark suburban hedgers) are a couple of very elegant, arching and free-flowering deciduous species valued for their conspicuous sprays of scented, creamy white flowers in midsummer and early autumn. But there are always two sides to the fence—or hedge. Both are environmentally disastrous

alien invasives in many states in the US: toxic to stock, freely self-seeding, robbing the soil of nutrients and creating such dense shade that nothing will grow beneath them.

They don't behave so badly in cool maritime climates. I grow them in dappled light in a woodland garden on chalk, and as a dark-leaved, late-flowering component of shrub and mixed borders. *Ligustrum quihoui* has very glossy, narrowly oval, dark green leaves, very strong but slender arching stems, and long, airy panicles of creamy white flowers in mid- to late summer. *Ligustrum sinense* has glossy leaves of a lighter green, and a great feathery profusion of white flowers in midsummer, followed by sprays of glossy black-purple fruits.

Twice head height. Fully hardy, z6–9. Any well-drained soil in sun or dappled shade.

Mahonia

Berberidaceae

I grow mahonias in cutting borders and in the woodland garden, the first group pillaged for whole branches, which are fabulous in large vases, and the latter left to be seen and admired, with berrying companions including hollies, and large cotoneasters. I love their scent so much that I have stuffed a few in out of the way places where the perfume catches attention on winter strolls; in milder years they flower from late autumn through early spring. The stuffed-in plants, which are neglected, develop a tall, gaunt and open habit, with most of the foliage in arching sprays atop thick, flexuous, ridged and furrowed stems, each rosette with a further spray of yellow plumes arising from their centre in winter. If you have space, they're very elegant like this; it approximates the natural habit seen in the shady woods and rocky places where they grow in the wild.

Mahonias bought from nurseries will have been pinched in their youth to ensure a denser, bushier habit, with an array of erect and leaning stems, densely clothed in dark, glossy sculpted pinnate leaves divided into spiny mar-

‹ *Mahonia lomariifolia*

▼ *Mahonia ×media*
'Charity', with *Euonymus*
europaeus 'Red Cascade'

▶ *Matteuccia*
struthiopteris

either parent, particularly so in *M. ×media* 'Buckland' and 'Charity'; in *M. ×media* 'Lionel Fortescue' they are long and densely packed but remain more or less erect. Without pruning, the hybrids reach three times head height, but have no objection at all to having their stems shortened immediately after flowering (be sure to wear gauntlets (long, heavy-duty gloves) to protect your hands); it's far better to keep at least some stems at head height or below so you can see and smell the flowers at close quarters.

Fully hardy, z6/7–10. Fertile, moisture-retentive soil, rich in humus, in shade or dappled shade, or part-day afternoon sun.

gined leaflets—an arching mound. It is those with long, spreading, terminal racemes of flower, rather than those with dumpy clusters, that have an arching line: *M. lomariifolia*, *M. japonica* and their hybrid offspring, *M. ×media* and its cultivars.

Mahonia lomariifolia has the finer foliage, with densely packed, upright racemes of small, cupped yellow flowers; it readily develops a gaunt elegant habit, and reaches twice head height if left to do so. At half that height, *M. japonica* has less finely divided leaves, and the spikes of pale primrose yellow flowers, longer than those of *M. lomariifolia*, are arching and spreading. Hybrids have upright, arching or spreading flower spikes, longer than those of

Matteuccia

Woodsiaceae ▪ ostrich fern, shuttlecock fern

Found in damp deciduous woodland, *Matteuccia struthiopteris* is a tall deciduous fern of great substance to be enjoyed for the lushness of its fleshy stipes as the crosiers unfurl in spring, and the translucence of the shuttlecocks of long, finely divided, brilliant green fronds when backlit by morning or evening sun. Unlike many other ferns that spread slowly by rhizomes, it produces a series of separate shuttlecocks, so doesn't lose its arching line. At the end of the summer, from the centre of the shuttlecock, a dark sheaf of fertile fronds emerges, persisting through the winter and becoming fabulous when rimed with frost. *Matteuccia struthiopteris* reaches almost head height in moist soils, is indispensable in woodland or damp and shaded borders, and looks particularly beautiful at the margins of open water or on the banks of bog gardens. Big enough to hold its own with gunneras, and very fine for textural contrasts with *Aruncus*, rodgersias, rheums, the whorled uprights of candelabra primulas and upright sheaves of *Iris sibirica*.

Fully hardy, z6–10. Moist, fertile, humusy, neutral to acid soils in part shade or light dappled shade.

Melianthus

Melianthaceae ▪ honey bush

Melianthus major actually looks like a designer's creation. It has huge arching, pinnate leaves, with sharply, very regularly toothed, ovate leaflets, the leaf surface covered with a fine, light-scattering wax so that it exhibits an array of colour from silver-green through jade to blue-green, depending on the age and angle of the leaf, and the angle and colour of the light that strikes its surfaces. Superb with blue and grey-leaved hostas, and the sheaves and fans of phormiums, irises, and kniphofias, it was once used in tropical bedding—and still is, to give a lush jungly feel to a composition.

The leaves have a unique aroma when brushed against, which I find muskily pleasant (some think it vile), and when it does bloom, it pushes up tall spike-like racemes of dark red-brown flowers that are so nectar rich that they drip. The flowers are unusual rather than exciting, and are borne on second-year growth; I wouldn't mind if it never flowered.

Melianthus major is by no means fully hardy, but neither is it as tender as usually implied, and it is eminently worth growing as a perennial rather than a shrub. It has hollow fleshy stems that collapse when frosted (a feature that isn't helped by its growth cycle). In its natural state on the Cape of South Africa, it grows in the relatively cool winters when moisture is plentiful, and sits out the hot summers. It confusedly

▲ *Melianthus major*

may try to do that in northern temperate gardens, putting on a spurt of growth as rainfall increases and temperatures cool in autumn. This soft growth is inevitably stricken by the first sharp frost, but if the rootstock survives the winter, it will resume growth in spring and make leafy stems to head height by the end of the season. I suspect that if it were fully hardy it would be in the same league as the noxious Japanese knotweed, *Fallopia japonica*—on its home ground, it suckers widely and colonizes ditches and riverbanks at a gallop.

Hardy, z8/9–11. Grow in a warm sheltered site in full sun in fertile, moist but well-drained soil. Mulch with garden compost or similar in spring for lush summer growth, and in cold areas, protect the rootstock with bracken litter, straw or a mound of conifer branchlets. If autumn growth appears and is frosted, ignore it.

▲ *Melica transsilvanica* 'Red Spire'

▶ *Neillia thibetica*

Melica

Poaceae · melick

Deciduous tufted perennial grasses of temperate woodlands and grasslands, the melicks have a delicate sort of beauty for plantings in wilder and more naturalistic parts of the garden. *Melica uniflora* forms open clumps of soft, arching, bright green leaves, never more than knee high, which emerge on shady hedgebanks with the primroses and violets in the sunny uplands of Yorkshire (it ranges from Europe to the Caucasus). The tiny purple spikelets are borne on hair-fine branchlets in nodding panicles in summer, a very fine haze en masse, with seeds like seed pearls when spangled with rain or dewdrops. *Melica altissima*, to waist high or taller, spreads rhizomatously, forming loose clumps of arching, pale greyish green leaves, above which emerge dense one-sided spires of tiny red-purple spikelets, a darker purple-brown in *M. a.* 'Atropurpurea'. *Melica transsilvanica* 'Red Spire' is taller, chest high and above, with dense spikes of red brown spikelets. If growing them in borders it makes sense to buy potted plants. If you want to naturalize them, seek out a specialist supplier of ornamental grass seed, and either direct-sow or start them in plugs.

Fully hardy, z4–11. Any moderately fertile, well-drained soil, in sun or light dappled shade.

Neillia

Rosaceae

One of life's little mysteries is why *Neillia thibetica* is not more widely grown. It occurs in the wild in rocky mountainous areas of Sichuan, western China, in scrub and by rocky mountain streams. The chestnut-coloured stems are arching but also endearingly flexuous having a zig-zag pattern of growth, with three-lobed, toothed and long-pointed, bright green leaves that turn golden yellow in autumn. The small, clear soft pink tubular bells are borne in long, slender racemes at the tips of the shoots in early summer. I grow it on a bank at the edge of a woodland garden, for although it will tolerate light shade, it flowers best in sun. It will

sucker once established, in time forming a thicket rather like *Rubus thibetanus*, except that the naked stems are bright chestnut brown. Thinning them out every second or third year when dormant shows the remainder off quite well, and keeps the arching line from becoming muddled.

Chest to head high. Fully hardy, z5–9. Moist but well-drained, fertile soil in sun or dappled shade.

Onoclea

Woodsiaceae

Enjoying the same conditions as *Matteuccia* and *Osmunda*, the sensitive fern, *Onoclea sensibilis*, is a perfect companion for either or both, being especially effective at the margins of pools, when the rhizomes sometimes grow out onto the water's surface. It is a spreading fern, eventually forming an undulating, thigh-high carpet of arching, pinnate fronds, pale green on emergence, often with pinkish bronze or red tints when young. In late summer it also produces fertile fronds, black and stiffly upright, revealed as the sterile fronds fall in the frost, and persisting through winter. Despite its obvious love of moisture, like *Dryopteris* it is remarkably tolerant of drier soils, not droughty ones, provided that it has shelter from drying winds.

Fully hardy, z4–9. Moist, fertile, humus-rich, preferably acid soils in part shade or light dappled shade.

Osmanthus

Oleaceae

The genus *Osmanthus* is a specialist in sweet fragrance, and although the tubular white flowers are small, they're borne in adequate sufficiency to scent the air for some distance around, and I site them where I pass them often. Most are beautiful but, like *O. yunnanensis*, almost tree-like; *O. heterophyllus* has a more rigid habit. But *Osmanthus* ×*burkwoodi* and *O. delavayi* are the hardiest and most resilient, both bearing their flowers in axillary clusters along the arching length of the previous year's shoots in mid to late spring. Both are dark, dignified shrubs when out of flower, providing a good backcloth for other, more colourful plantings in a mixed border. The tiny leaves of *O. delavayi* are very dark green and glossy, giving the whole plant a fine, glittering, light-reflecting texture after rain. *Osmanthus* ×*burkwoodii* is longer-leaved and more vigorous. I seldom prune freestanding specimens, but both tolerate clipping, immediately after flowering, and make dense flowering hedges, or more formal topiary forms, with a close, glossy surface studded with spring flowers.

◀ *Onoclea sensibilis*

▶ *Osmanthus delavayi*

Slow-growing, *O. delavayi* to head height, *O. ×burkwoodii* to one-and-a-half times head height. Fully hardy, z6/7–9. Any good, well-drained, fertile soil in sun or light dappled shade.

Osmunda

Osmundaceae • royal fern

Natives of boggy areas and watersides, the hardy osmundas are among the loveliest of ferns for damp areas, and with constant moisture they withstand both sun and shade. As companions to *Matteuccia* and *Onoclea*, they bring a quite different texture to a composition; the long arching fronds have broader pinnae, giving more heft and substance. *Osmunda regalis* forms upstanding mounds of massive fibrous rootstock (the source of osmunda fibre), above which fronds unfurl in spring to form a clump rather than a distinct shuttlecock of golden green, tinted russet and purple in *O. r.* 'Purpurascens'. They retain their pale golden green until they colour richly before dying back in autumn, in shades of raw sienna and old gold, leaving upright sheaves of tasselled chestnut brown fertile fronds standing. The crosiers, stipes and ribs of the shuttlecock-forming *O. cinnamomea* are densely covered in glistening rusty tomentum as they emerge, opening a rich

glaucous green, fading to cinnamon in autumn, with an erect central waist-high clump of fertile fronds crowded with a conspicuous mass of cinnamon-brown sporangia at the tips.

Fully hardy, z3–10/11. Constantly moist, fertile, humusy, preferably acid soils in part-shade, light dappled shade or sun (in cool summer climates).

Pennisetum

Poaceae • fountain grass

Natives of savannah grassland and woods in tropical, subtropical, and warm temperate regions, selected *Pennisetum* species have come into cultivation by virtue of the arching clumps of slender leaves and the shimmering, light-filtering, dew-glistening fountains of their inflorescences. In Latin, *penna* means feather, and *seta* bristle; the inflorescence is a long, tight, cylindrical panicle of spikelets, held at right angles to the stem, each with a ruff of long soft bristles.

As a species, the dark-green-leaved *P. alopecuroides* is variable in height depending on soil fertility and summer warmth—it reaches anywhere from knee to head high. *Pennisetum alopecuroides* 'Hameln', to mid thigh height, has the palest green spikelets with orange stamens, giving a foxy cast to the nodding flower-

◀ *Osmunda regalis*

▶ *Pennisetum alopecuroides* 'Hameln'

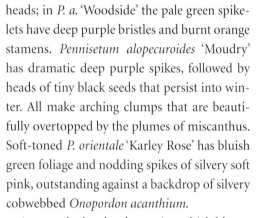

▲ *Pennisetum setaceum* 'Rubrum'

◀ *Pennisetum alopecuroides* 'Woodside' with *Miscanthus* 'Silberfelder'

heads; in *P. a.* 'Woodside' the pale green spikelets have deep purple bristles and burnt orange stamens. *Pennisetum alopecuroides* 'Moudry' has dramatic deep purple spikes, followed by heads of tiny black seeds that persist into winter. All make arching clumps that are beautifully overtopped by the plumes of miscanthus. Soft-toned *P. orientale* 'Karley Rose' has bluish green foliage and nodding spikes of silvery soft pink, outstanding against a backdrop of silvery cobwebbed *Onopordon acanthium*.

Among the less hardy species, which bloom in their first year from seed, *P. villosum* has feathery heads of honey blonde which are very satisfying with blue flowers, especially the metallic blues of eryngiums. *Pennisetum setaceum* and *P. s.* 'Rubrum' make waist-high fountains and have exceptionally long arching plumes, soft pink-purple in the species. In *P. s.* 'Rubrum', the leaves are red-purple and the flower spikes crimson. They're good in the ground, and excellent in tall containers.

Fully hardy, z5–9, to frost-tender. Full sun, with good drainage in light, moderately fertile soil.

▶ *Pennisetum orientale* 'Karley Rose'

▶ *Pennisetum villosum* with *Eryngium planum* 'Blaukappe'

Philadelphus

Hydrangeaceae • mock orange

In a Proustian way, the fragrance of philadelphus will always remind me of the birth of my midsummer baby (now long flown); the arboretum where she was born had a formidable collection of *Philadelphus*. There are forty species, and upwards of fifty cultivars, in the genus—so I will speak in generalities and with prejudice. Firstly, fragrance is less intense in double-flowered cultivars, and secondly, if your philadelphus become coarse and shapeless, it's usually your own fault for having relied on their tolerance of poor soils and because you've neglected their pruning. The ideal site is sun-dappled and sheltered, so that fragrance hangs heavy in the still air—perhaps an open glade in a woodland garden. The heady scent couldn't have been better designed to blend with that of the Old Roses, a carpet of clove-scented pinks beneath, and a stand of *Crambe cordifolia* beside.

The following are my best shots: of arching habit, well-scented, and mostly single-flowered, with double-flowered exceptions to the 'less fragrant' generality, and flowering in early and midsummer.

At waist to chest height, *P.* 'Belle Etoile' has large flowers marked mauve at the base, and is pineapple-scented; *P.* 'Manteau d'Hermine' bears double, fragrant, creamy white flowers; *P. microphyllus* is dainty, with small shining green leaves and delicate pure white flowers; free-flowering *P.* 'Silberregen' produces small, strawberry-scented flowers in masses; and *P.* 'Sybille' has large flowers, stained purple at the base and orange-scented.

At head height, *P.* 'Avalanche' bears small flowers in racemes, weighing down arching stems from midsummer; *P.* 'Bouquet Blanc' has semi-double or double flowers, orange-scented, in large clusters; *P.* 'Lemoinei' produces small flowers in many lateral clusters; and *P.* ×*purpureomaculatus* bears small single flowers, with purple-stained centres, in profusion.

◀ *Philadelphus* 'Belle Etoile'

Above head height, *P.* 'Beauclerk' has large, single or semi-double flowers, blushed pink at the centre; *P. coronarius* has small creamy white flowers in dense short-stemmed clusters; *P. delavayi* is vigorous, with large flowers in packed racemes, sometimes purple-flushed on the reverse; *P. delavayi* f. *melanocalyx* has deep maroon-purple stems and calyces; and *P.* 'Virginal' is very vigorous and highly fragrant, with pristine double white flowers.

Prune after flowering: thin out weak shoots, select and cut the strongest canes to pairs of buds low down near the base, and the following year they'll make a glorious fountain of russet-barked canes festooned with heavily fragrant flowers. Be fearless and ruthless in your pruning; once established, philadelphus are tough and willing to respond.

Fully hardy, z5/6–9. Moderately fertile, well-drained soil in sun or light dappled shade.

Polygonatum

Convalleriaceae • Solomon's seal

From temperate woodlands in North America and from Europe to the Himalayas and Asia, the polygonatums are a race of smooth-stemmed, spring- or early-summer-flowering herbaceous perennials for cool, damp and shady sites. The stems arch towards the tips in most, with pendent, waxy, tubular bells hanging from the

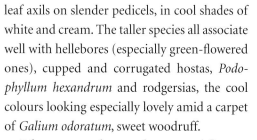

▲ *Polygonatum*
×hybridum 'Striatum'

◀ *Polygonatum*
odoratum var. *pluriflorum*
'Variegatum'

▼ *Polygonatum*
multiflorum (right)
with *Euonymus fortunei*
'Emerald Gaiety'

leaf axils on slender pedicels, in cool shades of white and cream. The taller species all associate well with hellebores (especially green-flowered ones), cupped and corrugated hostas, *Podophyllum hexandrum* and rodgersias, the cool colours looking especially lovely amid a carpet of *Galium odoratum*, sweet woodruff.

Polygonatum odoratum has scented flowers, white with green tips, in pairs, and *P. multiflorum* bears its white, green-tipped flowers in clusters of up to half a dozen. Both reach waist high or taller in optimal conditions. Their variegated forms are half that height; *P. odoratum* var. *pluriflorum* 'Variegatum' has red-flushed young stems and narrow, white margins outlining the leaves, while *P. ×hybridum* 'Striatum' has leaves irregularly striped with creamy white. The tallest include *P. hirtum*, and the most commonly grown, *P. ×hybridum*. *Polygonatum*

hirtum is distinguished from *P. ×hybridum* not only by its broader, longer and slightly pleated, shining leaves on slightly flexuous stems and later midsummer flowering time, but also by its angular habit; given good living, it arcs to head height. Very variable across its range, the dwarf form (to mid thigh) is more usually offered in cultivation.

Fully hardy, z3–9. Moist but well-drained, fertile, humus-rich soils in partial or deep shade. Saw fly larvae can strip the leaves overnight; females lay eggs in rows on the stems, as the plant comes into flower. Larvae can be removed by hand, or treated with a pyrethrum- or permethrin-based insecticide.

◀ *Polypodium vulgare*

Polypodium

Polypodiaceae

While many ferns used in gardens are strictly terrestrial in habit, needing their rhizomes in soil, the common polypody, *P. vulgare*, is surely one of the most adaptable of evergreen ferns. In the wild it is found as a lithophyte, on rocks and shady walls, on trees as an epiphyte, and as a ground-dweller, in open sites and in woodland. The arching pinnate fronds are bright green and thin-textured in moist shade, or darker and more leathery in drier and more open sites. An excellent colonizer for a range of situations where ferny textures are desirable but more moisture-loving ferns would fail, its greenery remains green even in the dog days of late summer. Once established, it may even be found colonizing wall niches of its own accord, and in higher rainfall regions it may take to the trees.

There are numerous fancy forms with crested and/or more finely divided fronds, although most are strongly prone to revert to type. Among the prettiest are *P. vulgare* 'Cornubiense' with lacy fronds of neatly and finely divided pinnae, and *P. v.* 'Cornubiense Grandiceps' with lacy fronds with conspicuous terminal crests.

Knee high. Fully hardy, z3–8. Full sun to dappled shade, in humus-rich, gritty or stony, well-drained soils.

Polystichum

Dryopteridaceae

The evergreen *P. setiferum* is a native of woods, shady rocks and hedgebanks and is distinctive due to the softness of its fronds, which form an arching shuttlecock of soft brilliant green, the stipes clothed in dense, golden brown scales. It retains luxuriance well into autumn and early winter, reaching waist high even in conditions rather drier than might be expected. In its many plumose, crested and more finely divided variants—some of the most elegant of hardy ferns—the fronds are often more sinuously arching, twisting towards the tip, and in some the pinnae and pinnules rise at an acute angle to their point of attachment, giving a depth of texture that is exceptionally beautiful. In *P. setiferum* 'Pulcherrimum Bevis', the pinnae are long and align themselves in a series of sweeping arcs towards the frond tips; in *P. s.* Plumosodivisilobum Group the fronds are almost mossy, four times divided, with pinnae overlapping at the frond base and becoming narrower and shorter towards the frond tips, giving a very distinctive outline.

Although tolerant of deep shade or part day sun, wherever you chose to grow them, in shady borders or the woodland garden, they

▶ *Polystichum setiferum*
'Pulcherrimum Bevis'

are at their most beautiful when patterned by the changing play of dappled light.

Fully hardy, z5–9. Humus-rich, fertile, well-drained soil in dappled shade.

Pyrus

Rosacaeae • pear

Under normal circumstances, I scorn the high clearing of lower branches from the boles of trees. It's a forestry practice which, when applied to many ornamental trees, gives the appearance of a municipal lollipop, and lifts the foliage, fruits and flowers too far from the eye and nose for my liking. However, the weeping willow-leaved pear, *Pyrus salicifolia* 'Pendula', is a tree for which I make an exception. So resolutely arching are its sinuous branches, clothed in narrowly lanceolate, silver-grey downy leaves, that they trail to the ground if left unattended. To avoid this the main stem needs to be cleared at least to between waist or head height, during dormancy. The actual length of clear stem depends on whether you intend to create an arching dome that weeps almost to the ground (which makes a great den under the canopy) or whether you want to plant beneath it, in which case, clear higher.

It is one of the most useful trees, even in smaller urban spaces, sustaining interest

through the year—from the emergence of its intensely felted leaves in spring, when the pendulous branches are wreathed in umbels of saucer-shaped creamy white flowers, through to its dark naked winter outline, which is sculptural when dusted with snow or rimed in frost. It makes a fine specimen, a pale backdrop to more colourful plantings, or an overarching canopy for sheltered arbours. I've seen it used in mediterranean-style plantings as a substitute for an olive, *Olea europaea*, in a garden too cold to countenance the survival of the real thing.

Incidentally, speaking of lollipops, *P. salicifolia* 'Pendula' withstands hard pruning, and can be trained and pruned as a globe-headed standard that is very attractive in formal knots and parterres.

Two to three times head height. Fully hardy, z4–9. Any fertile, well-drained soil in sun.

Salvia

Lamiaceae • sage

In a genus more often associated with dense upright spikes of flower, *S. uliginosa*, bog sage, is uniquely arching and very airy—so much so that can be used a transparent too. I have been charmed by it over long summer and autumn months, as its supple branching stems move in the breeze and are bowed over by the weight of bumble bees seeking nectar from the short racemes of two-lipped clear blue flowers. So airy is it that it's difficult to support unobtrusively, but so mobile that I feel it's better not to bother.

It's also unusual—the common name being a giveaway—in its enjoyment of very moist soils, so it is well placed in a sunny bog garden. But I have to say this: I am less than charmed by its invasive, rhizomatously spreading tendencies in the open, well-worked soils in my herbaceous borders. It is less rampant, and hardier, on drier, well-drained soils of lower fertility, and will thrive in a gravel garden or in a rain shadow beneath the study window, where bumble bee studies are my number one

▶ *Pyrus salicifolia* 'Pendula'

◀ *Salvia uliginosa*

▶ *Sorbaria sorbifolia*

▲ *Salvia uliginosa* in an autumn border with asters

displacement activity on sunny summer days. Its reputation for winter tenderness derives largely from the insistence on growing it in very moist soils—the cold and wet combo is the prime cause of winter fatalities in many so-called borderline hardy plants.

Salvia uliginosa 'African Skies' has deeper blue flowers, and both it and the species associate well with late-flowering echinaceas and asters, and look wonderful amid the shimmering golden plumes of deschampsias and stipas.

Chest to head high. Fully hardy, z6–10. Full sun, or light dappled shade in moist, moisture-retentive and well-drained, or fairly dry, fertile to moderately fertile soils.

Sorbaria

Rosaceae • false spiraea

Mostly native of riverbanks or from montane scrub and forest, all *Sorbaria* species bear arching, conical panicles of tiny white flowers late in the season, from midsummer to early autumn at the tips of the current season's growth. *Sorbaria sorbifolia* and *S. tomentosa* var. *angustifolia* reach head height, and have long, elegant leaves divided into slender, toothed and neatly veined bright green leaflets. Slightly shorter *S. sorbifolia* 'Sem' has foliage tinted in shades of bronze, plummy red and gold when young, with pink tints in the fluffy white flower panicles in late summer and red tints before leaf fall in autumn.

Where there is space, let them form thickets—they make a good wind-filtering screen, but benefit from thinning of the suckering canes, which displays their chestnut-coloured winter stems to better effect. They are equally at home as specimens in shrub borders, woodland or wild gardens or beside water, where their flowers echo the forms of the astilbes and *Aruncus dioicus*. In more confined areas, all of the top growth can be cut back to a woody framework in late winter or early spring, as for a buddleja, which results in larger foliage and longer flower panicles.

Fully hardy, z2–8, *S. sorbifolia*; z5–8, *S. tomentosa* var. *angustifolia*. Moderately fertile, moisture-retentive but well-drained, preferably neutral to alkaline soils in dappled shade or sun.

Spiraea
Rosaceae

Several spiraeas have a distinctly arching habit, a line that is strongly reinforced by the habit of flower production. They produce such dense corymbs of scintillating, clean white flowers, so close to the slender main stems that the foliage is almost invisible when they're in full foamy spate. Among the best are *Spiraea* 'Arguta' (bridal wreath) with small bright green leaves,

▶ *Stachyurus chinensis*

▶ *Stachyurus praecox*

◀ *Spiraea nipponica* 'Snowmound'

▼ *Spiraea* 'Arguta'

flowering in mid to late spring with the brunneras and single, late and lily-flowered tulips; and *S. nipponica* 'Snowmound', with blue-green leaves, flowering a few weeks later, in early summer, with the peonies, poppies and cistus.

Both flower on short sideshoots on the previous season's wood, and keep their form better and bloom quotient higher if some of the flowered shoots are cut back to within a few buds of their base immediately after flowering. This also disguises the fact that flowered branches look grubby as they fade. If they become untidy at maturity, assuming a shape other than the starburst you want, they tolerate hard pruning to a low framework and resume full flowering within a couple of seasons at most.

To head high. Fully hardy, z4/5–9. Any moderately fertile, moist but well-drained soil in sun.

Stachyurus
Stachyuraceae

Plants that bloom in late winter mark the lengthening days and signal the imminence of spring. *Stachyurus* species are excellent antidotes to the winter blues, bearing chains of tiny, bell-shaped flowers on naked branches from the leaf axils in late winter and early spring, *S. praecox* first, *S. chinensis* a couple of weeks later. Although the pendent racemes look as though they might quiver like catkins, they are actually quite stiff, more like beads on a wire. *Stachyurus praecox* has pale greenish yellow flowers on arching, dark claret red stems; the racemes of pale yellow flowers are longer in *S. chinensis*, and borne on smooth purplish brown shoots. They are lovely arching over a carpet of creamy- and dark-flowered hellebores. Both have long-ovate leaves tapering to a pointed tip, dark green and gracefully disposed along the stem in a quietly elegant array. Although I have a stubborn aversion to variegated foliage, the leaves of *S.* 'Magpie', with broad rose-tinted creamy margins on a grey-green ground, have a brightness that stands out in dappled shade.

very attractive and produce good autumn colour in shades of gold and scarlet. They flower in early summer.

Stephanandra incisa produces small, rounded terminal and axillary panicles of starry creamy yellow flowers, while *S. tanakae* is stouter-stemmed with larger sprays of pinkish white flowers. Neither is exuberantly showy in bloom, but shrubs that are so elegant in every season of the year hardly need to shout to warrant a place in the shrub border or woodland garden.

Remove some of the flowered stems after flowering to make room for the new. Thin out the stems of established clumps when dormant

They seldom need pruning, but regenerate freely from the base should replacement shoots be needed.

Slowly to head height. Fully hardy, z7–9. Fertile, humus-rich, moisture-retentive soils of open texture, in dappled shade or sun, in a site sheltered from cold, drying winds. They prefer lime-free soils, but will grow in almost any deep humusy soil.

▶ *Stephanandra tanakae*

▼ *Stephanandra incisa*

Stephanandra

Rosaceae

The multi-stemmed deciduous shrubs of the genus *Stephanandra* have particularly graceful arching stems—flexuous in *S. incisa*, like those of *Neillia thibetica*. They're coloured a warm rufous shade that makes them so attractive in winter. The deeply veined leaves, deeply and sharply lobed, bright green in *S. incisa* and larger and sharply serrated in *S. tanakae*, are

every second or third year, or as necessary to relieve congestion. If they become too untidy a thicket, they can be renewed by cutting to the ground in early spring.

To head high. Fully hardy, z4–9. Moist but well-drained, fertile soil in sun or dappled shade.

Syringa

Oleaceae

If the common lilac, *Syringa vulgaris*, and its cultivars are so loved, it's only partly because they are so reliable and easy to grow—they're beautiful trees, with colour and scent in abundance. If they seem rather stolid...well, perhaps that's the spur to seek out something a little more graceful in flower and a little more elegant in habit, maybe at half the height, so they're more suited to your smaller space or so you can extend lilac time into early summer?

Syringa reticulata subsp. *pekinensis* is late flowering and spicily scented, with arching shoots bearing large loose panicles of creamy flowers perhaps two weeks after the main flush of common lilacs; *S. reticulata* subsp. *pekinensis* 'Pendula' is a gracefully weeping form. *Syringa sweginzowii*, also late-flowering, bears narrowly tubular flowers in large lax branching panicles of soft lavender pink.

Twice head height. Fully hardy, z2/3–9. Full sun, in fertile, moisture-retentive, neutral to alkaline soils. See also page 230 (Clumps and Mounds).

Tamarix

Tamaricaceae

Since the tamarisks are notable wind-resisters and frequently found in the wild in coastal habitats, often on saline soils, they are commonly seen sheltering maritime gardens from wind and spray, and *Tamarix ramosissima* is sometimes used for stabilizing coastal dunes. This does not preclude their use in inland gardens; they are tolerant of a wide range of soils excepting shallow chalk.

◀ *Syringa reticulata* subsp. *pekinensis* 'Pendula'

▼ *Syringa sweginzowii*

Tamarix tetrandra bears tiny pale pink flowers in slender racemes on every lateral of the slender, arching, deep purple-brown shoots, the whole making sheer cascades of bloom in late spring. In *T. ramosissima* the red-brown shoots are crowded with dense, cylindrical racemes of flowers of a deeper, clearer pink from late summer to early autumn.

The tamarisks have a very interesting adaptive mechanism in regard to the salinity of soil; they actively use soil salts to help reduce transpiration in the face of strong maritime winds—so in coastal gardens they will grow on dry, freely draining, even very sandy soils. Inland, where soils are (one hopes) not saline, they need more moisture-retentive soils and some protection from cold, dry, searing winds.

▲ *Tamarix ramosissima*

There is often a fine line to be drawn between slender elegance and gaunt and straggly, and tamarisks cross it easily. They should be hard pruned on planting, to promote a well-branched habit and encourage good root establishment. As they mature they need pruning to keep them well furnished. Prune *T. ramosissima* in spring, shortening shoots to a permanent woody framework; prune *T. tetrandra* immediately after flowering, shortening flowered shoots to strong buds lower down on the shoots.

Fully hardy, z2–10, *T. ramosissima*; z6–10, *T. tetrandra*. Full sun. Moisture-retentive, moderately fertile, well-drained soils (but see above).

Teucrium

Lamiaceae

The shrubby germander, *Teucrium fruticans*, is one of the loveliest evergreens for late summer blues, on pure white shoots with aromatic grey-green leaves—exactly the thing for blue-, grey- and silver-themed plantings. Despite its being tarred with the 'warmer counties' brush, I have grown it for several years in hot sunny borders and in gravel gardens in 'colder counties', the keys to success being perfect winter drainage and maximum sunlight. The warmth of a

▶ *Teucrium fruticans*

sunny wall helps wood ripening and therefore hardiness. In these situations, it begins flowering in early summer, and continues unabated until autumn. Unfortunately, so thrilled was I by the mass of flowers, buzzing with bees, that I held back with the secateurs; if left unpruned it forms a really tangled mass, which is pretty enough, but rather formless. The best ascending fountains of white stems, studded with whorls of sky blue flowers, are had by cutting to a permanent woody framework, or to within three or four buds of the base, once growth is assured in early spring.

Fully hardy, z8–10. Poor to moderately fertile, neutral to alkaline, gritty, well-drained soil in full sun.

Clumps and Mounds

◄ *Hosta sieboldiana* var. *elegans*

Mounded and clump-forming plants are almost invariably the predominant mass, or masses, in any given planting scheme. They provide great opportunities for unifying a plant composition. By simple virtue of their green mass, their foliage is an element of unity and the effect can be stronger still if you select for tonal similarities in leaf colour, as in a silver-themed planting. Such bodies of colour are invaluable in exaggerating a spangling of stronger-hued flowers, or in separating rich tints, thus preventing them from being overpowering. I resist the temptation to call green a neutral colour, though; its array of hues, tones and tints, shaded with golds, greys, blues and blushes can form a diverse tapestry in its own right—a fabric of beauties that far outlast the more ephemeral virtues of flower. Similarly, such foliage mass provides unlimited potential for contrasts and harmonies in texture, both among themselves and with associates of stronger form.

The soft, rounded flanks of mound-formers and the more irregular masses of clumps give substance and structure to successive layers of height in a scheme. They form an essentially soft matrix against which plants of stronger line will make telling contrasts. They emphasize the lines of an accent plant, underscore the strength of vertical lines and the dynamism of diagonal ones, and are themselves anchored by the mass of low horizontals.

If evergreen, these plants' presence provides winter structure and frames the early bulbs that begin the season; if deciduous, they mask their early fading as new growth burgeons. They are the single most important component of any mixed planting, and although they may appear to play

◀ *Alchemilla mollis* (front) with geranium foliage

▶ *Anaphalis margaritacea* (centre left) with *Aster* 'Little Carlow', *Rudbeckia fulgida* var. *deamii* and *Plectranthus argentatus*

▶ *Anaphalis triplinervis*

a supporting role, their mass alone requires that they give great colour in flower, as well as good density, fine colour and a range of textures in foliage before and after flowering.

Alchemilla

Rosaceae ▪ lady's mantle

Useful as it as for borders and edging, the ubiquitous *Alchemilla mollis* is not the only alchemilla. There are others of greater refinement, most with a tang of lime in the froth of tiny yellow flowers of late spring or summer, and all with rounded, lobed leaves that gather mercurial dewdrops. The capture of perfectly spherical droplets with light-reflective qualities is a charm they all possess. Two near-knee-high mound-formers in particular are worth seeking out.

Alchemilla conjuncta has deeply seven-lobed, shining blue-green leaves, clearly outlined with the silver hair that clothes the undersides (not to be confused with the mat-forming *A. alpina*). *Alchemilla lapeyrousei*, beloved in eighteenth-century European gardens for its very neat habit; the velvety hairy leaves are more precisely lobed and a greyer green than those of *A. mollis*. Chic French gardeners regard the preference for *A. mollis* as an English folly.

Fully hardy, z4–9. Any moist but well-drained soil in full sun or light dappled shade.

Anaphalis

Asteraceae ▪ pearl everlasting

In general, white-, grey- and silver-leaved plants thrive in drier soils, demand good drainage and love full sun. *Anaphalis margaritacea* and *A. triplinervis* are exceptions, being suited to shady aspects and needing moisture-retentive soils. They have a quiet, old-fashioned charm, and thrive almost anywhere. Both make more-or-less knee-high mounds of more-or-less greyish foliage, with leafy stems in summer sporting more-or-less domed heads of more-or-less lustrous flowers with papery white bracts.

For more rather than less, be selective. For brighter foliage, choose *A. triplinervis*. It has the chunkier habit, downier stems and broader leaves of the two—pale grey-green above and densely white downy beneath, and flowers of more lustrous white. In *A. triplinervis* 'Sommerschnee' the flowers are shining white. In *A. margaritacea* the leaves are darker green, thinly white-downy beneath, and although flowerheads are broader, the bracts are a pearly, opalescent white. *Anaphalis margaritacea* 'Neuschnee' has an abundance of whiter flowers.

Fully hardy, z4–9. Moisture-retentive, but well-drained soil in sun, in light shade or indirect light.

Anthemis
Asteraceae

Dyer's chamomile, *Anthemis tinctoria*, grows wild in open, sunny and well-drained grasslands. Its cultivars make wide knee-high mounds of finely divided, aromatic foliage, with slender-stemmed daisy-like flowers with a mission to flower prolifically throughout summer, into autumn with a bit of management. It's best to curb this exuberance; it can lead to an early demise through exhaustion. Trim back in spring as growth commences, and you get denser mounds of healthy foliage. Trim again after the first flower flush to rejuvenate basal growth and you'll ensure a second.

You'll know, and indeed may love, the bright yellows that characterize many of the daisy family—at best, they're like sunshine on a stick; *A.* 'Grallach Gold' is one example. Where a softer moonshine-yellow is required, there are several candidates. Those with green or dark greyish green foliage include creamy primrose *A. t.* 'E.C. Buxton', *A. t.* 'Wargrave Variety' with cool lemon-yellow daisies; and *A. t.* 'Sauce Hollandaise' in pale cream. The more compact *A.*

SUSANNA MITCHELL 'Blomit' has soft creamy white flowers and silvery grey foliage.

As well as the usual border and edging sites, anthemis suit gravel plantings, and look lovely with airy grasses in the border, or among them in a meadow. Irresistible to lacewings and their larvae, which eat aphids, anthemis are a great aid in pest control.

Up to knee high. Fully hardy, z3/4–9. Any well-drained soil in sun or light part-day shade; the richer and moister, the soil the floppier the plant will be. Drought tolerant.

Artemisia
Asteraceae ▪ wormwood

The large, shrubby and subshrubby artemisias are characterized by billowing mounds of deeply cut or lobed, aromatic foliage, mostly in shimmering grey, silver and white. Those that branch from a woody base and don't have a creeping rootstock give a clearly delineated mound. Evergreen or semi-evergreen, in mild areas they retain good form in winter. They're not grown for their grubby flowers, but for the mass of pale colour and intricate textures the foliage brings to a composition, forming contrasts with strong shades and plainer surfaces. Some of the wildlings, such as the very silky *A. pycnocephala*, from California and Oregon, have this habit and one of them may be the wormwood of choice in your climate.

▲ *Anthemis tinctoria* 'Sauce Hollandaise' (front right) with *Campanula lactiflora*

Artemisia 'Powis Castle'

Artemisia arborescens
with alliums

knee-high mound, finer and brighter white than either the species or thigh-high *A.* 'Powis Castle', which is of the *A. arborescens* persuasion but hardier (z7–11), with filigreed silvery white foliage.

Fully hardy, z4–10. Full sun in well-drained or sharply drained, not-too-fertile soil. Drought tolerant. Leave top growth on over winter; cut back to buds on the lower stems in spring for a tighter mound of cleaner, brighter foliage. See also pages 44 (Horizontals and Tiers), 83 (Verticals and Diagonals) and 240 (Clouds and Transparents).

Ballota

Lamiaceae · false dittany

I've lost several *Ballota pseudodictamnus* specimens to heavy soils and cold, wet winters. It comes from dry, rocky places in the Aegean Islands, Crete and Turkey, where it lives in poor dirt with perfect drainage, and if you can offer similar conditions, it will thrive in them. White-woolly shoots rise from the base, clothed in wrinkled, heart-shaped, stem-clasping leaves—hairy as in the flock-like pilling on a woolly jumper (sweater), and a soft pale grey-green. Along each shoot, in midsummer, tight little whorls of tiny flowers appear; they have woolly green calyces from the centre of which sprout diminutive two-lipped, pink flowers.

Artemisia abrotanum, southernwood, forms a relatively narrow, waist-high mound. Deciduous in hard winters, it's a delicious rich sage green and finely divided into linear leaflets to give a very fine texture. It is one of most aromatic, lending a clean note to the perfume of Old Roses, both when cut and in the garden.

A. absinthium has silky grey leaves divided into quite broad lobes, but is a rather coarse and inveterate self-seeder. There are finer selections: *A. absinthium* 'Lambrook Silver' at waist high in pale, silvery grey-green, and the more finely cut *A. a.* 'Lambrook Mist' which forms a dense, lacy mound.

A. arborescens, from the Mediterranean, is slightly tender (z8–11), but its silvery white silk-lace filigree is worth a warm, dry, sheltered site. It's hardier on a lean diet with excellent drainage. *A. arborescens* 'Porquerolles' forms a neat

Ballota 'All Hallow's Green'

◀ *Ballota
pseudodictamnus*

▶ *Brunnera macrophylla*
'Dawson's White'

Ballota 'All Hallow's Green' (now *Marrubium bourgaei* var. *bourgaei* 'All Hallow's Green') makes a similar knee-high mound, but with a wash of lime green over stems, leaves and flowers. Both may resprout from the rootstock if felled by frost (or may not). Shorten the stems after flowering—enough to stop them from splaying in winter—but reserve harder pruning for spring.

Fully hardy, z7/8–10. Full sun in poor, open, sharply drained soil. Very drought tolerant.

Brunnera

Boraginaceae

From spruce forests and grassland on hills and mountain foothills in the Caucasus, and from Georgia to eastern Turkey, *Brunnera macrophylla* (Siberian bugloss) forms a knee-high, weed-smothering foliage mound that is absent only during the coldest months. The leaves develop fully only after flowering. In the wake of open sprays of small, intense blue forget-me-not flowers from spring to early summer (later in cool seasons), the heart-shaped, dark green leaves expand. They undulate at the margin, presenting different facets of their matt, rough-textured surfaces to the light, giving broad mounds of foliage of interesting and substantial texture when planted en masse. The species is a vigorous but slow-spreading rhizomatous perennial with green leaves, slightly paler beneath; extend interest by interplanting with *Brunnera macrophylla* 'Jack Frost', with green-veined silver leaves, or its silver-leaved sport 'Looking Glass'. Variegated forms of the species include 'Hadspen Cream' and 'Dawson's White' (syn. 'Variegata'), with cream-edged leaves, and 'Langtrees' with silver-white spotted ones. 'Betty Bowring' produces massed sprays of pure white flowers. All enjoy the same conditions as pulmonarias, dicentras, omphalodes and hepaticas at woodland margins and in shaded borders.

Knee high. Fully hardy, z3–8. Light or dappled shade and leafy, fertile, moisture-retentive soils; they withstand sun if soil is reliably moist.

Caltha

Ranunculaceae ▪ king cup

Having seen the king cup, *Caltha palustris*, in ancient water meadows, I know how heartstoppingly glorious it can be in vast swathes in wet soils or shallow water. In the wild, it associates with the marsh orchid, *Dactylorhiza fuchsii*, and the creamy plumes of meadowsweet, *Filipendula ulmaria*, the latter filling the air with sweet-sharp fragrance. It's a tapestry of contrasting scent, form and colour. In full light it flowers in carpets of shining gold in spring, later forming glossy mounds of leathery, rich green, almost

▲ *Brunnera macrophylla*
'Jack Frost'

▲ *Caltha palustris*

circular leaves. Though often recommended for partly shaded sites, they flower best in sun. At the water's edge or in bog gardens, the foliage is a great footnote for rodgersias or rheums, or fine-textured astilbes and actaeas.

Knee high. Fully hardy, z3–9. Consistently moist or boggy, humus-rich soil in sun or partial shade. *Caltha palustris* will grow in ankle-deep water.

Caryopteris

Verbenaceae • bluebeard

Forming a fragrant, grey-leaved mound with long, whorled wands of blue flowers with a brush of prominent stamens in the same shade, *Caryopteris ×clandonensis* has obviously inspired plant breeders. I've grown several variants, in herbaceous borders, on gravel banks and in other sunny sites, and the late summer flowers are much visited by bees and butterflies. *Caryopteris incana* and *C. mongolica*, the parents of *C. ×clandonensis* occur on steep slopes in dry scrub in eastern Asia, and although species and cultivars are fairly drought tolerant, they look sadly stressed if drought is prolonged. Although botanically a shrub, caryopteris may die back in hard winters, and is best treated as a woody-based perennial. The most definite mounds are to be had by cutting back to a low

▲▲ *Caryopteris ×clandonensis* GRAND BLEU 'Inoveris'

▲ *Caryopteris ×clandonensis* 'First Choice'

framework in spring; they flower late in summer on the current season's growth.

The best selections of *C. ×clandonensis* give more decisive blues than the simple hybrid. *Caryopteris ×clandonensis* 'Dark Knight' is compact and silver leaved with the darkest blue flowers; in 'Ferndown' they're a dark blue-violet; 'First Choice' has cobalt-blue flowers, and 'Heavenly Blue', clear sky blue. 'Longwood Blue' makes a taller than average mound with violet-blue flowers, and GRAND BLEU 'Inoveris' has more upright stems with short internodes so the mound is denser; it has darker green leaves and violet-blue flowers. It would be a sad thing if the first caryopteris you were introduced to was the gruesome 'Worcester Gold'; allegedly golden-leaved, it just looks chlorotic to me.

Thigh to waist high. Fully hardy, z5–9. Open-textured, moderately fertile, well-drained soil in sun.

Ceanothus

Rhamnaceae ▪ Californian lilac

When I went to California to see the Big Trees, I was stunned by the diversity of ceanothus along the coast—a fabulous variety seldom seen in European gardens. The Californian species range through coastal bluffs within reach of spray from big rollers, to chaparral and the dry slopes of the Coast Range. They fix nitrogen, control soil erosion, attract bees and feed a range of seed-eating birds; even the cultivated sorts are good for wildlife gardens.

I once designed a mixed border beneath tall windows, with the brief that nothing must be taller than head height, to leave the view unobscured. Good buns that kept their shape before and after flowering were among the first considerations, and preference was for evergreens. If they had scented blue flowers so much the better. There are several mound-forming ceanothus to fit the bill. The lowest, such as the knee-high *C. maritimus* 'Point Sierra', with lavender-violet flowers, or the equally low *C. gloriosus* 'Heart's Desire' in lavender blue, probably belong in the horizontal category, for they spread to several times their height. Both are wild selections introduced by Californian nurseries.

Nearly all of the newer introductions offer pleasing blues—not the insipid ones that some older cultivars display. In general, whatever their final height, those with smaller, thicker leaves (from botanical section Cerastes) are nearly all mounding in habit (and very drought tolerant). *Ceanothus* 'Blue Sapphire' is waist-high, with small, dark, glossy, chocolate-tinted leaves and intense violet-blue flowers in late spring-early summer. It's a bud sport of 'Blue Cushion' (same height, green leaves, sky-blue flowers). In my dry, sunny border, in not very fertile soil, both have a good dense habit. Other growers find 'Blue Sapphire' open and arching,

▶ *Ceanothus* 'Blue Cushion'

▶ *Ceanothus* 'Puget Blue'

but I am an avid pinch-pruner of young plants, and keep them tight by light shaping.

The following, head high or above, are irresistible owing to the intense hues of their prolific blooms: *Ceanothus* 'Blue Mound', 'Italian Skies', and 'Pin Cushion' produce so many clear bright blue flowers that you can hardly see the glossy foliage. In 'Cynthia Postan' and 'Concha' you get the anticipatory joy of tight magenta buds that burst into sheets of dazzling blue or blue-purple, and in 'Dark Star', which becomes more mounded as it matures, the tiny, very dark leaves are a perfect backdrop for radiant cobalt blooms. Among the hardiest, least temperamental and taller still is 'Puget Blue' in intense lavender blue, and with a reputation for longevity not shared by the genus as a whole.

Californian nurseries tell me that ceanothus are very accepting of pruning—as hedges, or even cushions—which we don't often do in the UK, being fearful of winter losses. No fear. The spring- and early-summer-flowering evergreens bloom on the previous season's growth and can be shaped *immediately* after flowering; cut back flowered shoots by about a third of their length. New growth then has time to ripen before the onset of winter.

Fully hardy, z7–10. Moderately fertile, emphatically well-drained soil in sun, with shelter from cold, drying winds.

Centranthus

Valerianaceae • valerian

When a plant is a garden commonplace—valerian is, after all, the ubiquitous cottage garden plant—it's as easy to grow as it is to overlook its virtues. It makes a rounded, open clump of fairly upright stems, with glaucous, bluish green leaves and dense, domed clusters of tiny white, dusky rose-pink, or red-crimson flowers throughout most of summer; they attract clouds of nectar-feeding moths and butterflies. 'Alba Pura' has blooms of a cleaner white than ever so slightly pink 'Albus'; *C. ruber* var. *coccineus* has carmine red flowers and 'Atrococcineus' deep scarlet red—none of the hues in the pink-red spectrum are pure, and they're all the more attractive for that.

On Lindisfarne, off northeastern England's Northumbrian coast, where Gertrude Jekyll designed her tiniest-ever garden, *Centhranthus ruber* is placed to perfection—not by Miss Jekyll, but self-sown wildly into shingle and wall, cliff and rock crevices. Since plants planted directly in dry stone niches often perish before they establish, one needs patience to achieve charming effects, I find. So did Jekyll: having allegedly dangled a lad from a rope with a basket of plants to place in the niches of Lindisfarne Castle walls—without success—she later resorted to chucking seeds from the Castle windows. If you establish a single plant in the

near vicinity of your walls, then sooner rather than later, you will discover niches that are colonized by wind-blown seed. Any plant that is so drought tolerant, thrives in poor dirt or spray-drenched shingle and sheds seed in great airborne clouds should alert you to its invasive capabilities.

Knee to thigh high. Fully hardy, z4–9. Any dry or well-drained soil in full sun; rich soils and partial shade result in leggy plants.

Ceratostigma

Plumbaginaceae • hardy or false plumbago

The hardy plumbagos give greatest pleasure towards the end of summer and into autumn. The foliage mounds begin to colour in shades of bronze and red as the days shorten, so their salverform blue flowers are borne against a constantly changing backcloth.

The lowest is the woody-stemmed perennial, *C. plumbaginoides*, a knee-high mound of bright green leaves on erect red stems that carry short spikes of rich blue flowers at their tips. It is a restrained spreader with slender rhizomes, sometimes used in the wider landscape

▲ *Centranthus ruber*

▶ Choisya 'Aztec Pearl'

for stabilizing banks. *Ceratostigma griffithii* is a dense, thigh-high, evergreen shrub with bristly red stems tipped with radiant blue flowers; its substantial, matt green leaves are margined purple and also bristle-rimmed, begging backlighting by low autumn sun. The deciduous, waist-high *C. willmottianum* has pale-bristled stems and shares with *C. griffithianum* the purple margins to its leaves; their texture is a little coarser but the terminal and axillary clusters of flowers more than compensate. In *C. wilmottianum* the flowers are a paler, slatey blue with red-purple calyces.

That irritating debate on the 'is it a shrub, subshrub or woody-based perennial?' theme is relevant here in practical terms if you want the best foliage. In cold areas *C. griffithii* looks sad at the turn of the year, and both it and *C. willmottianum* can be cut to the ground by hard winters—but resprout from the base. They flower late in the season, on the current year's growth, and there is a lot to gain by treating them as woody-based perennials and cutting them to the ground in spring. This way, you add a couple of extra hardiness zones (treat them to a winter mulch); not only are new leaves lovelier, you have space to fill with small spring bulbs. By the time late summer brings the first flowers and the colour changes of impending autumn, you can associate them with the

▶ Ceratostigma
plumbaginoides

autumn tints of gillenias, the late flower spikes of crocosmia and schizostylis, and they make good foreground for autumn colour maples. Late butterfly hatchings take full advantage of the flowers and it's a joy to watch them being worked over by hummingbird hawkmoths.

Fully hardy, z5–9, *C. plumbaginoides*; z7–9, *C. griffithii* and *C. willmottianum*; z5–9 as woody-based perennials. Full sun, in open, moderately fertile and moisture-retentive soil.

Choisya
Rutaceae ▪ Mexican orange blossom

If it should seem curmudgeonly to be indifferent to a sturdy, mound-forming evergreen shrub with dark, aromatic foliage and an exceptionally long season of white flowers scented of orange blossom, then so be it. For all that it offers, and it does make a good dark backcloth, *Choisya ternata* has a whiff of the Victorian shrubbery about it. Peter Moore, formerly of the Hillier Arboretum, used it in a cross with *Choisya dumosa* var. *arizonica* to bring us *Choisya* 'Aztec Pearl'—an elegant, well-bred plant with altogether more class. It has glossier, brighter green leaves with finer leaflets, and in place of plain white flowers it has fat cymes of pink buds that open to pristine white blooms. Although it is claimed that it bears them in two flushes in spring and late summer, each can be

so prolonged as to almost meet in the middle. I have two in a south-facing site that are seldom without some bloom, in some years even at midwinter solstice. They suffer a little winter windburn, but reward pruning out of damaged growth with glossy new shoots. Uncut, it makes a mound above head height; I trim in spring to keep a perfect chest-high mound and to bring bits in for the vase—flowers and foliage both smell good. One of the prettiest specimens I know is a close-cut sphere in a tiny urban garden, an orb of fine foliage, spangled with flowers, on a waist-high stem.

Fully hardy, z7–10. Any fertile well-drained soil in sun.

Cistus

Cistaceae • rock rose

The scrub, dry pinewoods, and particularly the maquis and garrigue found all around the Mediterranean, are full of cistus. They're a major contributor to the particular aroma you find in those habitats—gum labdanum, which several species produce, is used by parfumiers for woody, amber notes; would you still dab it on your pulse points if you thought it had been gathered from the beards of browsing goats, I wonder? If you've ever driven those narrow, white-knuckle roads in the foothills of the Sierra Nevada in Spain, with scary slopes falling away to either side, you know exactly the sort of terrain cistus enjoy.

They all bear shallowly cupped flowers with a central boss of liquid gold, and five lustrous petals the texture of crushed silk; several, such as *Cistus ladanifer*, have dark basal petal blotches that look as though painted by an exceptionally neat hand. That individual flowers open and fall on a daily basis is Zen on the cycle of life for the impatient; new blooms appear all through the summer days. Those with flowers in cymes give greater flower power than those that bear flowers singly.

I first saw the viscid *C. ladanifer* forming a dense mound of upright branches in the rain-

▲ *Cistus ×purpureus* 'Betty Taudevin' (front) with *Leptospermum scoparium* var. *incanum* 'Keatleyi'

◀ *Cistus ×aguilarii* 'Maculatus'

shadow of a sunny wall, where it was annually pinch-pruned by passing horticultural students for their summer identification tests. It gave me clues to the needs of cistus. They love well-drained, sunny and gravelly banks, terraces, wall tops, wall bases and borders; some growers recommend mound-planting to ensure perfect drainage at their moisture-sensitive necks. They die of fright if you try to restore a dense habit by hard pruning, so tip prune from early youth after flowering; even naturally leggy ones with upright branches have a mounded outline when treated this way.

The hardiest include *C. laurifolius*, head high, with aromatic, leathery, deep bluish green leaves and pure white flowers suffused with gold at the centre—and at waist to chest height: *C. ×aguilarii* with prominently veined leaves in brighter green and scintillating white flowers, *C. ×aguilarii* 'Maculatus' with a dark maroon petal blotch, and *C. ladanifer* with large, chocolate-blotched white flowers and sticky shoots bearing very dark green leaves that are clammy with labdanum.

The pink-flowered cistus include several that

seldom reach above waist height with flowers of girly silvery pink: *C. ×fernandesiae* 'Anne Palmer', rose pink; *C. argenteus* 'Peggy Sammons', pale lavender-pink; *C.* 'Silver Pink' is peachy pink, hardier than most and needs slightly more fertile soils if it is not to disappoint. In the head-high *C. ×purpureus* 'Betty Taudevin' the flowers are an altogether more vampish crimson-pink with dark basal blotches.

Fully hardy, z7–9/10. Full sun and poorish, dryish soils with excellent drainage; tolerant of limy soils but sometimes chlorotic on chalk. Site right the first time; they're unforgiving of being transplated.

◀ *Convolvulus cneorum*

Convolvulus

Convolvulaceae

The botanical descriptor for the foliage of *Convolvulus cneorum* (silver bush) is sericeous, derived from the Greek word for silk in (*serikos*). The narrow silver leaves of this knee-high bun do indeed have the feel and smooth, gleaming quality of fine silk; the fine hairs appear to be hot pressed to the leaf surface. It grows in the wild on hot, dry, limestone rocks of the Mediterraneanan coast. From early summer onwards, clusters of pink buds open to glistening white funnels, faintly lined on the reverse with pink. It's extremely covetable, but tarred with the too-tender brush if you garden in 'less-favoured climates'. Believing completely in its tenderness, I used to grow it in containers on a hot, sunny patio, but out of curiosity introduced it to a paving crevice there. It's still there five years later, in the company of its flat little friend, *C. sabatius* (see page 48), their roots protected from winter's worst by stone slabs. I also grow it on a hot, sunny bank in gravel up to its neck. Given perfect drainage, a lean diet, and maximum sunlight, it is hardier than you'd think, although doubtless a combination of winter cold with winter wet would kill it outright.

Knee high. Hardy, z8–10. Poor, perfectly drained soil in sun.

Corydalis

Papaveraceae

Once upon a time, corydalis were considered quite charming—faint praise and all that—but the dissemination and interbreeding of the blue-flowered corydalis, *C. elata*, *C. flexuosa* and *C. cashmiriana*, over the past decades has created a mania for them. *All* of the cultivated sorts make mounds or clumps of exceptionally pretty foliage: dainty, finely divided, filigreed (*C. ochreleuca*), sometimes ferny (*C. cheilanthifolia*), and often attractively bronzed (*C. anthriscifolia*), the leaves alone offer good potential for textural contrasts with smoother, plainer partners. And all bear racemes of small tubular, spurred flowers of intricate construction in spring/early summer or in summer, often for long periods, which adds to their distinction. They are fibrous-rooted or rhizomatous (blooming mainly in late spring or early summer), or tuberous (these being spring-flowering and summer-dormant).

Corydalis come from a range of shady and wooded habitats, from shaded cliffs or more open, rocky sites. In cool dappled shade with leafy, humus-rich, moist but well-drained soil, you can use any of the blues, and in a sheltered microclimate you may catch their elusive fragrance. *Corydalis cashmeriana* is tuberous, with bright green leaves and brilliant blue flowers, darker at the tips, with curved spurs; in *C. fumariifolia*, also tuberous, leaves are slightly glaucous and flowers azure, lavender-blue or violet. The fibrous-rooted *C. flexuosa* has enjoyed the attentions of breeders and selectors, and in several variants, such as 'Purple Leaf', the natural purple foliage flush is pronounced. The slender flowers are held almost upright, in dense, knee-high racemes in late spring, in shades from deep indigo blue ('Nightshade') to the clearest soft blue ('China Blue').

The translucent blues of *C. elata* tend to the electric—a piercing cobalt in late spring/early summer above blue-green leaves; it is increasingly used in hybridizing. Exquisitely dainty *C. anthriscifolia* suits these conditions too, with glaucous, faintly bronzed foliage and delicate, long-spurred flowers; a dusky mauve-purple fading to buff, like the effect you get pulling a laden watercolour brush across mulberry paper. You can enjoy an extended display of fresh foliage from non-tuberous species by shearing back after flowering.

If your site is slightly sunnier and very well drained, choose tuberous *C. solida*, with glaucous, grey-green leaves, reaching to about mid calf height. There are several colour selections: pale pinks in 'Sunrise'; deeper reds in 'Sunset'; 'Dieter Schact', apple-blossom pink; 'George Baker', in rich, bricky salmon-red, and 'Beth Evans', a pretty soft pink. The tuberous sorts don't enjoy summer baking, however, and most are perfect for naturalizing beneath a canopy of deciduous trees and shrubs. Include grit and leaf mould in the planting hole, and top dress with leaf mould to prevent summer desiccation. They do self-seed, and offspring give a spangling of various shades; select out deviants to maintain the colour you first thought of.

Easygoing non-tuberous species thrive in any fertile, well-drained soil in sun or shade, and include *C. cheilanthifolia*, with ferny plumes of olive green leaves and knee-high spikes of soft yellow flowers in spring and early summer. *Corydalis lutea* and *C. ochreleuca* look

▸ *Corydalis cheilanthifolia*

▸ *Corydalis flexuosa*

▸ *Corydalis solida* subsp. *solida* 'Dieter Schact'

alike, and bloom from summer to autumn, the former with clear yellow flowers and slightly glaucous leaves, the latter with creamier flowers and more markedly glaucous foliage. Both are evergreen, occurring naturally among rocks and screes, and are a refined addition to your wall flora, knee high in open ground.

Fully hardy, z4–9.

Daphne
Thymelaeaceae

A number of daphnes are evergreen mound-formers—neat and fine-textured in glossy leaf, and with glistening and fabulously fragrant blooms. Someone once described the scent as immoral, and I knew just what he meant. For me, the intoxicating scent is a close second consideration in siting; yes, they absolutely *must* be within reach of the nose—but foremost, they must be placed where they stand the best chance of thriving. With a notoriously picky genus like *Daphne* you mustn't give them any excuse to dislike you. Resentful and unforgiving of transplanting, they don't all enjoy the same conditions, and if stressed are more susceptible to diseases that cause sudden and tragic death.

Culturally, the most important differences within the genus derive from where they grow in the wild; some are mountain-dwellers, others woodland natives. The neatest mounds are those with small leaves of compact habit, a common characteristic in alpine plants. In high mountains, plants overwinter beneath an insulating snow blanket, cold but dry. At snowmelt they are treated to fresh water subject to sharp, gravity-assisted drainage, and to high light levels that are often ameliorated by low cloud, which shields them from the hottest sun. Their deep roots penetrate screes and fissures, which ensures cool roots and an equable moisture supply, never too wet in winter or bone-dry in summer.

While the most demanding alpine daphnes insist on exact replication of these conditions in cultivation, the mounding mountain daphnes described here thrive in an approximation: good light, in moisture-retentive, open-textured, really well-drained soil with some humus. Go easy on the humus and avoid too much moisture; wet organic soils encourage root-rotting fungi (*Phytopthera*) to which daphnes are vulnerable. A gravel mulch keep roots cool and moist in summer, but won't allow excess moisture to accumulate at the neck of the plant. I grow several fragrant mountain daphnes in gravelled gaps on a paved terrace, where their roots are cool beneath un-mortared slabs.

Daphne cneorum, at ankle to knee high, mounds up on itself, spreads slowly, and has

◀ *Daphne cneorum*

rose-pink flowers clustered close to the shining, dark green leaves in late spring/early summer. The following daphnes make dense, shapely domes, and bloom for several weeks around the cusp of late spring and early summer, then sporadically in several flushes till autumn: *D. sericea* Collina Group, almost knee high, with dense terminal clusters of rich rosy purple flowers; *D.* ×*mantensiana* 'Manten', to mid thigh, with flowers of deep rose-purple, pale lilac within; *D.* ×*napolitana*, slightly taller, longer and later in bloom, with rose-pink flowers; *D.* ×*susannae* 'Cheriton', with relatively large clusters of deep rose-purple flowers, to knee high and twice as wide as tall; and *D. tangutica*, which forms a more open, waist-high mound, blooming earlier in spring, with white flowers, purple within and flushed rose-purple without.

Unlike many other genera, in which hybrids are often bigger, brasher and more vigorous than the species, daphne hybrids retain much of the grace of their wild parents, unspoiled by hybrid vigour but often easier to grow as a result of it. Semi-evergreen *D.* ×*burkwoodii* is a good example; 'Albert Burkwood' forms a broad, waist-high mound with pale pink flowers flushed deeper pink without, while its taller sister seedling 'Somerset' is a narrower, vase-shaped mound with deeper pink flowers.

The second group of mound-formers are woodland natives, more lax and with larger

◀ *Daphne ×napolitana*

early spring; *D. laureola* subsp. *philippi* is similar but barely reaches knee high. Their scent can be a bit foxy by day, but becomes sweeter in the evening—they are moth pollinated. *Daphne pontica*, chest high eventually, has pointed, leathery, dark green leaves, with pale green flowers, in spring in paired clusters at the stem tips. These three are more tolerant than most daphnes of heavy soils and are useful for sites in fairly deep shade. Waist-high *D. odora* 'Aureomarginata' produces pink flowers at the stem tips from midwinter through spring. It has narrow, pointed, dark green leaves thinly margined in creamy yellow and is hardier than the plain-leaved species.

Fully hardy, z5–9, *D. ×burkwoodii*; z5–8, *D. caucasica*; z4–9, *D. cneorum*; z7–9, *D. laureola*, *D. ×napolitana*, *D. sericea* Collina Group, *D. ×susannae*; z7–8, *D. ×mantensiana*, *D. odora* 'Aureomarginata'; z6–9, *D. pontica, D. tangutica*. The sap of daphnes is highly irritant and all parts are toxic if eaten.

Dicentra

Papaveraceae

Closely related to *Corydalis*, dicentras are also plants of damp woodland margins and shady, rocky places in mountain woods. Like *Corydalis* they are valued for the textural intricacy of their finely divided foliage, often attractively glaucous in shades of bluish green or silvergrey. The panicles of pendent flowers, shaped like elongated hearts and pursed at the mouth, have a delicate charm, hanging from slender pedicels on upright, fleshy stalks; they come in shades of white through soft rose pinks to deep blood red.

The most commonly grown are selections and hybrids, mainly of *D. eximia* and *D. formosa*, which give a long season of interest in flower and leaf. *Dicentra formosa* has green leaves that are glaucous beneath and rosy pink flowers; *D. f.* 'Alba' has pure white flowers. Following the main display of spring and early summer, many give sporadic flushes of bloom

◀ *Daphne odora* 'Aureomarginata'

leaves than montane species. They need moisture-retentive, but well-drained, humus-rich soil in semi-shade; retain summer moisture with a leaf mould mulch, but avoid the stem base. They burn in too-high light levels, and need shelter from dry winds. *Daphne laureola*, a thigh-high evergreen, holds shining, dark green leaves in pleasingly symmetrical clusters at the stem tip and, almost hidden beneath them, yellow-green flowers in late winter and

till autumn, most reliably in good light with adequate moisture.

Dicentra 'Ivory Hearts', with strong-stemmed, ivory white flowers held well clear of substantial clumps of dense, blue-green foliage, is noted for its extended flowering period; in regions with cool summers it flowers almost continuously from spring to late summer. The following are clump-forming, mostly rhizomatous perennials, which, when they spread, give softly undulating mounds. It's easy to justify growing several cultivars together for subtle foliage contrasts in shades of green, blue-green and silver-grey. *Dicentra* 'Langtrees' has silvery grey-green leaves, and creamy, pink-tinted flowers; 'Pearl Drops' and 'Silver Smith' are similar, but with blue-green leaves. The foliage of 'Stuart Boothman' is blue-grey, the flowers deep pink; 'Bacchanal' is one of the darkest, with deep crimson flowers and greyish green leaves.

Knee high. Fully hardy, z4–9. Fertile, humus-rich, moisture-retentive soil in partial or dappled shade. See also page 155 (Arcs and Fountains).

Epimedium
Berberidaceae

The major charm of epimediums lies in their foliage—and indeed, they are notable for their mounds of overlapping, pointed, heart-shaped leaflets which, in the best, are beautifully tinted, mottled or outlined in shades of bronze, copper, russet or red when young, and often again in autumn. However, I feel cheated if a plant doesn't also have flowers that I can clearly *see*. Some epimediums have so few and such dainty pale flowers that they make little impact, but since the 1980s, epimediums of such exceptional grace have been introduced, mostly from eastern Asia, that they're now regarded as more than simply foliage plants.

In many Asian species, the tiny cupped flowers, suspended by fragile pedicels on the most slender of wiry stems, are adorned by long curving spurs, the whole inflorescence reminiscent of a cloud of diminutive, spidery aquilegias. Those from the Caucasus and around the Mediterranean have short-spurred or spurless flowers that are generally less showy. Both groups are perfect in shady corners and borders, or

◀ *Epimedium* ×*youngianum* 'Niveum'

▲ *Epimedium acuminatum* 'Galaxy'

◀ *Epimedium grandiflorum* 'Freya'

▶ *Epimedium wushanense* 'Caramel'

sheltered beneath a canopy of deciduous trees and shrubs; if shaded from early morning sun, they're less susceptible to spring frosts. Most epimediums are evergreen, but leaves retained through winter fade as the season progresses. The flower shoots arise in spring, as the new season's leaves begin to unfurl. This is the best time to clip away old foliage to reveal flowers and new foliage at their best, although it's not strictly necessary, and it does remove the modicum of frost protection that old leaves provide. The main exceptions to this pruning

recommendation are *E. perralderianum* and *E.* ×*perralchicum* because their wintergreen leaves are a glossy, brilliant green and remain so well into spring; clip them later if you must.

Epimedium perralderianum and *E. pinnatum* subsp. *colchicum* have long been grown in European gardens, the former with bronzed young leaves, the latter with good autumn tints, both with racemes of small, short-spurred yellow flowers in spring. Their hybrid, *E.* ×*perralchicum*, shares their best traits. Once established, they are more tolerant of sun and of drier soils in summer than the Asian species. *Epimedium* ×*versicolor* shares this tolerance; it has short-spurred, pink-and-yellow flowers, while *E.* ×*versicolor* 'Sulphureum' bears longer-spurred, soft, yellow flowers, and spreads more widely. *Epimedium ×youngianum* 'Niveum' is compact and deciduous, with rich bronze-red in both new and autumn leaves, and spurred white flowers like little bells.

The deciduous *E. grandiflorum*, from China, Japan and Korea, has bequeathed oriental grace to many selections and hybrids, with relatively large, long-spurred flowers in mid to late spring, and strong spring colour to their delicate, spiny-margined leaflets: 'Lilafee' has violet purple flowers; 'Saturn' pure white above dark-rimmed leaves; 'Freya' is very compact, lilac-purple with white-tipped spurs; 'Beni-Chidori', deep violet-pink with white-tipped spurs.

Among the influx of new Asian species, some are high on my wish-list: *E. acuminatum* 'Galaxy', with large white, long-spurred flowers; *E. wushanense*, with waist-high inflorescences of up to a hundred spidery yellow flowers; and *E. wushanense* 'Caramel', with caramel-amber flowers.

Fully hardy, z5–9. Fertile, humus-rich, well-drained soil, in semi-shade with shelter from dry winds. Adequate summer moisture ensures lush summer foliage, and is essential for Asian epimediums.

Erysimum

Brassicaceae/Cruciferae • wallflower

There are hybrid wallflowers quite unlike the *E. cheiri* cultivars that are grown as biennials. Forget spring bedding. The mound-forming, woody-based, subshrubby perennials have a shapely wintergreen presence, and dense spikes of fragrant, four-petalled flowers produced with scarcely a rest between early spring and autumn. *Erysimum* 'Bowles's Mauve' forms such a defined, thigh-high mound of narrow, grey-green leaves as to be almost orb-shaped if uncrowded. In early spring, long racemes of clear mauve flowers make a precocious companion for tulips and later an enduring one for Japanese anemones, *Anemone ×hybrida*. *Erysimum* 'Plant World Lemon', about the same size

▲ *Erysimum* 'Bowles's Mauve'

and height, features chameleon flowers in pale lemon yellow, bronze and mauve, each colour on every spike simultaneously. Most of the following are knee to thigh high or thereabouts: 'Apricot Twist' has vibrant orange to apricot flowers opening from dusky buds; 'Dawn Breaker' is well scented, in a mix of apricot, yellow and pale yellow; the flowers of 'Devon Sunset' open from mahogany buds, cream then grading to pale and deep lilac; 'Sweet Sorbet' has long spikes in creamy apricot, lilac and deep mauve.

They grow in any moderately fertile, well-drained soil in sun, but despite being best with adequate summer moisture, they dislike wet, cold winter soils. Give them a high-potash feed after the first flush of flowers. Take off spent flowered stems down to the next set of promising growth buds. If you let them become too tall into winter, they will fall over, having a relatively small root system. Having such reckless commitment to flower production, they are often short lived, but are easily propagated by heeled softwood cuttings in spring or summer.

Fully hardy, z6–10.

Euphorbia

Euphorbiaceae • spurge

There are two thousand or so species of *Euphorbia*, so let's concentrate on a few that are easily grown in a range of garden situations and form mounds or clumps. Some that I use for a

mounded outline also have upright stems that give strongly etched vertical lines. Euphorbias have complex inflorescences; male and female parts are visually insignificant, but cupped in a cyathium, the cyathia being held in cymes, umbels or clusters. The obviously ornamental parts are the coloured bracts or floral leaves surrounding the cyathia, which retain structure and colour for months. Add to that their attractive stems, foliage and architectural habit and these euphorbias give pleasure for many months of the year.

A number occur naturally in damp, wooded habitats and are suitable for moist but well-drained, humus-rich soil in dappled shade or part-day sun. The evergreen *A. amygdaloides*, knee to thigh high, has mounds of spoon-shaped, deep green leaves on pink-tinted stems that terminate in cymes of lime green flowers from spring to early summer. In some—*E. amygdaloides* 'Purpurea', with red stems and leaves, and *A. amygdaloides* 'Craigieburn', with leaves the colour of ruby port—the natural purple flush of the foliage is pronounced. The evergreen hybrid *E.* REDWING 'Charam' has densely leafy stems clothed in whorls of narrow blue-green leaves, flushed dusky purple in cold weather, with tight, deep red winter flowerheads that open in spring to large clear golden yellow; it thrives in drier soils with more sun than *E. amygdaloides*.

Among shade-lovers are several Himalayans, from rocky places and forest clearings, all winter dormant, forming clumps of vertical new stems annually. In loose, leafy, open-textured soils, some are invasive, but can be restrained by heavier soils and by cutting back. More or less thigh-high *E. griffithii* 'Dixter' has shining dark red stems clothed in narrow, deep coppery green leaves with red midribs, each stem terminating in a head of scarlet-vermilion bracts in late spring and early summer. In green-leaved *E. griffithii* 'Fireglow' stems and midribs are pink, with yellow cyathia surrounded by intense orange-red bracts. Not all plants so named

are the first-rate plant introduced by the late Alan Bloom; if seed-raised, offspring are variable and if they don't glow they're not the real thing. Both look really stunning in damp soils in a ferny sea of complementary green, with *Matteuccia*, *Onoclea* and *Osmunda*.

Euphorbia sikkimensis, from Sikkim, and *E. schillingii*, from Nepal, have stems that reach waist high by the time they flower in late summer. *Euphorbia schillingii* has long grey-green leaves rimmed red when young, on smooth pink stems that branch at their tips, each branchlet bearing broad cymes of luminous, yellow-green bracts. *E. sikkimensis* emerges in late winter with stems and leaves flushed deep pink. The dark green leaves pale as they mature but midribs and margins remain pink, and each stem terminates in flowers with pale yellow bracts. It's a slow runner, but even so I had to remove it from my borders, putting it instead among the ferns with *E. griffithii,* where it continues the interest where the latter leaves off.

The following euphorbias occur mainly in dry rocky places and in open scrub, and need light, open-textured, well-drained soils in sun or part-day shade. They don't like heavy soils, hate excessive winter wet, and taller sorts are best protected from strong wind.

Euphorbia polychroma is a neat knee-high dome covered from spring to midsummer in long-lasting clusters of sharp luminous yellow. Its perfect symmetry looks well for such a long time in classical urns and other containers; it dies back in late autumn.

Euphorbia characias scarcely needs introduction—sculptural and architectural are the usual descriptors. It and all its variants are taprooted shrubs with stout pale stems clothed in long narrow leaves in shades of blue-green and grey-green, each stem with a dense terminal cyme with green bracts, from late winter to early summer. The flowering stems form one year and flower early in the next; remove all flowered stems at the base in midsummer once flowers fade.

The cultivars and hybrids vary in leaf colour, in size, shape and density of the inflorescence, and in height. They are derived from *E. characias* subsp. *characias*, which has dark nectar glands on the cyathia, and is waist high, or *E. characias* subsp. *wulfenii*, with yellow-green nectar glands, which can reach head height, and has longer, glaucous blue-green leaves. Among the more dramatic are *E. characias* 'Black Pearl' with matt, bluish grey-green leaves, lime green bracts and very dark nectar glands; it makes a thigh-high mound with a pronounced dusky hue. Among the sturdiest of the variegated sorts is *E. characias* Silver Swan 'Wilcott' which reaches chest height, with blue-green leaves outlined in silvery white, the variegation repeated in the floral bracts. *Euphorbia characias* subsp. *characias* 'Humpty Dumpty' has pale grey-green leaves, and apple green floral bracts; both foliage and inflorescences are dense and the whole clump is a well-rounded, waist-high mound (not dumpy). *Euphorbia characias* 'Portuguese Velvet' makes a rounded thigh-high dome, with velvety blue-green leaves clothed in fine, silvery, light-reflecting hair.

Euphorbia mellifera, honey spurge, is much coveted. For a long time I was deterred by its reputation for tenderness, but having seen it gardens in the cold, wild hills of northern England, I'm not convinced this reputation is justified. It has a broad evergreen dome of long emerald green leaves, faintly outlined in dark red and with clean white midribs, and in spring or early summer it bears broad cymes of pale brown cyathia with bronze bracts, which emit a sweet, honeyed scent that travels for yards. In warm areas it can reach the height of a basketball ace, but in cooler gardens it seldom achieves more than (a normal person's) chest height unless it's very sheltered. *Euphorbia stygiana* is similar to *E. mellifera*, with paler but equally well-scented flowers. Its shapely evergreen mounds are now essential to the winter structure of my borders, and play host

to various compositions: with pleated leaved veratrums, the rosy young growth of *Paeonia mlokosewitschii*, and the tall, transparent candelabra of *Eryngium eburneum*. None of the plants have died of winter cold, nor have they reached much higher than my waist in ordinary well-drained garden soil.

I elaborate on the warning to avoid contact with the irritant milky sap of euphorbia; wash any inadvertent traces off thoroughly, especially beneath your nails. It will leave you prostrate with pain in a hospital emergency room if it comes in contact with your eyes.

Mostly fully hardy, z6–9, *E. amygdaloides*, *E. characias*, *E. polychroma*; z5–9, *E. griffithii*; z8/9, *E. mellifera*; z7–9, *E. schillingii*, *E. sikkimensis*; z8–9, *E. stygiana*.

Fatsia

Araliaceae ▪ Japanese aralia

For years I was blind to the virtues of *Fatsia japonica*, associating it with corporate atria, 1970s interiors and its aspidistra-like tenacity in the gloomy homes of aged relatives. Then one autumn morning I saw it above the white walls of an urban courtyard, all its glossy green glory adorned with huge creamy umbels; it was a revelation.

From humid coastal woodlands of the South Korea and the islands of Japan, it makes an evergreen mound from head height to three times that, depending on conditions. The thick, suckering stems patterned with leaf scars terminate in an array of huge, leathery, rich green leaves, palmately lobed and white veined, with a gloss that shrugs off urban pollution (and coastal spray). I concur with every recommendation for its use as an architectural specimen in courtyards, containers and city gardens. I also nominate it as a great backdrop in any shady green border, having cleared the lower stems to form a canopy for the contrasting textures of ferns, hostas and rodgersias, perhaps with a fountain bamboo such as *Chusquea culeou*.

Hardy, z8–11. Moisture-retentive soil in sun, shade or dappled shade, with shelter from dry winds.

Festuca

Poaceae ▪ fescue

Long before anybody thought of grasses as ornamentals, the fescues were used in fine-quality turf in cool temperate zones. I use them as the major seed component in my meadows, for they offer the least competition to wildflowers. Their very slender leaf blades, rolled around the midrib, lend the ornamental sorts an exceptionally fine texture to their neatly

mounded tussocks. The inflorescences often share the same hues as the foliage, in a range of glaucous blues, blue-greens, blue-greys and bronzes that inspire massed plantings as a foil of cool colour alongside flowers of brilliant blues, magentas and purples. Most are drought tolerant. Planting in gravel sets off their form, and helps retain moisture that keeps them in good condition throughout summer.

Festuca amethystina 'Bronzeglanz' has bronzed olive green leaves and golden flower spikes; *F. californica* forms a soft tussock of silvery blue-green, with tall, arching, violet-tinged inflorescences; and *F.* 'Siskiyou Blue' is spruce blue with erect blue inflorescences. Blue forms of *F. glauca* include 'Azurit', steely bright blue; 'Blauglut', intense silver-blue; and 'Elijah Blue', one of the most intensely coloured, in bright powdery blue.

About knee high. Fully hardy, z4–9. Well-drained to dry, low-fertility soils in sun, but water until established.

Geranium

Geraniaceae • cranesbill

I have eliminated huge numbers of geraniums from my palette, bypassing those that, though beautiful, flower for too short a period, have little to offer when out of bloom, or are a bit too particular in cultivation. Not so the sturdy, care-free stalwarts recommended here.

Geranium pyrenaicum, with low mounds of scalloped leaves and airy sprays of tiny purple flowers in flushes from early spring to autumn, is a versatile wildling; *G. p.* 'Bill Wallis', in richer violet purple, blooms for longer and comes true from seed. *Geranium sanguineum* is native to chalky turf and has a similar habit and flowering pattern, but with larger, cupped, glowing magenta flowers. At about half knee height, both self-seed and are meadow natives, naturalizing readily in turf that is cut as the narcissus and crocus fade. *Geranium sanguineum* has pretty foliage, deeply cut and fine textured, making a low-spreading mound at the border

◀ *Geranium sanguineum* 'Cedric Morris'

◀ *Geranium* 'Jolly Bee'

◀ *Geranium renardii*, with geums behind

front, for textural contrast. Its cultivars, such as 'Album', 'Ankum's Pride' (deep bright pink), 'Cedric Morris', and 'Nyewood' (clear pink-purple), bloom for extended periods and are a better choice in the garden.

On the same principle, double-flowered variants of the robust, thigh-high *G. pratense* are better suited to gardens than the rougher grassland in which the species thrives and blooms in midsummer: 'Plenum Album', violet-flushed white; 'Plenum Caeruleum', a loosely double lavender-blue; and 'Violaceum Plenum' in deep violet-blue. *Geranium* SUMMER SKIES 'Gernic' has pale sky blue flowers with ivory white centres.

The dusky wild woodlander *G. phaeum* is shade tolerant and naturalizes easily in the woodland garden, but for tamer shady spots, thigh- to waist-high selections such as the sterile, long-blooming *G. phaeum* 'Lily Lovell', with white-centred, rich purple flowers, and *G. phaeum* var. *phaeum* 'Samobor', with chocolate-purple flowers and chocolate-blotched leaves, are better value.

In sunny spots, I use prolific substitutes for the beloved blue-flowered *G. wallichianum* 'Buxton's Variety' and *G.* 'Johnsons Blue': *G.* 'Brookside', a long, knee-high mound sporting delicately nodding buds that open to cupped bright blue flowers; *G.* 'Jolly Bee', slightly taller and earlier in bloom, with large white-eyed blue flowers; and G. ROZANNE 'Gerwat', similar but slightly shorter. All three flower continuously till it's too cold and dark to carry on.

Queen of the summer border *G. psilostemon*, with black-eyed magenta blooms, gives three months of flower followed by a brief blaze of red autumn foliage. It's a waist-high mound with an imperious disregard for less robust neighbours. From the same dark-eyed mould, yet longer in bloom and better behaved, are G. PATRICIA 'Brempat', a long, thigh-high mound with larger, duskier flowers earlier and later in the season; *G.* 'Ivan', smaller, neater and knee high; *G.* 'Ann Folkard', a mounded, weaving, thigh-high

scrambler with yellow young leaves; and the similar but larger-flowered *G.* 'Sandrine'.

Those that edge the front of borders with exquisitely textured foliage include *G. renardii*,

▲▲ *Geranium* ×*oxonianum* 'Rose Clair'

▲ *Geranium phaeum* var. *phaeum* 'Samobor'

◀ *Geranium robustum*

a low hummock of scalloped, wrinkled, velvety grey leaves that long outlasts the brief early summer flush of palest grey-lavender flowers. *Geranium* 'Philippe Vapelle' is similar, with blue flowers; 'Sirak' is taller, with a prolonged flush of dark-veined, blue-lilac flowers. *Geranium robustum*, a delicately dissected mound of glistening silver grey leaves, to mid thigh, with an array of pale slender stems bearing delicate lavender pink blooms from early to midsummer, is almost transparent.

Some of the wintergreen hybrids of *G. ×oxonianum* are good ground coverers and summer-long bloomers; clear colours on knee-high mounds are had in 'A.T. Johnson', silvery pink; 'Rose Clair', clear deep pink; 'Patricia Josephine', palest silver-pink with darker veins; and 'Walter's Gift', palest grey-green veined pink.

Fully hardy, z4/5–9. Full sun or light dappled shade, any well-drained moderately fertile soil.

Geum

Rosaceae • avens

The crevices of the sunny terrace I care for are filled with self-sown clumps of the water avens, *Geum rivale*. They came from a nearby damp, natural meadow, which is flushed dusky orange-pink by the sheer mass of their nodding flowers in spring and summer, until they're shaded out by tall grasses. They're resilient, deep-rooted rosette-formers, thriving in dry, wet, sunny and shady sites, and have tolerated annual mowing since time immemorial. If only they weren't so dull...

Fortunately there are several garden hybrids close to *G. rivale*, with the same nodding flowers, yet more distinctively coloured petals and basal rosettes of pinnate green leaves; they can reach up to knee high (though usually shorter) in fertile soils. I use them in designed meadows, at woodland margins and in terrace plantings. *Geum* 'Herterton Primrose' has primrose yellow flowers with dark, violet-tinged calyces; in *G.* 'Farmer John Cross', stems and calyces are red and the petals buttercup yellow; in *G.*

▲ *Geum* 'Lemon Drops'

◀ *Geum* 'Prinses Juliana'

'Lemon Drops' clear lemon petals tone with green-brown calyces; and in *G.* 'Cream Drops' the petals are...as it says on the label.

The other group of garden hybrids, derived from *G. chiloense* and/or *G. coccineum*, have larger, upturned saucers in more exuberant colours, the parents having glowing scarlet or

brick red flowers. They're borne on long wiry stems, at knee to mid thigh height, in profusion over long periods in summer. Classically used in borders and as border edging, both parents occur naturally in meadows, and some of the loveliest compositions are to be had by allowing the brilliant flowers to weave artlessly through airy grasses such as *Stipa tenuissima*. *Geum* 'Mrs. J. Bradshaw' has double, glowing scarlet flowers, while 'Prinses Juliana' has golden orange flowers and 'Lady Stratheden' has beautifully poised semi-double flowers of clearest bright yellow.

Fully hardy, z5–9. Fertile, moist but well-drained, open-textured soil in sun.

Gunnera

Gunneraceae

From the streambanks and wet, mountain rocks of the Serra do Mar of southeastern Brazil, *G. manicata* forms a towering mound of magnificent leaves on immensely long stems, beneath which a woman and child could easily be sheltered from the rain. Its every part is a textural study, from the moment the prickly veined, deeply wrinkled, palmately lobed leaves

push up from damp earth in spring, expanding on thick, fleshy, prickled stalks until they reach two metres (six feet) or more across in summer, when tall, fat densely packed cones of tiny red flowers arise beneath the canopy. It's not a specimen for the small back yard, especially as it needs fairly hefty companions lest they be dwarfed into insignificance. The most suitable suspects—rheums, *Darmera peltata* and lysichiton, for example—enjoy the same damp, sunny waterside conditions. Sunlight brings gunneras alive, not only in the literal sense; the patterning of golden light and green shade as it filters through the canopy and picks out the outlining prickles on stems and leaves transforms *G. manicata* into a piece of living sculpture.

In colder regions, cover the dormant crowns with leaf mould or their own dead leaves to give winter protection; this becomes less necessary as plants mature, when they become more or less self-mulching.

Up to twice head height. Fully hardy, z7–9. Deep, humusy, wet or permanently moist soil in sun.

▲ *Gunnera manicata*

Helleborus

Ranunculaceae • hellebore

Hellebores range from Europe to western China, and are found in mountain woods, woodland glades, maquis scrub, and other open, rocky places, usually on limestone. Though often considered choice woodlanders for shady spots, I must say this: I was once upbraided by a hellebore specialist for emphasizing the need for dappled shade. While this need for shade is largely valid, several species—*H. lividus*, *H. argutifolius*, *H. foetidus*, *H. viridis* and *H. odorus*—also occur in habitats that are more exposed, on rocky slopes, sunny banks and in thin turf, and are more tolerant of sun than we usually allow.

With careful selection hellebores provide six good months of interest, spanning both winter and summer solstices, from the first, the Christmas rose, *H. niger*, to the last of the Lenten roses, *H. orientalis* and *H. ×hybridus*, which carry through well into late spring. They have no shortage of good companions, from the snowdrops, *Galanthus nivalis*; winter aconite, *Eranthis hyemalis*; wood anemone, *Anemone nemorosa*; and primroses through to hepaticas, pulmonarias, dicentras, brunneras, epimediums and euphorbias.

After flowering, the flowers stand, fruit, fade, and bleach to pale shades of buff. There are two main groups: deciduous, summer-dormant species, such as *H. viridis*, and evergreens with biennial, winter green foliage. The old overwintering leaves are best cut away to reveal the flowers; I have too many to do that, but have found that the old leaves bow out of their own accord and neatness doesn't matter in naturalistic plantings.

The white-flowered Christmas rose, *H. niger*, arises in midwinter or just after, and the best forms have long stems. These include 'Potter's Wheel', with large, green-eyed white flowers, and 'White Magic', with brighter green leaves and dark leaf and flower stalks, which offset the open-faced white flowers.

◀ *Helleborus foetidus* with snowdrops

◀ *Helleborus niger* 'Potter's Wheel'

◀ *Helleborus lividus*

Two of the larger species follow on to dispel the February blues, both forming sculptural, almost waist-high clumps. *Helleborus foetidus*, with leathery dark green leaves divided into seven to ten lanceolate leaflets, has stout stems with branched cymes of small, nodding, bell-shaped flowers in jade green, faintly rimmed with maroon-purple. In *H. argutifolius* the dark green leaves are divided into three leaflets margined with soft spines and the pendent flowers are a creamier green, larger and more open. These two, with *H. lividus*, belong to a group that botanists call caulescent hellebores; they share the characteristic of leafy flowering stems,

▲ *Helleborus ×hybridus* Ashwood Garden hybrid, anemone-centred

▶ *Helleborus ×hybridus* Ashwood Garden hybrid, black form

▼ *Helleborus ×hybridus* Ashwood Garden hybrid, double-flowered

which gives the inflorescences great substance. In knee-high *H. lividus* the leaves are bluish green with silvery venation, the stems and buds a bloomy pink and the open flowers creamy. At about the same size as *H. lividus* is *H. odorus*, which has green stems, leaves and outward-facing flowers; the dainty, nodding- flowered, celadon green *H. viridis* is slightly shorter.

I'm not convinced that a love of green flowers is sign of horticultural sophistication—who wouldn't love the play of dappled sun that splits simple greens into a whole array of shades?—but it's certainly a sign of decrepitude when you enjoy them in part because you don't have to bend to look into their pretty faces. The Lenten rose, *H. orientalis*, and hybrids derived from it such as *H. ×hybridus*, all have nodding flowers and some—those with speckled, freckled or blushed interiors—hide their most charming assets when you can't see inside. You either have to stoop to cup them in hand, or better yet...grow them on a slope or terrace that you can look up to. The hybrids come in a range of colours, white, cream, apricot, yellow and green, marked or unmarked; in some strains, such as the Ashwood Garden hybrids, there are doubles and anemone-centred forms. At the other end of the spectrum are the dark ones, in shades of red, purple, slates and near black, the darkest having a pruinose bloom, like that of an untouched plum, and these I place where I know they will sit in a pool of light.

Fully hardy, z4–9, *H. niger*, *H. orientalis*, *H. ×hybridus*; z6–9, H. *argutifolius*, H. *foetidus*, *H. odorus*; z7–9, *H. lividus*, *H. viridis*. Most of the hellebores described here will thrive in a deep, fertile, moisture-retentive, neutral to slightly alkaline soil, rather heavy and with plenty of humus, and in dappled shade or part-day sun; *H. odorus* prefers sunny sites.

Heuchera
Saxifragaceae

Heuchera is a North American genus of evergreen and semi-evergreen perennials found mainly in damp, shady, rocky places and in woodland. Many of the wild ones are low-mound-formers of singular grace. Although not well known in European gardens, several of the wildlings deserve to be more widely grown. For instance, *H. pilosissima*, shaggy alum root—as seen among the redwoods, and so named because it's covered in rusty-velvety hair—has dark knee-high stems of tiny bell-shaped, pink-white flowers. Perhaps the best known in Europe is *H. cylindrica*, poker alum root, usually in its green-flowered form, 'Greenfinch', which has rounded, wavy-margined green leaves with pale metallic marbling, and dense spikes of green flowers on tall, finely hairy flowering stems which, when side lit, are haloed in silver.

▶ *Heuchera* 'Chocolate Ruffles' with *Tulipa* 'Orange Princess'

▶ *Heuchera* 'Plum Pudding' (front right) with *Stipa gigantea*, *Phormium* 'Sundowner' and *Hakenochloa macra* 'Aureola'

▶ *Heuchera* 'Rachel' (foreground)

◀ *Heuchera cylindrica* 'Greenfinch'

The species have been elbowed out of gardens in favour of coloured-leaved, evergreen hybrids, which make low, ground-covering mounds of rounded, lobed, toothed and often ruffled leaves. Individual flowers are too tiny to catch the attention of any but bees and hummingbirds, but make an airy haze above the foliage from late spring to late summer. The slender-stemmed, loose racemes or panicles in shades of coral, buff or greenish pink are lovely when glistening in dappled light after rain. The high sheen of the satiny leaves, too, is light reflecting, especially in the ruffled sorts, and particularly when the gleaming metallic overlay that so many possess is pronounced.

There have many new introductions since *H. villosa* 'Palace Purple', with jagged leaves of burnished bronze on a dark red ground. Some of the best are from Dan Heims, in Portland, Oregon, though several come in psychedelic hues of orange, peach, lime and hot pink, which my uptight English reserve cannot countenance.

The burgundy- and metallic-leaved cultivars give the opportunity for weaving together the colours of nearby plantings. For instance, the rich reds and silvers of *H.* 'Persian Carpet' echo the translucent canopy of mahogany red in *Cercis canadensis* 'Forest Pansy', and the bronzed silver of *H.* 'Quick Silver' complements the lush dark reds of *Penstemon digitalis* 'Mystica'. *Heuchera* 'Chocolate Ruffles' has dark green leaves, overlaid with a glaze of shining chocolate, with a dark-stemmed haze of white flowers. There may be impostors on the market; the true plant has fluted and fantastically ruffled leaves that display glowing burgundy undersides. The rounded leaves of *H.* 'Obsidian' are a uniform burnished pewter, a dramatic foil for lacy artemisas or dusky *Euphorbia characias* 'Black Pearl'. Those of *H.* 'Pewter Moon' are scalloped, marbled heavily with silvery pewter, with red-purple veins and undersides. *Heuchera* 'Plum Pudding' is dark plummy red, silvered all over, with darker pewter veins and dark-stemmed maroon and green flowers. *Heuchera* 'Rachel' forms a mound of burnished red-purple on a dark green ground, with leaves that are red beneath, while *H.* 'Stormy Seas' is a ruffled red, the underlying tints washed with silver, pewter and charcoal. And there are fresher, brighter flavours: *H.* 'Mint Frost' in bright silver over mint green; *H.* 'Quick Silver', silvered all over

and patterned with bronzed veins; and *H.* 'Cinnabar Silver', metallic purple with an almost completely silver overlay.

Fully hardy, z4–9. Sun or part-shade or dappled shade in any good, fertile, well-drained soil with adequate summer moisture. An annual mulch ameliorates the tendency of the woody rootstock to thrust above ground, but eventually you'll need to lift and replant.

Hosta

Hostaceae ▪ plantain lily, giboshi

There must be close to four thousand registered cultivars of *Hosta*, many on offer from a single source, many of little presence or stature, and some surely scarcely distinguishable except by those who love them obsessively. How to choose?

My brief for hostas is unequivocal. I want noble mounds of sumptuous overlapping leaves that cover the ground completely; they should be corrugated, cupped, puckered, waved or waxed to cause rain or dew to pearl upon them, and if they produce tall spires of flowers of opalescent colour and ethereal scent in summer, so much the better. Yuccas and irises, lilies, hemerocallis and tree peonies, astilbes, corydalis, *Myrrhis odorata* and ferns are classic companions—the heft and textural strength of hostas associates as well with bold, sword-shaped diagonals as with strong verticals and almost anything that can be described as filigreed, feathered or finely divided.

My choices below are mainly giant and large cultivars, though many of the medium hostas fit the brief in all but size. Excluding the flower scapes, medium is knee high, large is mid thigh high, and giants are taller than that. Mature mounds are frequently three times as wide as tall and leaf sizes show a corresponding scale of magnificence.

Green Giants: 'Birchwood Elegance', with heart-shaped, mid-green leaves with deeply impressed veins, arching downwards, with flowers of white to palest lavender; 'Colossal', with

long heart-shaped, sheeny green leaves, deeply ribbed, slightly puckered, downward arching, with dense spikes of funnel-shaped lavender flowers; and 'Domaine de Courson', with soft olive green, broadly heart-shaped leaves, with deeply impressed veins, slightly waxy and wavy-margined with pale lavender flowers.

Blue Giants: 'Big Daddy', with broadly heart-shaped, chalky deep blue, cupped, puckered leaves, and bell-shaped ivory-white flowers, with good fragrance and some slug resistance; 'Bigfoot', with narrowly heart-shaped leaves—waxy, intense blue-green, ribbed, with rippled margins—and lavender-tinted white flowers, with some slug resistance; 'Blue Angel', with pointed, heart-shaped, heavily bloomed, intense blue-grey leaves, deeply veined and downward pointing, with large grey-lavender flowers, very drought tolerant when established; and 'Prince of Wales', with deeply impressed, slightly corrugated and waxy, rounded heart-shaped blue-green leaves, each with an acute drip tip, and pure white flowers.

Golden Giant: 'Sum and Substance', with heart-shaped leaves, white waxy beneath, deeply veined, slightly cupped, lightly corrugated when mature, glossy chartreuse in shade, golden in sun, with funnel-shaped pale lavender flowers. Slug resistant.

Variegated Giant: 'Lady Isobel Barnett', with heart-shaped, thick- textured, strongly ribbed,

▲ *Hosta sieboldiana*

▶ *Hosta* 'Halcyon'

▶ *Hosta fortunei* 'Albomarginata'

◀ *Hosta* 'Sum and Substance'

shining deep green leaves with narrow golden margins fading to cream, and large pale lavender flowers. Slug resistant, with good sun tolerance

Large Greens: *H. plantaginea* 'Aphrodite', with long, narrowly heart-shaped, deeply ribbed, glossy dark green leaves and very fragrant double white flowers, tolerates sun; and *H.* 'Jade Cascade', with long, narrowly ovate, deeply veined, glossy olive green leaves, with ruffled margins, arching, downward pointing and overlapping, with pale lavender-blue flowers.

Large Blues: *H. sieboldiana*, with ovate-heart-shaped, cupped, puckered, bluish grey-green leaves, paler beneath, with lilac-grey to white flowers, slug resistant; *H. sieboldiana* var. *elegans*, with rounded heart-shaped, cupped, dimpled and deeply corrugated, very glaucous blue-grey leaves, and white flowers; and *H.* 'True Blue', with pointed heart-shaped, leathery, deeply puckered, very glaucous grey-blue leaves, and white flowers.

Large Gold: 'Zounds', with heart-shaped, slightly twisted, deeply puckered, metallic chartreuse to bright golden yellow leaves (in sun), with lavender-blue flowers. Slug resistant.

Large Variegated Hostas: 'Frances Williams', with broadly heart-shaped, cupped, corrugated, blue-green leaves with margins broadly and irregularly margined gold, and white flowers; 'Frosted Jade', with pointed, long heart-shaped leaves with deeply impressed veins, deep jade green with grey-green frosting and narrow white margins, and white, lavender-tinted flowers; and 'Sagae', with broadly ovate, prominently veined leaves, glaucous moss green at first, with golden margins, later frosted grey-green, margined white—leaves have a satin texture, and are distinctively poised on erect stalks. Its long racemes of large white flowers are suffused with violet and it has good slug resistance.

Medium-Sized Hostas: 'Abiqua Drinking Gourd', with rounded, very deeply cupped, heavily corrugated, very waxy blue-grey leaves, tubular white flowers and good slug resist-

ance; *H. fortunei* 'Albomarginata', with ovate, deeply veined, slightly corrugated dark green leaves with irregular cream margins and pale lavender flowers; *H. fortunei* var. *albopicta*, with narrowly heart-shaped, pale yellow leaves with irregular dark green margins, entirely green in summer, and pale lavender flowers; *H.* 'Halcyon', with narrowly heart-shaped, heavily ribbed, glaucous, bright grey-blue leaves, and pale lavender-grey flowers; and 'Krossa Regal', with leathery, heart-shaped, heavily bloomed, blue-grey leaves with undulating margins, and pale lavender flowers.

Hostas are quite satisfied by any deep, fertile, moist but well-drained soil, but repay the liberal incorporation of well-rotted organic matter before planting and an annual mulch of the same with larger and lusher foliage. Including

▲ *Hosta fortunei* var. *albopicta* (left), with *Rhododendron* 'Colyer'

◀ *Hosta* 'Krossa Regal' (front left) with rodgersias and calthas

some larger-grade stuff such as matured, well-composted bark keeps soil open and friable. Although many become more drought tolerant with age, they always do best with adequate summer moisture, and the sunnier the site the more moisture is needed. Both warm and cold dry winds will sear them, especially those with variegated margins, so provide some side shelter.

Hostas are well known as shade plants. It may seem pedantic, but shade-tolerant is not the same as shade-demanding. They grow slowly and don't flower so well in the dark; some of the golden forms positively need higher light levels to develop good colour, and all grow best with a few hours of sunlight each day. The moving dappling light beneath a high canopy can be sufficient, as can the bright but indirect light you might get beside walls that don't directly face the sun. Avoid the direct searing of hot midday sun. Your supplier should give you guidelines—many of the newer hybrids are much more sun tolerant than the hostas of old. If you do grow hostas beneath a canopy of taller shrubs or trees, site them away from shallow roots. Those that are cupped and corrugated accumulate falling debris, which spoils the show; in such sites, those with smoother, downward arching leaves serve better.

The primary desecrators of hostas are slugs, which emerge from dormancy at the same time as hostas come into growth. You have provided perfect conditions for slugs, and if you lose the battle in spring, that's it for the season. Use copper bands, parasitic nematodes or slug pellets (put them safely in a jar on its side as a trap).

Fully hardy, z3–8.

Kalmia
Ericaceae

When I was a small child, I was enamoured by the tiny biscuits known as iced gems, with a piped rosette of sugar icing on top. The exquisite, crimped flower buds of *Kalmia latifolia*, calico bush, look exactly like them (though all

Kalmia latifolia

▲ *Kalmia latifolia,* flower

◀ *Kalmia latifolia* 'Minuet'

parts of kalmia are toxic).

Among the most charming of evergreen shrubs, *K. latifolia* forms mounds of lustrous, elliptic, dark green leaves—mound upon mound as it reaches twice head height, though most cultivars grow slowly to a much more manageable size. All are a joy in early summer, especially beautiful in bud with the anticipation of the opening flowers, when many reveal a ring of colour at the centre of each cupped bloom. They are borne in dense corymbs at the branch tips and can almost obscure the leaves when in full sail.

The species occurs on streambanks, rocky cliffs and in the mixed forests of eastern North America and, being a sometimes-woodlander it has acquired a reputation as a deep-shade-lover. They need sun to flower well, and—at least in cool temperate areas—thrive in full sun with consistent moisture. Failing that, give them the dappled light at the margins of sheltered glades or bright light beneath a high canopy. In too-deep shade, they become rangy and open.

Kalmia latifolia 'Carousel', to waist high, has white flowers heavily banded and intensely marked with deep cinnamon red inside; 'Elf' is dense, rounded and knee to waist high, with small glossy leaves and pale pink buds opening white; 'Minuet' is similarly diminutive with pale pink buds revealing pale pink interiors banded with maroon-pink. 'Pink Charm' makes a head-high mound eventually, but flowers freely when young, bearing rich pink flowers with a narrow dark pink band at the base inside. 'Richard Jaynes' has lustrous foliage and is free flowering, chest high, with intense red buds opening to relatively large, pale pink flowers. 'Snowdrift' and 'Silver Dollar' are slightly taller. 'Snowdrift' is pure white in bud and faintly marked pink when open, and has a very dense habit, with very dark green, thick and leathery leaves. The glistening white flowers of 'Silver Dollar' are larger than most, opening from pale pink buds.

Fully hardy, z4/5–9. Humus-rich, moisture-retentive, neutral to acid, lime-free soils. Mulch annually with leaf mould or pine needles. Dead-head carefully to avoid damaging new growth buds. Provide shelter from strong winds.

Kirengeshoma

Hydrangeaceae

I often forget about my kirengeshoma (*K. palmata*) until late summer, and then each year it astounds me anew with its sheer grace. The mound of foliage quietly assumes its full stature before it flowers; the clear soft green leaves, shaped like those of an oriental plane,

◀ *Kirengeshoma palmata*

are borne in well-spaced pairs on strong but slender ebony stems, poised so that they overlap without touching. As summer draws to its end, the dark stems extend, each arching branch bearing cymes of perfectly symmetrical buds, like tiny acorns in a cup, which then gradually elongate before finally opening to nodding bells with waxy, gently recurved petals in cool pale yellow. It occurs in woodlands in Japan and Korea, and it seems obvious to look for other damp-shade-lovers as companions: ferns, hostas, podophyllums, tricyrtis, perhaps one of the green-striated snake bark maples?

Waist to chest high. Fully hardy, z5–9. Moist, deep, humus-rich acid soil in dappled shade with shelter from dry winds.

Lamium

Lamiaceae ▪ dead nettle

Lamium orvala is as different from the creeping little thugs that belong under *L. maculata* as can be imagined. It is vital to distinguish it from the wilding white dead nettle, *L. alba*, so that you don't rip it out in its youth when weeding. Unlike many lamiums, *L. orvala* is neither stoloniferous nor invasive; the stems arise from a central crown to form a shapely, almost orbicular dome of at least knee height. Its toothed, broadly ovate leaves are deeply veined, dark green and softly hairy—very attractive and of substantial texture. In *L. orvala* 'Silva' they have a central silvery stripe, which looks good

◀ *Lamium orvala*

with spotted-leaved pulmonarias. The upper stem bears whorls of large two-lipped flowers, pink-purple to soft coppery pink, the hooded upper lip softly hairy, the lower lip marked with darker streaks; in *L. orvala* 'Album', they're white blushed pink.

These lamiums flower from spring to early summer, in one big hit for about six weeks, along with dicentras, pulmonarias and brunneras. Inch-for-inch, *L. orvala* is every bit as effective as weed-smothering ground cover as cultivars of *L. maculata* are, but you won't have to pull it out by the armful to keep it in check. In fertile soils, the stems may splay by midsummer, but that's easily fixed by cutting back after flowering. This prevents self-seeding and induces a new flush of foliage.

Fully hardy, z5–9. Any moist but well-drained soil in sun, dappled or deep shade.

Lavandula

Lamiaceae ▪ lavender

Long ago, I sat on a shaded Provençal terrace sipping anisette, in shock at the stark severity of the residual mounds of lavender after harvest. But it was a good lesson in how to create dense, perfect mounds in the garden, on which I rely for edging and for winter structure in borders and gravel banks.

I modify that fearless technique to suit damp English winters, never daring to take lavenders

as low as they do in a continental climate where hot, dry summers ensure full ripening—and hence hardiness—of the wood. I don't grow hopelessly gnarled lavenders with tufts of foliage atop old woody branches, from which new growth never breaks. Each year, I cut back to within a few centimetres of last year's growth. I do it in two stages, the first when harvesting the flowers, taking about two and a half centimetres (one inch) of the current year's growth with them. This neatens the mound and forestalls splaying in wild winter weather. In spring, as new buds break into growth, I cut back again, leaving about five to ten centimetres (two to four inches) of strong new shoots on the previous year's growth. The flowers are borne at the tips of the current season's growth.

My brief for lavenders demands dense, pale grey, grey-green or silvery foliage, and long, strong stems, with long, dense heads of intensely coloured, highly fragrant flowers to make a halo that echoes the mound. If I'm using them formally I want good uniformity, which means vegetatively propagated rather than seed-raised plants, and I need to be certain that they'll all survive the winters, so I buy locally or root my own of proven provenance. There are white- and pink-flowered lavenders, but dilly-dilly: as far as I'm concerned, lavender's blue. The sweetest scents are in *L. angustifolia*, but all those here fit the brief.

Lavandula angustifolia cultivars are usually the first to flower: 'Folgate' is grey-leaved, to mid thigh, with violet-blue flowers; 'Hidcote' is knee high, with dark blue-purple flowers and a uniform habit (beware: many plants offered are seed-raised and variable); 'Loddon Blue' is knee high, with silver-grey leaves and deep blue-purple flowers; and 'Twickel Purple' is a neat, thigh-high mound of broad, grey-green leaves with long-stemmed, very long spikes of deep violet-purple.

Lavandula ×chaytoriae hybrids are knee high and long-flowering with excellent scent, and their aromatic, silvery white foliage is the palest

of all lavenders. They take their pale colouring from *L. lanata* and their hardiness from *L. angustifolia*, but don't enjoy excessive winter wet. 'Richard Gray' has deep purple spikes, while 'Sawyers' has long, narrow spikes of violet-blue.

Among the *L. ×intermedia* hybrids, these selections are particularly well scented and long-stemmed: 'Gros Bleu', with dense spikes of deep blue-purple; 'Grosso', with deep purple flowers; and late-flowering 'Seal', with dark blue-purple spikes. (*Lavandula ×intermedia* 'Grosso' is the most commonly grown lavender in Provence for oil extraction, and one of the toughest and most tolerant of winter damp.)

Fully hardy, z5/6–9. Full sun, very well-drained, lean to moderately fertile soil; thrives on chalky soils.

Luzula

Juncaceae · woodrush

Let's not pretend that woodrushes are in the highest rank of grass-like ornamentals. However, several are evergreen, tolerant of shade, and have a breadth of leaf that gives their rounded tussocks substance—their beauty is subtle, their grace much enhanced by the play of dew and dappled light upon them, for side lighting illuminates droplets trapped on the flexuous hairs on the margins of their shiny leaves and on

the soft heads of tiny summer flowers. In the wild garden, they make delightful companions to ferns, forget-me-nots, sweet violets, *Viola odorata*, and other spring ephemerals, and in more contrived plantings associate quietly with other shade-lovers such as euphorbias, hostas or heucheras. Both species described here are rhizomatous but slow spreading.

Luzula nivea, the snowy woodrush, has shining dark green leaves and a haze of tiny white flowers in midsummer; the higher the light levels, the more freely it flowers, provided soil moisture is adequate. *Luzula sylvatica*, which is ideal also for waterside plantings, forms denser, deep green tussocks, and has less showy

◀ Mounds of lavender with silvery *Stachys byzantina*

▲ *Lavandula*

◀ *Luzula nivea*

▼ *Luzula sylvatica* 'Marginata'

conker-coloured flowers on taller stems. Both *L. sylvatica* 'Hohe Tatra' and *L. s.* 'Marginata' bring light to dark places. In the former the leaves emerge lime green, fade to yellow-green and remain golden yellow through winter; the latter has dark green leaves rimmed with white and nodding panicles of glistening, golden brown spikelets.

Fully hardy, z4–9. Humus-rich, moist but well-drained soil in dappled or deep shade.

Myrrhis

Apiaceae ▪ sweet cicely

Standing in dappled light beside a purling beck amid a natural drift of sweet cicely, *Myrrhis odorata*, after rain, inhaling its anise aroma in cool humid air: this is how I would introduce it to those innocent to its charm. Of all the plants in its vast family, few possess such softness of leaf, brightness of green or purity of white. The fern-like leaves emerge very early in the year, unfurling emerald green, then forming a rapidly growing mound to waist height before producing broad, flattened umbels of starry white flowers in spring or early summer.

If *M. odorata* has a fault, it lies in its profuse self-seeding, but this is easily avoided by brutal deadheading—cutting the whole plant to the ground ensures there will be a fresh crop of both flowers and foliage. (The seeds are chewable and refreshing.)

I grow it in wild and woodland gardens, with sweet woodruff, *Galium odoratum*, and white dame's violet, *Hesperis matronalis* var. *albiflora*, and in mixed and herbaceous borders. Not only does its soft lacy foliage provide a good and easily refreshed colour foil for other plants, but it is also invaluable in masking the fading foliage of early bulbs.

Fully hardy, z3–9. Moist but well-drained, preferably deep and humus-rich soil in sun or dappled shade.

◀ *Myrrhis odorata*

Nepeta

Lamiaceae ▪ catmint

The grey-leaved, blue-flowered catmints are among the most aromatic of mound-forming perennials, and if they are ubiquitous it is for good reason. They form a clearly delineated mound, and their soft greys and blues associate well with almost any other colour. They are easily grown in almost any well-drained soil, are very hardy and drought tolerant, and have a naturally long flowering season that can be easily induced to last most of summer. And they bring sound and motion to the garden, as their long spikes of two-lipped flowers nod under the weight of bumble bees.

Nepeta 'Six Hills Giant' is more tolerant of damp winters than most; it would form a waist-high mound were it not so determined to fall apart under the weight of its lavender-blue flowers. A patient gardener might give it the support of twiggy pea sticks, but life's too short; there are newer and better catmints. *Nepeta racemosa* 'Walker's Low', at mid thigh, has firmer stems and is less susceptible to splaying, bearing dense spikes of blue-violet flowers that give a neat uniformity that is especially good for edging. *Nepeta* 'Dropmore', an exception-

◀ *Nepeta* 'Six Hills Giant'

◀ *Nepeta racemosa* 'Walker's Low', with *Geranium ×oxonianum* 'A.T. Johnson' and *Papaver orientale* 'Allegro'

ally hardy hybrid (to z2) from Manitoba, is dense, compact and knee high, with very long spikes of bright blue-violet flowers. *Nepeta grandiflora*, from grassy meadows of the Caucasus, has more olive green foliage and elongated spikes of flowers with dusky calyces, and *N. grandiflora* 'Pool Bank' has rich blue flowers with blue-purple calyces—very effective with pale-stemmed spires of *Perovskia*—and in 'Dawn to Dusk' they are earthy pink with smoky violet calyces. Both make neat mounds to mid thigh.

Catmints, to a greater or lesser degree, contain nepetalactone which is highly aphrodisiac and addictive (to cats), provoking unhinged, licentious behaviour during which they roll catmints flat. Planting a diversionary clump of fully potent catnip, *N. cataria*, may help keep cats off the border. Failing this, a low dome of wire netting stops them from damaging the crown (although disentanglement at the end of the season is a chore). All nepetas are amenable to shearing back hard. If cut back immediately after the first flush of flower, new shoots at the crown are revealed; they will flower later in the season whether you cut them back or not, but this pleasurably aromatic intervention will keep mounds round and tight.

Fully hardy, z3/4–9. Well-drained soil in sun or light dappled shade; leaner soils and full sun ensure more compact growth, but in warmer climates provide some shade from the hottest midday sun. See also page 262 (Clouds and Transparents).

Paeonia
Paeoniaceae

There is more than one kind of floral splendour to be had from the herbaceous peonies, from the graceful species and from the more familiar, sumptuous garden hybrids largely derived from the Chinese peony, *P. lactiflora*. Although the flowering period of all herbaceous peonies is short, they have beautiful lobed and divided foliage, too, often coloured on emergence and in autumn, which provides good ground cover until late in summer, when fertile species and cultivars develop seedpods with very ornamental seeds in cerise, blue or glossy black. They make fine hosts for early bulbs, and for summer ones, such as the lilies, fritillaries and galtonias, and can do good service for up to fifty years. Whatever: why try to justify the indispensable?

Paeonia lactiflora was already a venerable and highly bred garden flower in China and Japan when it was introduced to Europe in the late eighteenth century, and there are now thousands, bred on both sides of the Atlantic. In early summer, they bear deeply cupped or bowl-shaped flowers, single, semi-double or fully double, all with the sheened texture of silk and a colour range from pure white to deepest crimson.

I have a cutting bed for peonies, and my selections are big, beautiful, strong-stemmed and fragrant. By spreading my choices across early, midseason and late cultivars I can be picking the flowers (or enjoying them in the borders) for six to eight weeks. My favourites are nearly all fragrant, double, Victorian and Edward-

ian peonies; I'm an old-fashioned girl, and in any case, the singles neither cut well nor last very long in the garden. *Paeonia* 'Duchesse de Nemours' is very double, with pure white petals tinted lemon at the base; *P.* 'Sarah Bernhardt' is a double in clear pink, with ruffled inner petals touched with silver; and *P.* 'Karl Rosenfield' has deep velvety crimson double flowers with golden stamens. The anemone-centred (Japanese or Imperial) peonies have a crowd of narrow ribbon-like petaloids at the centre of their flowers. *Paeonia* 'Bowl of Beauty' has creamy petaloids in a cup of rich carmine-pink petals, and *P.* 'Kelway's Majestic' is a rosy, cherry pink, with silvered petaloids of the same hue.

Grow them in deep, fertile, humus-rich and moisture-retentive soil in sun or light dappled shade. (Joy of joys for the gardener on chalk, the lactifloras prefer slightly alkaline soils.) Prepare the soil deeply before planting, incorporating well-rotted organic matter, and feed annually in early spring with general-purpose fertilizer. The primary cause of failure to flower is planting too deeply; the top of the crown should be no more than five centimetres (two inches) below soil level, and this applies when planting, moving or mulching. If you attend to this rule, you can move your peonies with impunity in autumn (best) or very early spring (if you must), and you can mulch annually if you avoid the immediate crown.

Many of the species, including *P. emodii* and *P. mlokosewitschii*, grow in similar conditions but have a grace that lends them well to less formal uses. *Paeonia emodii*, from mountain forests in the western Himalayas, is perfectly adapted for plantings in dappled light or part-day shade in open glades in a woodland garden. The lush brilliant green leaves are finely divided, forming a mound that long outlasts the arching stems of scented, slightly nodding white flowers of spring. *Paeonia mlokosewitschii*, Caucasian peony, from sunny slopes in forest glades, is equally suited to sun or part shade. It is fair to complain that its flowering

period is short, but don't dismiss it on that account. At winter's end it pushes pointed red buds above the soil, extending to bloomed, dark red-pink stems, which slowly unfurl into broad, blunt blue-green leaflets, deeply pleated at first, heavily bloomed and flushed with deep dusky pink. The tight, round, deep red buds eventually open to deep bowls of soft ethereal yellow, revealing a dense boss of golden stamens, and when the petals fall, the silky hairy seedpods swell, to burst open in late summer to reveal brilliant magenta seeds. That takes eight months.

Paeonia mascula, Balkan peony, and its subspecies range from southern Europe to northern Iran, occuring on sunny, rocky slopes, or in open scrub and forest. They have smooth, slightly shiny, sometimes bluish green leaves and exquisite single bowl-shaped flowers with golden stamens and petals in shades from rose pink to glossy deep carmine—perfect for hot, dry, sunny banks in very well-drained soil.

Knee to thigh high. Fully hardy, z3–8, *P. lactiflora*; z7–9, *P. mascula*; z6–9, *P. mlokosewitschii*.

Papaver

Papaveraceae • poppy

From rocky mountainsides and meadows in the Caucasus, to northern Iran and northeastern Turkey, the Oriental poppy, *Papaver orientale*, has produced a garden race of mound-forming herbaceous perennials bearing huge flowers with crumpled silk-satin petals. Undisputed highlights of the herbaceous border from early to midsummer, the major drawbacks are that they can be so heavy headed as to sprawl under their own weight, and they enter summer dormancy after flowering to leave gaps in the border. Since poppies are gorgeously indispensable, solutions have been found.

The classic Jekyllian response was to grow them with cascading plants to fill the space later in the season; the old-fashioned *Gypsophila paniculata* was a favourite and in *Colour Schemes for the Flower Garden* she wrote:

> *Each plant of* Gypsophila paniculata *when full grown covers a space of a good four feet wide. On each side of it, within reasonable distance of the root, I plant oriental poppies.*

Astrantias are good, too.

But since these robust perennial poppies are naturally denizens of grassland, their summer dormancy can be turned to advantage by growing them among grasses, either ornamental types such as *Panicum virgatum* 'Hänse Herms', or in the wild meadow, where *P. orientale* will hold its own and tolerate a high mowing-over with impunity when fully dormant. They are deep rooting and the rootstock is hard to budge once established. In borders, cutting hard as soon as the blooms go over and feeding with high-potash fertilizer promotes good regrowth of foliage after dormancy and, with luck and a good summer, a second crop of flowers.

Although scarlet was once the predominant hue in many *P. orientale* offspring—difficult to place in softer-toned plantings—breeders have extended the spectrum from the black-blotched

▲ *Papaver orientale* 'Cedric Morris' with *Digitalis purpurea* f. *albiflora*

◀ *Papaver orientale* 'Patty's Plum'

pure white of *P.* 'Black and White' through to the soft corals of 'Cedric Morris'. There is a way to go, however, before some of the newer ones live up to the hype. I am unswayed by allusions to the faded silk of old ball gowns, or comparisons with the graceful fading of the Old Roses.

P. orientale 'Patty's Plum' has dusky, greyish, maroon-purple blooms, but unless carefully placed its beautiful tones bleach too quickly; similarly, its offspring 'Lilac Girl' displays an outstanding lavender pink at first but rapidly becomes pasty if overexposed to hot sun. Some nurseries in the Netherlands list them as plants for part shade, and I concur. Place them out of the full glare of midday sun, into the lee of taller plants—cardoons, bronze fennel, *Crambe cordifolia* and *Phlomis fruticosa*—where colours fade more gracefully.

Some newer cultivars have been bred to hold their foliage longer, and with much stronger stems. The Dutch hybridizer Eleanore de Koning has concentrated her efforts on these two characteristics, and many of her raisings give a second flush of bloom. Her sumptuous New York and Parisienne Series share a common ancestor in *P. orientale* 'Royal Chocolate Distinction', a glossy, intense chocolate-maroon, extravagant but disappointing in its colour-fastness, and this she addressed in subsequent breeding from it. Among the New Yorkers 'Brooklyn' has black-blotched, ruby red flowers; 'Harlem', rich rosy burgundy; and 'Staten Island', black-blotched,

▲ *Papaver* 'Lilac Girl'

◀ *Papaver* 'Black and White'

rich red-purple. *P. orientale* 'Manhattan' is rose-lavender, not unlike 'Patty's Plum', but more colour-fast. The Parisienne Series plants are shorter and very strong stemmed, which reduces problematic flopping of the heavy-headed blooms: 'Louvre' is pink-tinted soft white with central

221

◀ *Phlomis fruticosa* with blue-flowered geranium

black blotch, 'Place de Pigalle' is white with a ruffled margin of pink, and 'Clochard' is double, frilled, soft apricot pink.

Thigh high. Fully hardy, z3–7. Any deep fertile soil in sun; avoid full midday sun for dusky-hued variants, or better, try them in light shade.

Phlomis

Lamiaceae

The mounded, evergreen subshrub *Phlomis fruticosa*, Jerusalem sage, is found around the Mediterranean, growing in poor dry dirt, in cliff crevices and among limestone rocks. The botanical description of the plant is a prose poem on plant hair. Pubescent to floccose throughout, it has dense, tawny hair on the stout, square, olive-yellow stems—floccose, like little pills on fine wool—from which sprout pairs of broadly lance-shaped, rugose, felted, pale olive-grey-green leaves that are hoary beneath with minute starry hairs, in flocks on the pale conspicuous veins. The leaves are muskily aromatic when bruised (and make you sneeze). As stems elongate, in early and midsummer, they produced tight whorls of hooded, two-lipped, deep yellow flowers.

Phlomis fruticosa tones perfectly with *Euphorbia stygiana*, and I also grow it with the blue-purples of *Nepeta racemosa* 'Walker's Low' and the purples of *Allium giganteum*. Nevertheless, I like the foliage more, and I discourage flowering by cutting back in late spring so that, from each leaf pair, two new shoots emerge with newly pubescent leaves. It gives great textural contrast with *Ballota pseudodictamnus*, and filigreed santolinas such as *S. pinnata* subsp. *neapolitana* 'Edward Bowles'. Speaking of which, there is an eponymous shrubby hybrid, *Phlomis* 'Edward Bowles', with softer sulphur yellow flowers.

To chest high, but usually shorter. Fully hardy, z7–10. Full sun, any well-drained, not-too-fertile soil. Being very drought tolerant, it needs little if any supplemental water in summer. See also page 126 (Verticals and Diagonals).

Phlox

Polemoniaceae

From the eastern United States, on streambanks, in open woodland and thickets, often on limestone hills, the midsummer- to autumn-flowering *Phlox paniculata* (garden or fall phlox) has given rise to hundreds of highly coloured cultivars. The wild ones have diffuse, almost transparent heads of small, white, pink, or pale lavender flowers, quite different in effect to the cultivated sorts. Ethereal and graceful, these upright wildlings are very fragrant and particularly lovely in dappled light or partial shade in the wild and woodland garden, all the more useful there because they flower so late.

I don't use cultivars of *P. paniculata* for their vertical lines because, although their stems are erect, this is not their most immediately striking feature; rather, they are striking for their billowing masses of relatively large flowers, borne in broad, branching cyme-like panicles, at waist to chest height. *Phlox paniculata* 'Norah Leigh' is an obvious exception, for the vertical stems are highlighted by the cream-variegated leaves. The whites, amethysts and lilac-blues are luminous at twilight when I stalk the garden in search of balmy evening fragrances. *P. paniculata* var. *alba*, 'Mount Fuji' and 'David' are among the best of whites; 'Eventide' is pale lavender,

◀◀ *Phlox paniculata* var. *alba*

◀ *Phlox paniculata*

▼ *Phlox paniculata* 'Eva Cullum'

'Prospero' pale lilac, 'Mother of Pearl' the palest of pinks and 'Eva Cullum' a stronger pink. They all attract butterflies and hummingbirds.

Phlox paniculata 'David' is said to be mildew resistant, and for the rest, good culture in regard to adequate moisture, nutrients and air circulation reduces the risk. Even so, be prepared to treat powdery mildew as soon as seen by removing affected leaves and spraying with sulphur or a suitable fungicide. Give supplementary water regularly in dry conditions, but avoid the foliage as fungal spores are spread in water splash.

Fully hardy, z4–8. Full sun or light shade on fertile, humus-rich, moisture-retentive soils. An annual mulch of leaf mould or similar helps to conserve moisture. See also page 61 (Horizontals and Tiers) and page 126 (Verticals and Diagonals).

Podophyllum
Berberidaceae ▪ may apple

Both Asian and American species of *Podophyllum* are herbaceous, rhizomatous perennials, denizens of scrub, moist meadows, and damp open woodland. They are grown mainly for the drama of their large, shining, palmately lobed leaves, which offer sculptural contrasts to other damp shade-lovers such as rodgersias, epimediums and ferns. The spring flowers are fascinating, beautiful but ephemeral, and give rise to interesting, egg-shaped fruit (which are mainly hidden by the foliage) in late summer. The flower, fully formed and tightly packed into its pointed bud, springs into action as soon as conditions allow.

In *P. hexandrum*, Himalayan may apple, the flower pushes up from the earth, pulling folded leaves behind it, looking for all the world like a cocktail umbrella, perhaps a winged woodland sprite—or something more rudely sinister if you have a grubby mind. The glistening, cupped pink or white flowers open between each pair of lobed green leaves, which later expand to reveal

Rheum

◄ *Podophyllum peltatum*

Polygonaceae ▪ rhubarb

This gigantic rhubarb emerges from a massive rootstock in spring, the huge jagged leaves springing from a vast and bulbous bud, unfolding red, creased and pleated, rich purple red beneath, heavily veined and most splendid as sunlight filters through them. Majestic, architectural and stately are all descriptors that truly apply. At full stretch, palmately lobed and deeply toothed, each leaf can be a metre (three feet) across, overlapping to form a chest-high mound. That's even before they push up stout, fleshy stalks bearing plumed panicles of starry, creamy white, or pink flowers in early summer, which tower above the foliage.

In *R. palmatum*, Chinese rhubarb, leaves mature relatively quickly to dark green, retaining but a vestige of red beneath. In *R. p.* 'Atrosanguineum', the buds are a vivid scarlet, the leaves a sumptuous, burgundy purple when

▶ *Rheum* 'Ace of Hearts'

▼ *Rheum palmatum*

markings and mottlings of brown-purple. Later still, it bears bright red fruits the size and shape of a bantam's egg. It will spread very slowly to form small patches where suited.

Although plain in comparison, *P. peltatum*, may apple, is more vigorous and wide spreading, and forms colonies in time. The long-stalked, shining, dark green lobed leaves, which are fairly well-developed at flowering, form attractive cover and glittering textural contrasts to ferns such as *Onoclea* or *Matteuccia*. They expand as the fragrant, waxy, cupped pink or white flowers, which are held beneath the leaves, begin to fade in early summer.

Knee to thigh high. Fully hardy, z5/6–8; z4–8, *P. peltatum*. Partial to deep shade on moist, leafy, neutral to acid soil. Treat all parts as toxic if eaten; *P. peltatum* was part of the native North American pharmacopoeia, as a purgative and emetic.

young; the flowering stems, wrapped round with red bracts, bear plumes of deep pink or crimson flowers. *Rheum* 'Ace of Hearts' is better suited to smaller spaces, reaching about chest high, including the open airy panicles of pink-flushed white flowers of mid- to late summer. The deeply wrinkled, heart-shaped leaves emerge red, maturing to dark green with a network of red veins, and russetted red-purple beneath.

Grow rheums in wild and woodland gardens, bog gardens and water gardens, in company with gunneras, *Darmera peltata*, lysichiton and rodgersias, the swords of water irises—perhaps along with actaeas, astilbes and ferns as light-textured relief to all the drama. They might be used in borders, too, if you have one large enough, as a darkly sculpted backdrop, at least until they become tattered and jaded as they fade back in late summer.

Chest high and above. Fully hardy, z5–9. Plentiful moisture essential. Deep, fertile humus-rich soil in sun or dappled shade, with well-rotted organic matter incorporated at planting, and with an annual spring mulch of the same.

Rodgersia
Saxifragaceae

If space does not permit, as the well-worn horticultural saying goes, use *x* instead of *y*. Although the alternative usually has the whiff of the poor man's substitute about it, that's not the case when you use rodgersias in place of rheums; they're actually better value because the leaves look good for longer, and they're later flowering, from mid- to late summer. Associate them with big hostas, the slender arching stems of *Polygonatum* ×*hybridum*, and candelabra primulas such as *Primula bulleyana*—soft orange on a backcloth of bronze.

Rodgersia aesculifolia has leaves like those of a horse chestnut (*Aesculus*): palmate, wrinkled and dark green, with stalks and veins covered in woolly russet indumentum, and tall panicles of starry white flowers in midsummer. In *R. pinnata* the leaves are rugose and with deeply impressed venation. The species has dark green leaves and tall panicles of white, pink or red flowers, while in in *R. pinnata.* 'Superba' the leaves are coppery purple in youth, and the inflorescence is a splendidly dense array of starry, rich pink flowers.

▲ *Rheum palmatum* 'Atrosanguineum' with tulips and forget-me-nots

225

mahogany when young; 'Braunlaub' has very dark young leaves of a bronzed chocolatey brown.

Rodgersias are frequently recommended as bog garden plants, but just as shade can be a matter of fine degree, so can moisture. They like consistently moist but not wet soils. They are just as suited to a reliably moist border, will thrive in part shade or in sun—the best leaf colour, at either end of the season, will be had with at least part day sun.

Waist to chest high. Fully hardy, z4/5–8. Sun, dappled or part-day shade in fertile, humus-rich soil.

Santolina

Asteraceae

In the case of the button-like flowerheads of santolinas, you might have wondered how anyone could think that that shade of yellow goes with silver-grey; it's as brassy as a badly bleached blonde. As Graham Stuart Thomas says, "this bright colour is at variance with most colour schemes for which grey foliage is used".

For years I cut off the vile yellow flowerheads of cotton lavender, *Santolina chamaecyparissuss*, for the sake of the neat dense foliage hummocks that I love. It has the least filigreed foliage of the three most useful santolinas, each subdivision of the finely divided, ash-grey leaves having fat little marginal teeth, giving a rather knubbly texture. The following offer a much more acceptable range of yellows in their flowerheads. *Santolina chamaecyparissus* 'Lemon Queen' is altogether easier to place, having soft lemon flowerheads. *S. pinnata* subsp. *neapolitana* has silver-grey, pinnate leaves with longer, cylindrical leaflets which give a finer texture and more graceful demeanour, and offers two pale-flowered variants in 'Edward Bowles', pale creamy yellow, and 'Sulphurea', primrose yellow. *S. rosmarinifolia* is a fine-textured mound of rich mossy green; 'Primrose Gem' has soft primrose yellow flowerheads. It is less reliably hardy than the other two, being more suscepti-

Rodgersia podophylla sports leaves divided into five leaflets, each with three to five jagged lobes at the tip, wrinkled and bronzed when young, then glossy dark green, but by late summer they're flushing bronze again, with full-blown colour in oranges, reds and crimsons by autumn. The inflorescence comprises tiny, long-pointed stars of pale creamy green. The leaves of *R. podophylla* 'Rotlaub' are a coppery

▲▲ *Rodgersia aesculifolia*

▲ *Rodgersia podophylla* (front right), with forget-me-nots

ble to winter wet and drying winter winds, but the green and the grey do look great together when forming an undulating, pillowy ground as the backbone of a border.

Santolinas occur on limestone hills and other dry, rocky mediterranean habitats, and their cultural needs and mounded forms are a good match for those of lavenders. If dead-headed just as the flowerheads begin to fade—cutting flower stems back to the foliage, and a little beyond to neaten the mound—santolinas provide evergreen winter structure, as hedges, edges, in borders, or dry or gravel gardens. They need a few weeks of good growing weather before autumn to make sure this happens. I prune hard in spring to redefine and keep them dense once new growth is well underway.

Knee high. Fully hardy, z7–10. Full sun, very well-drained, lean to moderately fertile soil; thrives on chalky soils.

Sedum

Crassulaceae ▪ ice plant, orpine

It seems wrong, very wrong, that a succulent should be so hardy—one of life's mysteries to be thankful for, since the plump, bloomed, fleshy foliage of the larger mounding sedums is so unlike anything else in the palette. It is infinitely useful for contrasts in colour and texture, with the woolly felted leaves of stachys and phlomis, the dimpled leaves of hostas, the filigrees of artemisias and santolinas. It offers glaucous grey-greens or plummy grey-purples in leaf for many months as a rising mound before midsummer, when it begins to flower, in a range of pale and deep pinks, port and claret, a nectar-rich treat for bees and butterflies. As they fade, flowerheads bring autumn tones of russet, chestnut, bronze and golden brown, toning with the sere panicles of flowering grasses and the standing candelabra of veronicastrums.

◀ *Santolina* (front), with achilleas

▲▲ *Santolina pinnata* subsp. *neapolitana* 'Edward Bowles'

▲ *Santolina chamaecyparissus* with lavender and box hedging

◀ *Sedum telephium* Atropurpureum Group 'Purple Emperor'

▶ *Sedum spectabile* 'Iceberg' with *Sedum spectabile* 'Brilliant'

◀ *Sedum* 'Matrona' with nepeta and stachys

▶ *Sedum* 'Munstead Red'

◀ *Sedum* 'Sunset Cloud'

▶ *Sedum telephium* 'Strawberries and Cream' (left), with *Stipa calamagrostis*

Defer deadheading until late winter, and they become ice sculptures after frost, as well as winter nests for hibernating ladybirds.

In *Sedum spectabile*, the terminal cymes of small starry flowers are broad and flattened, giving a subsidiary horizontal line; in *S. telephium*, cymes are terminal and axillary, smaller and more rounded, more like a tiny well-fluffed duvet. The latter forms a more open plant. If these two and the hybrids between them have a fault, it is the inability of the stout, fleshy unbranched stems to remain firm in the face of heavy summer rain. The plants are very hard to support unobtrusively. Cutting a third of the stems back to the base in late spring helps; they provide support when they grow back and flower later, thus prolonging the display. The other recourse is to starve them into submission, either by planting in lean, gritty soils to begin with, or by lifting and dividing every second or third year and replanting into the same hole without the customary amelioration.

Among *Sedum* hybrids, 'Matrona' has silvery green leaves flushed plummy red on the midrib and margins, and pale smoky pink flowers on tall upright grey-burgundy stems; *S.* 'Munstead Red' has grey-green leaves heavily flushed deep red purple, and red-stemmed cymes of deep red-purple flowers—the red suffusion throughout is the mark of the true plant, as opposed to the variable seedlings derived from it. *Sedum* 'Sunset Cloud' has blue-grey leaves suffused plum-purple, and branched cymes of vibrant deep red-pink flowers.

Sedum spectabile cultivars include 'Iceberg', with leaves of pale sage green and broad flat heads of white flowers; 'Stardust', similar but with pale grey-green leaves and silvered white flowers, sometimes blushed pale pink; and 'Neon', a vibrant, almost luminous magenta—one of the Brilliant Group, derived from rose-magenta *S. spectabile* 'Brilliant', all of which sport sharper pinks.

Of the *S. telephium* cultivars, 'Purple Emperor' is one of the duskiest of sedums, a fairly upright mound of satiny, bronzed deep purple leaves with red stems and deep red-pink flowers, sturdy with less tendency to flop than most. 'Strawberries and Cream' has red-stemmed cymes of deep pink buds that open to reveal creamy centres; the leaves, at first bluish green, become increasingly plummy as they mature.

Knee high or a little taller. Fully hardy, z3/4–9. Full sun, in dry to well-drained, poor to moderately fertile, neutral to alkaline soil.

Syringa

Oleacae • lilac

There are tree lilacs of the *Syringa vulgaris* ilk with which we are familiar, and for which gardeners on chalky soils are particularly grateful. But when a plant we admire proves too big for the site we can provide, it's a near certainty that others in the genus will fit the bill. We got lucky with the lilacs. Some make a moderate-sized, deciduous dome, and better still, some are repeat flowering. If you want to bring the fragrance of lilac closer to home and nearer to the nose than tree lilacs allow, try the following.

Syringa meyeri forms a chest-high mound of many slender twigs, with delicate panicles of tiny, very fragrant pale lilac to violet flowers in spring, and sometimes again in late summer or early autumn; *S. m.* 'Palibin' is a more compact selection with lavender pink flowers. The Persian lilac, *S.* ×*persica*, has small, narrowly ovate leaves and rather slender twigs, and makes a compact, bushy mound, chest to head high. The flower panicles are as wide as long, and densely packed with small lilac flowers—or alternatively, in *S.* ×*persica* 'Alba', white ones—with the typical sweet lilac scent, and so freely produced in late spring as to almost obscure the foliage. If you made a case for treating this as as an arching line, I wouldn't disagree.

Syringa pubescens subsp. *microphylla* makes a broadly conical mound to head height, but very slowly. It is fine textured, with small leaves and short, dense panicles of very fragrant, pale

▲▲ *Syringa meyeri* 'Palibin'

▲ *Syringa ×persica* 'Alba'

lilac-pink flowers in early summer and autumn. Both this and its cultivar 'Superba' produce flowering panicles in pairs at the shoot tips, and sometimes in the leaf axils below them as well; 'Superba' is particularly free flowering, with darker rosy pink flowers in early summer, and flushes of bloom on the current season's growth until autumn.

Syringa pubescens subsp. *patula* has very attractive leaves, matt green, flushed maroon-purple when young, on sturdy purple-tinted young shoots that tone with the gracefully nodding, open panicles of pale lilac-purple flowers of early summer. It is strictly speaking rather too large and open to be included here, but *S. pubescens* subsp. *patula* 'Miss Kim' forms

a shorter, chunkier mound, to chest high, with fatter panicles of deep purple-pink buds that open purple but fade to a blue-lilac tinted white. It has a spicy scent and the matt-textured, wavy-margined leaves are large, dusky green, purple when young and red-purple in autumn.

I make a point of deadheading these smaller lilacs, an enjoyable job for an early summer day, and I take the opportunity to do a little surreptitious shaping, taking the spent flower heads off to a promising pair of growth buds further down the stem than is strictly necessary. Then I feed with high-potash fertilizer to egg on the later flowers.

Chest to head high. Fully hardy, z4/5–9. Full

sun, in fertile, moisture-retentive, neutral to alkaline soils. See also page 178 (Arcs and Fountains).

Tradescantia

Commelinaceae • spiderwort

The wild spiderwort, *Tradescantia virginiana*, is a native of damp, shady bluffs, meadows, thickets and woodland margins of eastern North America. It was first introduced to Europe in 1629, by the elder John Tradescant and named for the Tradescants, father and son, by Linnaeus. Hybrids from *T. virginiana*, *T. aspera* and *T. ohiensis* are known as the Andersoniana Group, which have largely superseded the species in gardens. All three of the supposed parents have a place in the wild, woodland and native plant garden. Their offspring are an extraordinarily long-flowering group of clump-forming herbaceous perennials, blooming from early summer till cut by frosts. They have sheaves of arching, grass-like, mostly bright green leaves, and terminal cymes of flowers with three triangular petals, from blue-eyed white in 'Alba' and 'Osprey', through carmine red in 'Karminglut', purple in 'Purple Dome' and deep blue-violet in 'Zwanenburg Blue'. The furry anther filaments at the flower centre are often in a contrasting colour. Among newer cultivars with more distinctive blue-green foliage, are 'Blueberry Ice' with silvery mauve flowers and 'Concord Grape' with deep magenta blooms. The tendency for the foliage to look a little tatty by midsummer can be reduced by ensuring adequate summer moisture, or subverted by cutting back flowered stems after the first flush, or if desperate, by cutting the whole plant back before midsummer and give it food

and water, they resprout willingly. If they have a slight propensity to wander, confine them by digging out pieces from the margins and give them away to friends.

Knee high. Fully hardy, z3/4–9. Any fertile, moisture-retentive but well-drained soil in sun or dappled shade.

▲▲ *Tradescantia*
(Andersoniana Group)
'Purple Dome'

▲ *Tradescantia* 'Alba'

▲ *Trillium grandiflorum*
f. *roseum*

◀ *Trillium rivale*

Trillium

Trilliaceae ▪ trinity flower, wake robin

Most trilliums emerge in spring from damp leafy earth in the shady woodlands of North America; a scattering of species also occur in the western Himalayas and northeastern Asia. *Trillium grandiflorum* grows in the wild with *Osmunda cinnamomea* and *Veratrum viride*, a tip to take up in cultivated surroundings, for the simple trinity of trillium leaves looks fabulous with the pleated silk of veratrum foliage and the emerging crosiers of osmunda. *Trillium nivale* is frequently found pushing through snow in humus-filled rocky niches, and often flowers before snowmelt in the wild. All are shade lovers, for damp shady borders, for underplantings between shrubs, and for the wild and woodland garden.

They form clumps of upright stems, each terminating in a simple whorl of three lance-shaped to diamond-shaped green leaves sometimes marked, marbled or mottled in other shades. They die back in autumn. Each three-petalled flower has a whorl of three green, leafy sepals. I apply a little ornamental sub-classification to the trilliums, based on the visibility of the flowers, not being one who likes to lie down to see them. Some, such as *T. cernuum*, have nodding flowers that appear below or among the leaves, while others, like *T. luteum*, present an upturned flower like a posy upon the whorl of three leaves, and the rest, like *T. grandiflorum*, have stalked flowers above the leaves. My choices here are from the two latter types.

Trillium albidum bears fragrant, stalkless white flowers nestling upon the slightly silvered foliage in spring. One of the most beautiful compositions I have ever seen of this was as an underplanting beneath the tiers of *Cornus controversa* 'Variegata', its mounded foliage offset against the verticals of *Leucojum aestivum* with the nodding bells of the white form of the snake-shead fritillary, *Fritillaria meleagris* var. *alba*.

Trillium chloropetalum forms a sturdy clump of red-tinted stems, with leaves variously marbled in creamy grey and maroon, and erect, stalkless, fragrant flowers in deep glossy red, white or yellow. One of the largest-flowered trilliums, *T. grandiflorum*, blooms in late spring, presenting its stalked flowers wide open above a mound of dark green leaves; they are usually a crisp crystalline white, but in *T. grandiflorum* f. *roseum*, a soft pink. *Trillium luteum* is sweetly scented with golden or bronzed green petals nestling directly on top of the leaves, which are marbled and mottled in deep and pale green. Most of the above make knee-high mounds.

Knee high. Fully hardy, z6–9, *T. albidum*; z4–9, *T. chloropetalum*, *T. grandiflorum*; z5–9, *T. luteum*. Shade, part-day shade or dappled shade in open-textured, moist but well-drained soil with plenty of leafy organic matter. They prefer slightly acid to neutral soils, but *T. chloropetalum*, *T. grandiflorum*, and *T. luteum* occur on soils slightly to the alkaline side of neutral.

▲ *Trillium albinum*, with *Fritillaria meleagris* var. *unicolor* subvar. *alba*

▼ *Trillium chloropetalum*

Clouds and Transparents

◀ *Thalictrum*
dipterocarpum with
Catananche caerulea

In many ways, the plants I classify as clouds and transparents bring the most decorative of finishing touches to a plant composition. They are light, airy and graceful, lacking solidity even when of substantial volume. Glistening, gauzy, often adorning themselves with raindrops, dew and frost rime, and usually mobile in the slightest breath of breeze, they are ethereal in effect, though often exceptionally tough.

Transparent or sufficiently translucent to permit light and sight to filter through them, their height is no bar to using them as foreground. They can bring height to the fore, where their fragility can be appreciated intimately, without obscuring what lies behind them. In this way they are a most useful group, especially when you wish to avoid the bank of ascending height that characterizes the more traditional border, or if perhaps you wish to frame a part of your planting as a cameo or composition within a composition. Transparents allow you to play with the theme of partial concealment and gradual revelation.

Miniscule, minute or simply small flowers are the essence of most clouds and transparents; in most cases they have fine foliage, too. These are often the sort of plants that will weave themselves through companions of greater substance—coreopsis, cosmos, gauras and nigellas—creating a unifying thread as they embroider their way through a planting. But I also include here those that might be called seasonal transparents: *Daphne bholua*, *Corylopsis* species and glorious *Hamamelis* cultivars, for example. These are transparent only when in winter bloom, on bare winter branches, when low glancing sun filters through a veil of tiny blooms—thus creating chiaroscuro, capturing the play of light and shade as an integral part of your compositions.

◀ *Alisma plantago-aquatica*

▶ *Ammi majus* with *Consolida ajacis* (larkspur)

Alisma

Alismataceae

Alisma plantago-aquatica (water plantain) is among the earliest water plants to emerge in spring, when rolled up, pointed tips of the rosettes of straight-stemmed leaves rise vertically from the water's surface. They open into deeply ribbed lance-shaped, bluish green leaves, like those of plantains. In midsummer, leafless greens stems rise well above the leaves, bearing lax and airy pyramidal panicles of tiny, white or pink-flushed, three-petalled flowers at the top. Excellent for wild water gardens; birds and small mammals feed on its abundant seed. Widespread from North America through Europe, to Africa and Asia, in still and slow-moving freshwater, bogs, marshes and ditches. A successful species, spreading from a fleshy rootstock and self-sowing. If you don't have lots of space, deadhead ruthlessly and lift and reduce the rootstock every second or third year.

Waist to chest high. Fully hardy, z3. Grow in full sun, in heavy, permanently wet soils as a water marginal, or in mud at the bottom of ankle- to knee-deep water.

Ammi

Apiaceae

If you long for something white and lacy, *Ammi majus* is just the thing. One of slenderest of cultivated umbellifers, it's at its loveliest when drawing a translucent veil through summer borders. A much-branched annual with fresh, finely divided, bright green ferny leaves,

the flowerheads are domed, delicate, finely wrought umbels of pure clean white.

A native of bare and rocky Mediterranean habitats, often used in cottage gardens, refined and never brutish, it is a perfect filler plant in mixed borders. As the sap can cause photosensitivity, avoid contact with it if cutting for the vase. Direct-sow in drifts in spring, or in plugs under glass in early spring.

Knee to thigh high. Fully hardy, z6–10. Full sun or dappled shade in any moderately fertile, moist but well-drained soil.

Anemone
Ranunculaceae ▪ windflower

From high altitudes in the Himalayas in northern India, Kashmir and Nepal, to Tibet and southwestern China, in meadows and open forest glades, and on stream- and hedgebanks, *Anemone rivularis* is among the most aristocratic of the buttercup family. It blooms in late spring and early summer above the basal mounds of rounded, three-lobed, dusky green leaves, on stiffly branching stems in few-flowered umbels, each floret on a stalk of different length—creating a shower of luminous, satiny white flowers, flushed metallic blue on the reverse, with purple-blue anthers at the centres: exactly the right shade for light shade. A beautiful woodlander...place where you can take a peek at twilight.

To thigh high. Fully hardy, z5–9. Sun or light dappled shade in open-textured, moist but well-drained, leafy, humus-rich soil.

Anethum

Apiaceae • dill

If you grow dill (*A. graveolens*) for culinary purposes—baked with salmon in olive oil with white vermouth, perhaps—you may not have noticed how ethereally airy it becomes when it flowers and goes to seed. A fountain of filiform blue-green leaves with open umbels of tiny yellow flowers, it's a shame to confine it to the herb border. Sow a few in early summer to create a haze among late perennials such as *Helianthus* 'Lemon Queen', *Echinacea pallida* or *Rudbeckia occidentalis* 'Green Wizard'.

Waist high. Fully hardy, z8–10. Sun and fertile, moisture-retentive, well-drained soil.

Anthriscus

Apiaceae

Common cow parsley, *Anthriscus sylvestris*, ubiquitous in meadow and woodland, has ferny fresh green foliage and umbels of tiny white flowers; it is the creamy froth that brightens hedgebanks in spring and early summer. Although it works well in rough meadows, where more desirable flowers cannot compete with coarse grasses, it outlives its welcome in short order unless the first cut is made before it goes to seed. Then its invasive ambitions can be controlled; as it resprouts, it's easy to see and spot-spray or dig out.

The chocolate-purple-leaved variant *A. sylvestris* 'Ravenswing' has white flowers with pink bracts. More often used in border plantings, where it associates dramatically with

► *Anthriscus sylvestris* 'Ravenswing'

dark-hued tulips such as 'Queen of Night'. It too is a self-sower. If cut back to base to prevent self-seeding, a second flush of richly coloured foliage arises, probably coinciding with the flowering of *Cerinthe major* 'Purpurascens'.

Waist to chest high. Fully hardy, z4–9. Any well-drained soil in sun, or partial or dappled shade.

Aquilegia

Ranunculaceae • columbine

There isn't a single aquilegia species, cultivar or hybrid that I cannot love. I'm fond of the singles with bell-shaped flowers, spurred petals and self-coloured tepals, or with petals and tepals in a wide range of contrasting colours, as well as the doubles with fluted tepals, and those like *A. vulgaris* var. *stellata* Barlow Series, which are so doubled that they take the form of starry tepalled pompons. They bloom between spring and midsummer—with alliums, peonies, roses and bearded irises—and are classics of the herbaceous border.

The more delicate-flowered species display flowers on long, strong stems well above the basal rosettes of lobed leaves—an airy, waist-high transparency. Although they are lovely in borders, their natural grace makes them perfect for more naturalistic plantings, too.

Wild columbine, *A. vulgaris*, is native to grassland, open woodlands and hedgebanks; I grow it in my wild meadows. It has a deep rootstock and withstands mowing. And like other tough variants of *A. vulgaris*, it is glorious among slender young grasses and in the dappled light of woodland. The species has terminal racemes of short-spurred bells, usually in shades blue and violet, although pink- and white-flowered forms also occur. In *A. vulgaris* var. *stellata* several beautiful colour forms are offered: 'Ruby Port', glowing wine red; 'Black Barlow', deep plummy maroon; 'Blue Barlow' and 'Rose Barlow' in shades of blue and rose pink.

Aquilegia canadensis has scarlet tepals and lemon yellow petals with upright red spurs. Natural woodlanders for dappled shade, with delicate blooms and fine foliage, include *A. chrysantha*, with spurred pale yellow petals and darker yellow tepals, and *A. longissima*, with fragrant, exceptionally long-spurred yellow flowers. All self-sow; you can transplant seedlings when tiny to exactly where you want them.

Thigh to waist high. Fully hardy, z3–10. Moist but well-drained soil in sun or dappled shade.

▶ *Aquilegia vulgaris*

▼ *Aquilegia vulgaris* var. *stellata* 'Blue Barlow'

▲ *Aquilegia longissima* with forget-me-nots

▲ *Aquilegia vulgaris* var. *stellata* 'Ruby Port'

◀ *Artemisia lactiflora*
Guizhou Group with
sidalceas

Artemisia

Asteraceae

There is an artemisia for every purpose. *Artemisia lactiflora* has the some of the most acceptably coloured flowers in the genus, and they're borne in tall, upright, branching plumes—airy and light-filled at waist to chest height. It forms clumps of jaggedly cut, grey green leaves and bears tiny creamy white flowers in late summer and early autumn, quite unlike the grubby browns and yellows of other artemisias. They're excellent with the blues and purples of the asters, and with the stronger-hued echinaceas, but not next to pure whites, where the off-white risks becoming reminiscent of poor laundry practices. *Artemisia lactiflora* Guizhou Group, with leaves of a pewter-tinged green, flushed dark red when young, has mahogany flower stems, against which the white flowers stand out well.

Waist to chest high. Fully hardy, z4–10. Reliably moist but well-drained, moderately fertile soil in full sun or light dappled shade. See also page 44 (Horizontals and Tiers), page 83 (Verticals and Diagonals) and page 183 (Clumps and Mounds).

Aruncus

Rosaceae • goat's beard

The collocation of tough with graceful applies to the *n*th degree to *Aruncus dioicus*. A statuesque head-high clump-former with billowing mounds of large leaves divided into fresh green leaflets, it bears huge, hazy plumes of many tiny starry flowers in creamy white, from early to late summer. It occurs on damp streambanks and shady woodland throughout northern temperate regions, even in the subarctic. Equally at home in wild and woodland gardens, in bog gardens echoing astilbes, in shady borders with rodgersias and big-leaved hostas or in sunnier borders with tall campanulas, *Crambe cordifolia* and roses.

In the best nurseries, it is the male form that's stocked; the female plant is much less showy, with droopy, greenish white tassels. *Aruncus dioicus* 'Zweiweltenkind' is shorter than the species, with mahogany stems and plumper

▼ *Aruncus dioicus*

plumes of creamy flowers. *Aruncus* 'Misty Lace', at about thigh high, has more ferny leaves and more open plumes—starry flowers are borne in long narrow spikes held horizontally on glossy deep red stems. It's also more tolerant of both drought and hot, humid continental summers than *A. dioicus*.

Fully hardy, z3–8. Dry or moist, fertile soil in sun or light dappled shade.

Aster
Asteraceae

From the dry, dappled shade of open woodland in eastern North America, *Aster divaricatus* is a rhizomatous herbaceous perennial bearing clouds of tiny white daisies in very lax corymbs on wiry, deep black-purple stems above clumps of long-heart-shaped leaves from midsummer to autumn. Long used as an airy edger—in homage to Gertrude Jekyll, let it fall in among *Bergenia cordifolia*. It creeps slowly and is especially lovely weaving through the sere golden inflorescences of deschampsias or among woodland grasses such as *Melica uniflora*.

Knee to mid thigh. Fully hardy, z4–9. Fertile to moderately fertile, moist but well-drained to dry soils, in dappled shade. See also page 45 (Horizontals and Tiers).

◀ *Aster divaricatus* with *Deschampsia*

▼ *Aster divaricatus*, close up of flowers

Astilbe
Saxifragaceae

Early, midseason and late; ankle high to head high; airy plumes, dense plumes, arching plumes and upright ones; pure white through ethereal pinks to vivid reds. Such is the choice in the genus *Astilbe*. It is possible to select for interest with astilbes almost throughout the year, from the emergence of the beautifully tinted young growth, some blooming almost from the last spring frost, others to the first frost of autumn, followed by sere nut-brown seedheads which stand though winter—until it's almost time for their re-emergence the following spring.

They have in common a bomb-proof hardiness, a love of moisture and a dislike of drought and summer heat. They reach perfection in bog gardens and on stream- and poolsides, look beautiful in damp, shady borders and in dappled woodland shade, and are exquisite in rocky niches in damp shade that approximate the habitat of *Astilbe japonica* in mountain ravines.

Dwarf cultivars of *A.* ×*arendsii* and *A. simplicifolia* give me the impression I'm not doing enough for them. I want the more substantial presence of the taller astilbes that reach waist high and above. They might have the open, elegantly arching panicles that are truly transparent and typified by *A. thunbergii* and its hybrids, such as 'Professor van der Wielen' with green leaves and white flowers from midsummer on, 'Betsy Cuperus' in pale pink, or 'Straussenfeder' in deep coral, from late summer to autumn.

For a line that is strong, vertical and semi-transparent, choose cultivars of *A. chinensis*, with slender, steepled plumes, from mid- to late summer and early autumn; *A. chinensis* var. *taquetii* 'Purpurlanze', in deep magenta purple; and 'Superba', in rich violet-pink. *Astilbe chinensis* 'Diamonds and Pearls' has exceptionally long plumes in silvery white, and *A. c.* 'Milk and Honey', with silver marbled young foliage, has green buds and white flowers flushed soft

pink. *Astilbe* 'Jo Ophurst' in deep rose-lilac is a very late bloomer.

Many *A. japonica* hybrids are on the short side, but have great midsummer presence with dense, upright, pyramidal panicles and, in the darker-flowered sorts, foliage with bronze or mahogany tints. For fabulous contrasts, 'Montgomery', with dark red plumes, has red-bronze foliage, and 'Red Sentinel' has full-packed heads of red-crimson.

With the *A. ×arendsii* hybrids, anything is possible. The parents include *A. astilboides*, *A.*

◀ *Astilbe* 'Ceres'

▲ *Astilbe* 'Hyazinth'

▶ *Astilbe* 'Red Sentinel'

japonica, *A. thunbergii* and variants of *A. chinensis*. The darker the flower colour the duskier the foliage, with emergent tints in crimson-mahogany and red-bronze; paler and white-flowered sorts have lush green leaves, amber and gold on emergence. Early summer bloomers include 'Rhythm and Blues' in raspberry pink and 'Fanal' in deep crimson red. The lilac pink of 'Hyazinth' and ethereally pale pink of 'Ceres' appear in mid- to late summer, the pure white of 'Weisse Gloria' in late summer and autumn.

◀ *Astilbe* 'Weisse Gloria'

▶ *Astilbe* 'Fanal'

Fully hardy, z3/4–8. Reliably moist, fertile, humus-rich soils in dappled shade, light shade or in wetter soils in sun—but absolutely with shade from hot midday sun: too much sun and too little moisture leads to crispy leaves and a rapid demise.

▶ *Astrantia major*

Astrantia

Apiaceae • masterwort, Hattie's pincushion

A denizen of woodland and meadows, *Astrantia major* has been valued for centuries for its delicate airy presence and long summer blooming period. It has a pincushion of tiny flowers upon a pale ruff of bracts, borne on long, branching, wiry stems well above the basal rosettes of palmately lobed leaves; in *A. major* subsp. *involucrata*, the bracts are longer, white with green tips and veins. *Astrantia maxima* has neat, broadly triangular bracts in dusky pink and a soft pink pincushion; the umbels are borne singly on unbranched stems, giving it a more transparent effect than *A. major* and its cultivars.

▶ *Astrantia major* 'Rosensinfonie'

Spreading slowly from the rootstock, all are great weavers—dispersed through other plants, they tie a scheme together very satisfactorily. They associate so well with grasses, a transitional texture between translucent haze and more solid forms: the clear pinks of *A.* 'Roma' and *A.* 'Rosensinfonie' work well with the smoky pinks of *Sedum* 'Matrona', *Calamagrostis brachytricha* or *Pennisetum orientale* 'Karley Rose'. Pale-flowered cultivars, such as *A.* 'Buckland' and *A. major* subsp. *involucrata* 'Shaggy', make ethereal compositions among bronze fennel (*Foeniculum vulgare* 'Purpureum'), or actaeas.

▶ *Astrantia* 'Roma'

There are now several strong-hued astrantias in the sultry spectrum once represented only by *A.* 'Hadspen Blood'. Among them are *A. major* 'Claret', in sunlight-shot ruby port; *A.* 'Moulin Rouge', deep maroon with dark-tipped bracts; and *A. major* 'Ruby Wedding', in ruby red with dusky foliage. The most beautiful by far is *A. major* 'Gill Richardson', with maroon-purple new leaves, black stems, and blood red flowers upon black-tipped bracts.

▶ *Astrantia* 'Buckland'

Astrantia 'Hadspen Blood'

◀ *Briza media*

Deadhead to prolong flowering; while I'm reluctant to spoil the early summer show, I know I must be ruthless if later flowers are to give their best with sedums and the second show of New York poppies (see page 221).

Knee to thigh high. Fully hardy, z4/5–9. Reliably moisture-retentive but well-drained, humus-rich, fertile soil in light dappled shade or sun. Best in sun in cool-summer gardens, but shade from hot sun in warmer climes.

Briza
Poaceae ▪ quaking grass

When I was small, my grandmother and I would hunt for quaking grass (*Briza media*) in the fields and hedgerows, entranced by the rustling of the tiny heart-shaped spikelets trembling on hair-fine stalks in summer. In the intervening years, it has become increasingly scarce with agricultural intensification and the decline in 'unimproved' species-rich chalk and limestone grasslands. At least we still grow it in gardens. It's too slender and diffuse to use as a single specimen, but perfect in drifts, when it can even be used as ground cover in the dappled shade beneath trees—in which case it needs to be grown from seed. You get about 250 plugs from a gram of seed.

Knee high. Fully hardy, z4–10. Well-drained, poor to moderately fertile, freely draining soil in sun.

Calamagrostis
Poaceae ▪ reed grass

Substantial perennials of some height and upright habit, calamagrostis are particularly useful as an overtopping backdrop in border or prairie plantings, for in spite of their committed verticality, their plumy inflorescences are soft, airy and enchantingly light-filtering. *Calamagrostis ×acutiflora* makes sheaves of arching, grey-green leaves topped by erect, stiff-stemmed plumes of silky, silvered bronze to pale bronze-purple in mid- to late summer. *C. ×acutiflora* 'Overdam' has leaves margined and lined with yellow, and purplish plumes, which fade to a dusky grey pink; in *C. ×acutiflora* 'Karl Foerster', open pink-bronze plumes age to tawny buff, closing up as the leaves assume foxy autumn tints, to become narrow and stiff, in which state they persist through winter, to be rimed by hoar frosts. At chest high, *Calamagrostis brachytricha* is shorter than *C. ×acutiflora* but has longer flower plumes in silvery grey-pink. Giving good contrast with the arching stems of *Pennisetum*, the calamagrostis tone with the candelabra of

◀ *Calamagrostis acutiflora* 'Overdam'

veronicastrums, the airy horizontals of *Aster lateriflorus*, *A.* 'Ringdove' and rubicund echinaceas.

Chest to head high. Fully hardy, z5–9. Full sun, in dry but not arid, moisture-retentive or damp soil.

Chaerophyllum

Apiaceae

If you like *Anthriscus sylvestris* 'Ravenswing', you'll love *Chaerophyllum hirsutum* 'Roseum'— a herbaceous perennial with ferny green, apple-scented foliage; stems that are flushed strongly red-purple when young; and lacy, dark-stemmed umbels of deep pink flowers from spring to midsummer. I first saw it stylishly underpinning airy sprays of *Thalictrum* 'Elin'

◀ *Calamagrostis brachytricha*

▶ *Chaerophyllum hirsutum* 'Roseum'

◀ *Calamagrostis* x*acutiflora* 'Karl Foerster'

against the emerging inflorescences of *Molinia caerulea* subsp. *arundinacea* 'Transparent' and *Astrantia* 'Roma'. It also looks lovely with globe-flowered alliums (see page X), and *Papaver orientale* 'Manhattan' and 'Lilac Girl'.

Thigh high. Fully hardy, z4–9. Any damp, moderately fertile soil in sun, partial or dappled shade.

Cirsium

Asteraceae • plume thistle

Among the legion ranks of thistles found in meadows and grasslands and as nuisance weeds in neglected pastures throughout the northern hemisphere, some two hundred are *Cirsium* species—which gives a clue about their tendencies; in cultivation, they should not be allowed to self-sow. Nevertheless, several are handsome additions to borders and cutting borders, with sculptural mounds of divided, spine-tipped and often densely hairy leaves, and thistly flowerheads with upstanding ray florets. They are borne on tall stems, which makes them useful for arranging a scattering of more or less intense colour at about chest height in a composition, without obscuring neighbours in the fore- or background.

Cirsium japonicum branches from a basal mound of dark green leaves, the upright slender stems tipped by pink or purple flowerheads in summer and early autumn. A number of named selections are popular florists' flowers: *C. japonicum* 'Rose Beauty' has deep carmine pink flowers, while those of 'Pink Beauty' are a softer pink. The species is also grown as a border perennial, but *C. rivulare* 'Atropurpureum' is preferred, having greater colour intensity in its tight, almost-spherical, deep crimson flowerheads in early to midsummer, and again later if deadheaded. It lacks the egregious habits of its wild cousins, doesn't spread rampantly and, at least in cool maritime climates, is not a notorious self-seeder.

The Himalayan thistle, *C. falconeri*, takes the prize for the spiniest and most woolly-hairy of all the thistles. The leaves are deeply and variously lobed, adorned with glassy marginal spines, and surfaced with long, glistening spines and silvery hair. The head-high flowerheads and rigidly upright stems are densely white-woolly and the ray florets are creamy white. Unlike its close competitor in the architectural beauty stakes, the biennial *Onopordum acanthium*, it is perennial. Bees and other beneficial insects regard these (and most other thistles) as the nectar of the gods.

Fully hardy, z5–9. Full sun, in any moist but well-drained soil.

Coreopsis

Asteraceae • tickseed

A race of meadow, prairie and woodland natives, with golden daisies on long upright stems, several of the tickseeds are used for cutting. Some, such as *C. auriculata*, with solitary, sunny yellow daisies on erect thigh-high stems, and the similar but larger-flowered *C. grandiflora*, are eminently suitable for meadow and prairie plantings. I value *C. verticillata* for its hazy mounds of very finely divided leaves with almost thread-like brilliant green leaflets, and *C. verticillata* 'Moonbeam' even more for its many small pale lemon yellow flowers from early to midsummer. It's a soft colour that

▲▲ *Cirsium rivulare* 'Atropurpureum'

▲ *Cirsium falconeri*

◀ *Coreopsis verticillata* 'Moonbeam'

▶ *Corylopsis glabrescens*

associates well with the blues of nepetas, eryngiums and nigellas, and tones with the whorls of *Phlomis russeliana*, making excellent textural contrast to all of the above.

Knee high. Fully hardy, z6–10. Any moderately fertile, well-drained soil, in full sun.

Corylopsis

Hamamelidaceae · winter hazel

Without exception the cultivated species of *Corylopsis* are exquisite in bloom, bearing pendent chains of fragrant, bell-shaped primrose yellow flowers on bare branches in early spring. They are rather open, mostly deciduous shrubs, with *C. pauciflora*, *C. spicata* and *C. sinensis* var. *calvescens* f. *veitchii* being the best choices for smaller spaces—they reach head height, but slowly (though twice that eventually). At their best beneath a high canopy of deciduous trees that shelters them from cold dry winds, frost and hot summer sun, in full flower they create a cloud of translucent pale gold that is glorious in the dappled low light of morning and late afternoon. Their fragrance is not forthcoming unless warmed by spring sunshine or the huff of your own warm breath upon them. The foliage is often bronzed, purple or tawny red on emergence, subdued in summer but with respectable autumn colour in shades of old gold. All are delicately beautiful and generous in flowering—the longest catkins are borne by *C. spicata*, those of *C. pauciflora* are shorter and

▶ *Corylopsis sinensis*

▶ *Corylopsis pauciflora*

plumper, and those of *C. sinensis* var. *calvescens* f. *veitchii* are long and slender, the pale yellow petals surrounding conspicuous brick red anthers. *C. glabrescens*, taller at five times head height, has plump pale primrose catkins.

Fully hardy, z6/7–9. Dappled shade, moist but well-drained, open-textured, humus-rich soils, preferably neutral to acid. All except *C. pauciflora* will grow on chalk providing there is a good depth of woodsy soil on top.

Cosmos
Asteraceae

A tuberous perennial from Mexico, *C. atrosanguineus*, the chocolate cosmos, is so named not for the chocolate-maroon velvet of its petals, but for the elusive scent of dark chocolate that it exudes only when you're not actively seeking it. It forms clumps of shining pinnate green leaves, and from midsummer to autumn long dark stems with solitary, single, cupped daisies at knee to thigh high. It's a terrible flopper—an unattractive trait if you want a continuous

▼ *Cosmos atrosanguineus* with *Agrostis nebulosa*

swathe of rich colour, but a great virtue with close companions for support so that they interlace. Grasses can be among the loveliest of companions. If you intend to lift *C. atrosanguineus* in autumn, use an annual grass such as *Agrostis nebulosa*; otherwise, allow it to weave through hazy perennial grasses, such as *Stipa tenuissima*, *S. calamagrostis* 'Lempberg' or *Deschampsia cespitosa* 'Goldtau'.

The tubers of *C. atrosanguineus* are not fully hardy, but life is too short to lift and store them every autumn—so I give them a deep leafy winter mulch that won't become too soggy in the cold and damp.

Hardy, z8–10. Full sun and well-drained, moisture-retentive, moderately fertile soil.

Crambe
Brassicaceae

Crambe cordifolia forms an enormous mound of large, shining, heart-shaped leaves, puckered and undulating, above which, in early and midsummer, appear billowing, semi-transparent

▶ *Crambe cordifolia*

clouds of blossom on stout stems that branch exponentially into finer and finer branchlets until each minute cross-shaped, creamy white flower is suspended on an infinitely slender pedicel. Strange that a member of the cabbage family should have such sweet fragrance? No, think of that sickly scent from oilseed rape— fortunately, that of crambe is much more honeyed. It's a traditional companion to the Old Roses and philadelphus, adding a light note to the admixture of their sensuous fragrances.

The foliage dies back soon after flowering, and in spring pigeons can strip them to the stalks. Even I, a very lazy gardener, am bound to cover the emergent clump with a cage of bamboo canes and string to deter them. The leaves grow through but it's not pretty, not even in a boho-chic kind of way. So I always use crambes behind other plants that disguise both the support and the die-back gap.

To twice head height. Fully hardy, z6–9. Full sun and fertile well-drained soil.

Daphne

Thymeleaceae

From the eastern Himalayas, *Daphne bholua* is one of the most exquisite of a superlatively lovely genus. Evergreen, semi-evergreen or shortly deciduous shrubs, forming an open mound of upright branches, they have glossy, narrowly elliptical, dark green leaves, and small tubular flowers in terminal clusters. They open from deep red-purple buds, the flowers white with a red-mauve reverse, and you know they're in bloom before you set eyes upon them; the sweet, heady scent is pervasive, carrying for yards on still winter days.

In my favourite client's arboretum, we made a small glade of *D. bholua*, open to late morning and afternoon sun, but sheltered from cold, dry northeasterly winds that are the kiss of death to marginally hardy evergreens in early spring. The hardiest of *D. bholua* are high-altitude selections that become completely deciduous in winter. The deciduous habit highlights

▶ *Daphne bholua* 'Jacqueline Postill'

their extraordinary beauty: blooming on bare branches gives them an enchanting transparency not seen in the evergreens. The evergreen or semi-evergreen *D. bholua* 'Jacqueline Postill' has a reputation for hardiness, and so it has proved, although it tends to produce its red-mauve flowers among the leaves. The very hardy, deciduous *D. bholua* var. *glacialis* 'Ghurka' bears fat clusters of deep pink buds, opening to white, on each branch tip, with a glorious fragrance from January to March.

Hardy, z7–10. In sun, but sited to avoid early morning sun, in deep, freely draining, moisture-retentive, moderately fertile soil of good open texture, enriched with plentiful leafy humus, and mulched with the same.

Deschampsia

Poaceae

These tussock-forming perennial grasses inhabit meadows, moors and woodland glades throughout temperate and arctic regions. They're among the easiest of grasses to identify in the wild, forming distinct tussocks of rigid,

249

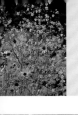

narrowly linear leaves—evergreen in the case of *D. cespitosa* and *D. flexuosa*. If you have ever seen a natural stand of *D. cespitosa*, you'll appreciate its garden virtues: fine dark green mounds appear early in the season; by midsummer they form a transparent haze of silver-purple spikelets; by late summer, they make a stand of shimmering tawny blonde at chest height, aching to be decorated with veronicastrums. The sere

◀ *Deschampsia* 'Goldschleier' with *Monarda* 'Squaw', *Achillea* 'Walther Funcke' and *Phlox ×arendsii* 'Luc's Lilac'

▲ *Deschampsia* 'Goldtau' with *Verbena bonariensis*

inflorescences stand though winter, glistening with frost, and only have to be cut down before growth begins again in early spring.

Cultivated selections are similar to the species, but vary in detail. *Deschampsia cespitosa* 'Goldtau' is a warmer blonde and reaches to mid thigh; 'Goldschleier', waist to chest high, is a more silvery platinum blonde at about the same height; 'Bronzeschleier' is a darker bronzed gold. 'Goldegehänge' is a taller selection, with a haze of golden yellow at head height.

Fully hardy, z4–9. Sun or dappled shade, moisture-retentive but well-drained soils.

Dierama

Iridaceae • angel's fishing rod, wandflower

Dierama pulcherrimum is found in the wild in damp flushes and among rocks on steep grassy mountain slopes in South Africa, with their heads in the sun, and their corms cool and evenly moist. If that sounds like a recipe for growing an alpine plant, well so it is. It's very hardy, which makes its tremendous appeal all the greater.

◀ *Dierama pulcherrimum*

▶ *Erigeron karvinskianus*

◀ *Deschampsia* 'Goldtau' in frost

It forms a sheaf of sharp-edged grey-green leaves, and, in summer, long strong stems rise up, arching at the tips, and from them hang sprays of silk-crêpe-textured, tubular bell-shaped flowers on the most slender of pedicels. It brings such graceful movement and transparency to a composition; the stems and flowers shimmer and tremble in each breath of breeze, and despite their slender and delicate appearance, they're remarkably resilient in the face of stronger wind. In the species, flowers range from pure white through magenta to purple; cultivated selections include *D. pulcherrimum* var. album and *D.* 'Guinevere' in pure white; *D. pulcherrimum* 'Merlin' in blackberry purple; and *D. p.* 'Blackbird', deep wine purple.

Waist to head high. Fully hardy, z7–10. Full sun, in deep, humus-rich, moisture-retentive but freely draining soils.

Erigeron
Asteraceae

Almost every gardener who sees the hazy little Mexican daisy, *Erigeron karvinskianus*, covets it and needs one or half a dozen or so for

themselves. I first saw it on a sunny paved terrace, self-sown into every crevice and scattered charmingly and randomly through the borders. Its charm lies in the lax and open sprays of small, grey-green leaves and the mobile haze created by a profusion of tiny white daisies that turn pink soon after they open. Although it sows itself freely, and I have given bags of the fresh seed away, it seems determined not to germinate when placed where it's wanted by the hand of the gardener; it's easier to dig up and distribute your unwanted seedlings.

Ankle to knee high. Fully hardy, z8–11. Any well-drained soil in sun, or in dirt, or in gravel.

Ferula
Apiaceae • giant fennel

Ferula communis is a magnificent specimen with the architecture of angelica—a huge mound of finely divided leaves with very slender, linear bright green segments, fennel-like but much larger. It grows high on rocky Mediterranean hills and mountain slopes, often making prolific foliage growth in soils moistened by snowmelt and spring rains. By summer, stout branching stems rocket skywards, each branch with a broad, open umbel of tiny yellow flowers. It takes a great deal of energy to produce towering inflorescences, to twice head height, and it may take three to four years before the plant gathers sufficient strength to flower. The plants

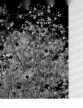

◀ *Ferula communis*

These tough and hardy rhizomatous herbaceous perennials are appreciated for their handsome foliage and the plumes, feathery sprays or great cumulus clouds of tiny flowers in summer, many with a fresh, sweet-sharp fragrance. *Filipendula rubra* forms a statuesque mound of large pinnate leaves with jaggedly lobed leaflets. The towering red-stemmed flowerheads, with crowded clouds of fragrant, peach-pink flowers, can reach almost twice head height in early and midsummer. *Filipendula rubra* 'Venusta', equally majestic, bears flowers of deep clear rosy pink. Short of moving to a house with a few acres and a lake, those of us who garden on a less grand scale will probably prefer *F. purpurea*, a more modest chest-high mound of gracefully disposed, palmately divided, fresh green leaves, with more open sprays of glowing crimson-cerise flowers on deep crimson stems in mid- to late summer. *F. purpurea* f. *albiflora* bears elegant airy sprays of crisp white, and *F. ulmaria* 'Flore Pleno' gives a similar effect at waist height. *Filipendula purpurea* 'Elegans', on the same scale, has plumes of deep rose pink. Where space is really tight, *F.* 'Kahome', the

▼ *Filipendula rubra* 'Venusta' with astilbes

▶ *Filipendula* 'Kahome' with *Hemerocallis* 'Dresden Dream'

often die after flowering—but be philosophical: you will have enjoyed several years of great billowing mounds of fabulous foliage. If you want to grow it purely as a foliage specimen, cut out the flower stems as soon as they show.

Fully hardy, z6–9. Full sun and deep, fertile, well-drained soil. Protect the crown with a deep, dry mulch in winter.

Filipendula

Rosaceae

Filipendula is native to flushed wet meadows, streambanks, marshes, fens or damp woods and prairies. Some, notably *F. ulmaria*, meadowsweet, have long been grown for herbal use. In his *Herball* of 1597, John Gerard described its habitat thus: "It groweth in the brinkes of watery ditches and rivers sides, and also in meadows." Aspirin, the natural medicine, was first isolated in 1837 from its flowerheads.

dwarf meadowsweet, makes a knee to thigh high mound with feathery sprays in deep rose pink, from early summer to early autumn.

Whatever their heft and height, all of these can be grown in damp borders, at the margins of pools and bog gardens, and in moist woodland sites. *F. rubra* and *F. ulmaria* thrive in wet boggy soils.

Fully hardy, z3–8/9. Sun or dappled shade in moist but well-drained, humus-rich soils.

Foeniculum
Apiaceae ▪ fennel

Fennel brings to mind the aniseed-scented and -flavoured foliage used for cooking with plump pink trout. But who has ever grown *Foeniculum vulgare* and not pondered the translucent beauty of its fresh green, hair-fine leaves fanning from smooth, jointed stems, and wondered how might it be exploited to ornamental effect elsewhere? I often include the bronzed form, *Foeniculum vulgare* 'Purpureum', as a fine-textured fountain in borders, along with the purple sage, *Salvia officinalis* 'Purpurascens', for contrasts: rather an unimaginative

▼ *Foeniculum vulgare*

under-exploitation of its potential, I think. Imagine that fresh green interlaced with the deep blues of *Echinops*, or pierced by the spires of foxgloves, the bottlebrushes of sanguisorbas, or threaded through with aquilegias or tickseed daisies, *Coreopsis*. Both the fresh fine green or purple-bronze forms complement the sharper limes of the euphorbias, or the alchemillas. You can lift self-sown seedlings from the herb garden and experiment.

Fully hardy, z5–10. Any fertile moist but well-drained soil in sun.

Gaura
Onagraceae

From open coastal prairies in Texas and Louisiana, and in Mexico, usually on mineral soils that are low in organic matter, the rise of *Gaura* as a garden plant corresponds closely with the interest in naturalistic plantings. You know when a plant has 'arrived' when you are greeted by a mass of humanity trailing away from the flower shows, all but hidden by their hoard of 'Whirling Butterflies'.

Gaura lindheimeri forms a rosetted basal clump of narrow leaves, with long, arching, slender stems, bearing lax panicles of pale flowers, each irregularly starry with four petals and conspicuous anthers. The effect is a transparent cloud, gracefully mobile and responsive to breeze, in much the same way as *Dierama*. The flowers open at dawn, enjoy the day, and quickly fall, but in continuous succession from summer until autumn. The species reaches head height, as does *G. l.* 'Siskiyou Pink', with vivid raspberry pink flowers on crimson stems. At thigh to waist high: *G. l.* 'Whirling Butterflies' and KARALEE WHITE 'Nagauwhite', with white flowers and red sepals; at knee high: *G. l.* 'Crimson Butterflies' with pale crimson flowers and crimson-flushed foliage; *G. l.* 'Passionate Blush' in deep blush pink. The dwarf cultivars will be enjoyed by tidy-minded gardeners. Taller ones flop and weave among neighbouring plants and are beautiful spangling the late summer

◀◀ *Gaura lindheimeri*

◀ *Gaura lindheimeri*
'Siskiyou Pink'

golds of airy grasses. If you plant your new gaura in spring, it is apt to become lost among neighbours; in cool climates, grow it on until it achieves some substance before setting out.

Fully hardy. z5/6–9. Full sun, in any well-drained soil, whether dry or more moisture-retentive. Tolerant of poor soils including sandy and chalky ones. *Gaura* are deeply tap rooted, and once established, very resistant to drought and heat.

Gillenia

Rosaceae

Found in rocky, open woodland in eastern North America, *Gillenia trifoliata* (bowman's root or Indian physic) was introduced to Europe in the seventeenth century. We generally grow it in borders and love it there—it associates so well with other border stalwarts such as astrantias, cirsiums, sedums, nepetas and Old Roses. But its airiness can equally be appreciated in more naturalistic plantings in light-dappled woodland among ferns, foxgloves, sedges (*Carex*) and woodland grasses such as the melicks (*Melica* species), or in prairie plantings with *Stipa tenuissima* and *Deschampsia*.

Gillenia trifoliata is a rhizomatous herbaceous perennial, with handsome sheaves of three-palmate leaves, deeply veined, conspicuously toothed, and in a beautiful shade of bronzed green. The lax panicles of irregularly starry white flowers have crimson calyces and are borne on wiry crimson-red stems, from early to midsummer or a little later, but the show's not over until you've enjoyed the standing red-crimson stems with the persistent red calyces, followed by the vivid autumn foliage tints. Slugs will undermine your attempts to get *Gillenia* established.

Waist high. Fully hardy, z4–9. Any fertile, near-neutral, well-drained but retentive soil, in light shade, dappled shade or sun, with protection from the hottest sun.

▶ *Gillenia trifoliata*

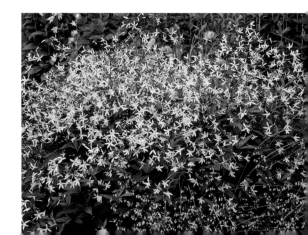

◀ *Gypsophila paniculata* 'Bristol Fairy'

◀ *Gypsophila paniculata* with digitalis

Gypsophila

Caryophyllaceae ▪ baby's breath

From dry grasslands and stony slopes of central and eastern Europe, usually on alkaline soils, *Gypsophila paniculata* is one of the best exemplars of the transparent cloud. Arising from a robust rhizome, from a semi-woody base, it branches diffusely, the fleshy branches sporting narrow, grey-green leaves and, in mid- to late summer, a massed profusion of light-filled panicles of very tiny white flowers. The flowers are larger and pale pink in *G. paniculata* 'Flamingo', double white in *G. paniculata* 'Bristol Fairy', and double in *G.* 'Rosenschleier', opening white and then blushing soft pink.

Well grown, gypsophila will form a mound to chest height and as much across, but how many times have I inadvertently hoed off the new growth of gypsophila? It is brittle, fleshy and snaps easily from the rootstock, so mark its position well.

It is the classic disguiser of gaps left by early summer bloomers, such as *Papaver orientale*, and it masks the fading foliage of spring bulbs. Its delicate mass is fabulous draping the tops of stone walls, and spilling down from terraces, pierced by the spires of sidalcea, arching over rising mounds of sedums, or flanked by eryngiums and echinops. Its diffuseness inspires thoughts of growing among grasses, but so pale is it that it is easily lost among soft silvers and golds; it does, however, associate with grasses of more definite colour such *Pennisetum orientale* 'Karley Rose', or the strongly upright forms of *Panicum virgatum*.

Fully hardy, z4–9. Deep, open-textured, sharply drained, preferably alkaline soil in sun.

Hamamelis

Hamamelidaceae ▪ witch hazel

If it seems a little odd to include witch hazels among the transparents, it's because I try to categorize plants by the effect they have when at their peak of interest. But although the most obvious feature of the hamamelis is the haze of flower on bare winter wood, they do have other strong features too. *Hamamelis ×intermedia* 'Aphrodite', for instance, has a tiered and spreading habit of growth; *H. ×intermedia* 'Aurora' has ascending branches and a vase-shaped habit. Most have wonderful autumn colour in luminous shades of scarlet, crimson, orange and gold.

The flowers comprise fine ribbons of petals held in dense axillary clusters along the bare branches between midwinter and early spring; they're spidery and exquisitely scented—neither primrose nor honey, but redolent of both. They are also resistant to cold, and continue blooming even if frosted, or capped with snow.

Once available in any colour as long as it was yellow, the range in *H. ×intermedia* is now much wider, from the palest of primrose yellow, in 'Pallida' and 'Moonlight', through deep yellows

in 'Arnold Promise' and 'Ripe Corn'; fiery orange in 'Glowing Embers', 'Vesna' and 'Winter Beauty'; orange-tinted copper in 'Jelena' and 'Feuerzauber'; and glowing reds in 'Diane' and 'Ruby Glow'. They all look best against a dark background, but beneath a canopy of deciduous trees, all colours take on a translucent glow when illuminated with slanting winter light.

Grows slowly to twice head height. Fully hardy, z4–9. Fertile, moist but well-drained, leafy, humus-rich soils, in dappled shade or sun. They prefer slightly acid or near-neutral soil, but thrive in deep soils over chalk if the soil is rich in leafy organic matter.

Hesperis

Brassicaceae ▪ dame's violet, sweet rocket

So long and widely cultivated and such a frequent escapee from gardens, dame's violet is now found in hedgebanks and woods, and on streambanks and roadsides far beyond its natural range from southern Europe to Asia. With sweet heady evening fragrance from the open heads of four-petalled flowers in white, lilac or pale purple, in late spring and summer, *Hesperis* is nectar rich and attracts bees, moths and butterflies.

The species, *H. matronalis*, and white-flowered *H. m.* var. *albiflora* suit naturalistic plantings in the dappled shade of the woodland garden with brunneras and dicentras, where they self-sow gently making drifts that glow in the half-light. Double-flowered variants, pure white in *H. m.* 'Alba Plena' and stronger-coloured ones like *H. m.* 'Lilacina' in soft lilac and 'Purpurea' with red-purple flowers, have sufficient heft to hold their own in mixed borders. They consort naturally with foxgloves, and wonderfully with the ball-headed alliums. Short-lived perennials or biennials, if allowed to self-sow, they'll pop up unexpectedly in random clouds of soft colour.

Waist high. Fully hardy, z3–10. Moist but well-drained, moderately fertile, neutral to alkaline soil in sun or dappled shade.

▲ *Hamamelis xintermedia* 'Jelena'

▶ *Hamamelis xintermedia* 'Vesna'

▶ *Hamamelis xintermedia* 'Pallida'

▶ *Hamamelis xintermedia* 'Diane'

◀ *Hesperis matronalis*
with alliums

◀ *Hesperis matronalis*
'Alba Plena'

its neighbours and reaches twice the expected size. It self-sows freely where conditions suit. Although I still love it, I'm now more realistic—I like its deep colouring and the way it can weave through a planting. I allow it to sow in the crevices of a terrace, where low nutrients and physical constriction control its exuberance. I grow it among grasses, I grow it in gravel banks. And in borders,

I grow it with hefty associates, such as the silver-leaved *Artemisia ludoviciana*, buxom nepetas, *Onopordum acanthium*, and stands of foxgloves. I supervise it closely, surgically with secateurs if necessary. I can spot a seedling a mile off.

To thigh high and above. Fully hardy, z6–10. Poor to moderately fertile, well-drained soil in full sun.

Knautia

Dipsacaceae

▶ *Knautia macedonica*
with *Campanula latiloba*

Growing wild in woods and scrub across the Balkans into Romania, *Knautia macedonica* is a robust perennial with a basal mound of rough-textured, greyish green foliage above which rise wiry stems supporting deep maroon pincushion flowerheads from mid- to late summer, often later. For me it was love at first sight, but with familiarity came obvious character flaws; many wild plants become brutish given rich living, and *K. macedonica* is one of them. In good soil in a sunny border it sprawls over

Limonium

Plumbaginaceae • sea lavender

With a basal rosette of long, leathery dark green leaves held close to the ground, and stiff wiry stems that branch freely to hold aloft airy panicles of tiny, papery lavender blue flowers from mid- to late summer, *Limonium platyphyllum* is one of the prettiest of cloud-formers for dry gardens. The flower sprays, which can be cut for drying or flower-arranging, are everlasting, retaining their form in the garden for many months. It thrives in gravel, or among rocks and cobbles, even in shingle coastal sites, and is heat and drought tolerant once established. *Limonium platyphyllum* 'Violetta' has deep violet flowers; *L. p.* 'Robert Butler' is a knee-high selection with intense violet purple flowers.

To mid thigh. Fully hardy, z3–9. Full sun, freely draining, dry or moist, preferably sandy or stony soils, but fine too in any acid or alkaline, moderately fertile border soil.

▲ *Lychnis coronaria*
Oculata Group

▶ *Lychnis coronaria*

◀ *Limonium platyphyllum*

Lychnis

Caryophyllaceae

Lychnis coronaria, rose campion, is one of the most welcome of self-seeders—not least because it can be short-lived and I wouldn't want to be without it. It has basal rosettes of white woolly-hairy leaves, and tall white stems, each with an open terminal raceme of flowers in glowing magenta. It's a very strong colour,

but cooled by the contrast to its own silvery white leaves and stems, a self-contained object lesson in how to use intense hues without letting them overpower—so that they're like points of light.

Lychnis coronaria 'Alba' is pristine in silver and white. If you dither between cool white and hot magenta, then the only choice is the exquisite *L. coronaria* Oculata Group, which has white flowers with glowing pink centres. These plants self-sow, but hybridize, and the magenta proves dominant.

These are see-through plants for the front or middle of a border, but they also find special niches in gravel, paving crevices and dry stone walls—adding accidental incidents that you can claim as your own. With excellent drainage, they survive wet winters, but don't like them; they look shabby after a hard winter but usually recover their good looks once new growth gets underway.

Thigh high. Fully hardy, z4–10. Full sun in well-drained soil.

◀ *Macleaya cordata*

Macleaya
Papaveraceae ▪ plume poppy

Tall, stately, rhizomatous herbaceous perennials from open meadows and grassland in China and Japan, both *Macleaya microcarpa* and *M. cordata* have handsome foliage—broadly heart-shaped, deeply lobed, prominently veined and heavily bloomed olivine grey-green. Leaves climb the stout pale stems, and in a modest

breeze ripple upwards to reveal the downy white surface beneath. The majestic plumes of mid- to late summer, far above the leaves, create a scintillating haze of creamy buff, or a muted coral pink in *M. microcarpa* 'Kelway's Coral Plume'. Traditionally used as back border plants in mixed borders, they need a significantly lower or transparent foreground so as not to obscure their foliage. They also make an excellent sculptural contrast for larger grasses; several of the larger *Miscanthus* are eminently suitable, especially those with pink or coral tints to the inflorescences, such as *M. sinensis* 'Flamingo' or 'Silberfeder'.

Above head height. Fully hardy, z3–10. Moisture-retentive but well-drained soil in sun. Can be invasive, especially in rich, open-textured soils.

Meum
Apiaceae ▪ baldmoney, spignel

A modest umbellifer from screes, thin grassland and montane meadows, usually on limestone, in central and western Europe, *Meum athamanticum* resembles a happy cross between fennel, *Foeniculum vulgare*, and sweet cicely, *Myrrhis odorata*. The aromatic fresh green leaves are divided into thread-like leaflets, giving a light feathery effect, and the umbels of

▶ *Meum athamanticum* with *Viola cornuta*

tiny starry flowers in early and midsummer are a bright clean white. It happily cohabits with *Viola cornuta*, either in white or blue, which will wreath through its stems, and is an excellent host to nodding alliums such as *Allium carinatum* subsp. *pulchellum*.

Thigh high. Fully hardy, z6–9. Well-drained, poor to moderately fertile, near-neutral or alkaline soil in sun.

◀ *Milium effusum* 'Aureum' with hostas and violas

Milium

Poaceae

Milium effusum is a graceful grass sometimes seen in open oak or beech woodland; *M. effusum* 'Aureum', Bowles's golden grass, is the one to grow in gardens. Its new spring leaves are a golden yellow, fading to a bright golden green— a useful colour with green-flowered hellebores, euphorbias, golden hostas and flowers of blue or blue-violet, as with the more delicate flowered aquilegias. The flowering stems, the slender hair-fine branchlets of the open nodding panicles, and the tiny spikelets are all golden, making a very delicate haze above the foliage from late spring to summer.

Knee to thigh high. Fully hardy, z5–10. Moist but well-drained, humusy soil in dappled or light shade. Comes true from seed.

Miscanthus

Poaceae

Miscanthus is one of the most versatile of grassy genera, both in prairie plantings and in more traditional beds and borders. The grasses are imposing in height, late-flowering, with good autumn colour, standing firm through winter, rimed by frost or spangled with dew. They vary in habit from erect to gently arching, and despite being substantial in size, the inflorences are delightfully airy—open panicles with silky hairy spikelets that shimmer in low, golden autumn and winter light. If their differences are subtle, it might just be one particular subtlety that gives you precisely what you want. It takes patience. They seldom establish fully until their third year, but then give increasing pleasure year by year throughout their long lives.

Miscanthus sinensis is the most valuable of all, with a huge range of cultivars that all have flat, linear, usually bluish green leaves and long pyramidal panicles of silky spikelets to head height or above: 'Flamingo' has leaves with a silver midrib and long, open, silvery grey-pink inflorescences; 'Graziella', is upright with open plumes of warm golden pink ageing silver; 'Grosse Fontäne' is very tall, arching, with red panicles aging silver; 'Kleine Silberspinne' is compact, arching, with open panicles of pink-tinted white, ageing silver; 'Malepertus' has bronzed, arching leaves, and metallic, crimson-tinted golden plumes in upright tassels well above the foliage; 'Silberfeder' has arching panicles, silvery pink ageing to silver, well above the foliage; 'Undine' has arching leaves, with silver midribs, and upright stems with open inflorescences in silvered deep crimson ageing silver-pink.

Fully hardy, z5–9. Full sun, moderately fertile, moisture-retentive but well-drained soil.

◀ *Miscanthus sinensis*
'Undine'

◀ *Miscanthus sinensis*
'Flamingo' with
Miscanthus sinensis
'Graziella'

◀ *Miscanthus sinensis*
'Silberfeder'

◀ *Miscanthus sinensis*
'Kleine Silberspinne'

Molinia

Poaceae • moor grass

Purple moor grass, *Molinia caerulea* subsp. *caerulea*, is the dominant species on the high damp acidic moorland, from Europe to Asia, where it forms low tussocks of flattened linear leaves that are flushed purple at the base. In mid- to late summer, the moorland takes on a purple haze as flower stems elongate to bear a long spike-like panicle of compressed, purple spikelets at each tip. The stems are rigid and rise clear of the basal foliage, and as autumn approaches the whole plant turns gold with an array of inflorescences becoming a gauzy golden halo.

Tall moor grass, *Molinia caerulea* subsp. *arundinacea*, is found at lower elevations, in fens and marshes, and on less acidic soils. Whereas the purple moor grass seldom exceeds waist height, tall moor grass is just what it says on the label. It has a similar habit, but with much more impact—its glistening halo of stiff slender stems makes a perfectly transparent echo of the basal mound at head height and above. In both subspecies, the inflorescence holds dew and raindrops so that the haloes are scintillating against a backcloth of sunny sky (we hope).

So diffuse and perfectly transparent in flower, these grasses' height is no bar to including them in mixed perennial plantings, whether you place them fore or aft. *Molinia caerulea* subsp. *arundinacea* will accommodate the tall cymes of *Verbena bonariensis*, the butterflies of the gauras, the sinuous narrow spikes of *Persicaria amplexicaulis*, or the spires of perovskia; *M. c.* subsp. *caerulea* is more in scale with the bottlebrushes of the sanguisorbas, or the violet racemes of *Salvia sylvestris*.

Among the *M. c.* subsp. *arundinacea* cultivars, 'Karl Foerster' is very erect, with deep purple inflorescences on bright golden stems, and red-gold autumn colour; 'Sky Racer' is probably the tallest, with purple inflorescences on a fan of stiff stems, all turning clear gold in autumn; 'Transparent' has fine, stiffly erect stems supporting

◀ *Molinia caerulea* subsp. *arundinacea* 'Transparent'

◀ *Molinia caerulea* subsp. *arundinacea* 'Windspiel'

▶ *Nepeta govaniana*

deep purple spikelets; and 'Strahlenquelle' has a distinctive arching habit, with a fountain of long, slender purple inflorescences.

Thigh high to sky high. Fully hardy, z4/5–8. Moist but well-drained, low-nutrient to moderately fertile soil in sun or light shade.

Nepeta

Lamiaceae

From moist, open woodland in the Himalayas, *Nepeta govaniana* bears little resemblance to the catmint nepetas. It forms basal mounds of aromatic, soft bright green leaves, and elongated racemes of long-tubed, soft yellow flowers, mobile and trembling on long pedicels, spaced widely along graceful stems from early summer to autumn. Elegant, tall and light, it makes a softer punctuation than a spire of the same height in a border, but still serves to draw

an array of large, very open plumes on which spikelets are sparse and tightly compressed, hence one of the most transparent of haloes; and 'Windspiel' has erect, slender stems with very dense inflorescences, that are very mobile in breeze.

Molinia caerulea subsp. *caerulea* cultivars: 'Moorflamme' at knee to thigh high, with dark purple-brown inflorescences and particularly good autumn colour in orange, gold and red; 'Moorhexe' is thigh high, with stiff dark green foliage, dark flower stems and tight heads of

the eye along a planting. The flowers tone well with the pale pokers of *Kniphofia* 'Percy's Pride' or 'Green Jade', and complement all shades of blue and violet; the foliage has a hint of lime that looks well with euphorbias. It prefers a cool position, and looks frazzled pretty quickly in hot and droughty soils. I've never used it in the dappled shade of the woodland garden, but some do, and it is certainly a pleasure to see in a lightly shaded border, with golden and variegated hostas and arching ferns.

Chest high. Fully hardy, z5–9. Sun or light

dappled shade in moderately fertile, moisture-retentive but well-drained soil.

Nicotiana

Solanaceae

Few annuals can be described as majestic or even architectural, but *Nicotiana sylvestris* (flowering or woodland tobacco) is one of them. It rockets to head high in a season—by summer, the basal rosettes of large dark green leaves produce a towering stem with a starburst of pendent, long-tubed, pure white trumpets. The right size and height to group at the back of border, where they look best with a dark background, but not so far away as to deny yourself the pleasure of their fabulous perfume. In shade or on a cloudy day they scent the daytime, but when it's warm and sunny they save their best till dusk. Squeeze in a few near doors

▶ *Nigella damascena* with *Alchemilla mollis*

▼ *Nicotiana sylvestris*

and open windows so that the scent will waft inside, save some for the terrace or patio and site others to be seen luminescent at dusk. It is a woodland native, and flowers usefully late—many shade-lovers have passed their peak by the time tobacco plants hit theirs.

It's not difficult from seed, and if you grow your own you will have more than enough for all of the above places.

Head high. Any moderately fertile, moist but well-drained soil in sun or light shade. Don't smoke it, don't eat it; all parts are poisonous.

Nigella

Ranunculaceae • love-in-a-mist

Misty and transient, *Nigella damascena* is a hardy annual with feathery bright green foliage and terminal saucers of pointed, pale blue petals with a filigreed bright green ruff beneath. Call it a permanent annual; once sown, it's self-perpetuating if you don't cut all the seedheads for arranging. In traditional cottage gardens it would be allowed to pop up wherever it chose, and that's how I like to use in more modern plantings. Its strength is as a filler, not a feature,

and once you have established drifts in the first year, you take or leave the seedlings as you will. Very easy to recognize, they look like incipient carrots. It grows wild in subalpine meadows in southern Europe and North Africa, and looks very beautiful when scattered through drifts of *Melica uniflora*, *Milium effusum* 'Aureum' or *Stipa tenuissima*. And any seedlings that find their way into clumps of fennel like *Foeniculum vulgare* or *F. v.* 'Purpureum' should be allowed to stay. You might sow a few when you sow *Ammi majus*, too.

There are several seed strains: *N. d.* 'Miss Jekyll' in a clear light blue, 'Miss Jekyll White', and 'Oxford Blue' in dark blue. The impartial might select the University strain, which includes 'Oxford Blue' and 'Cambridge Blue', a lighter bright blue.

Mid thigh high. Any well-drained soil in sun.

◀ *Oemleria cerasiformis* with snowdrops, hellebores and winter aconites

Oemleria

Rosaceae • oso berry, Oregon plum

A suckering understorey shrub of the margins of damp forests of the Pacific Northwest, *Oemleria cerasiformis* is one of the earliest plants to leaf up in late winter, and it bears pendent chains of delicate white flowers as it does so. As the leaves open they are considerably folded upwards, so don't obscure the flowers; rather, they contribute to the delicate lightness of the affair, being a translucent, intense sea green. Male and female flowers are borne on different plants, the male flowers being more attractive, but the females give rise to bloomy, sloe-black fruit like tiny plums. In the oso berry, scent is a gender-sensitive issue—males smell of tomcat, while females have a light sweet scent—but the scents are neither carrying nor pervasive. You need both to produce fruit but you'll be lucky to find a nursery that sells by gender (buy in flower and take a hand lens with you—the males have stamens).

▶ *Origanum laevigatum* 'Herrenhausen'

Oemleria cerasiformis is a specimen for the shady border or beneath a light canopy of deciduous trees. Arrange, if you can, for it to be illuminated by bright shafts of winter sunlight so that leaves filter the light and white flowers glisten. Its tendency to sucker seems marked only in very moist soils, and I like to keep it as a rather open specimen, which means thinning out shoots as necessary after flowering.

Fully hardy, z6–10. Moisture-retentive but well-drained, moderately fertile, humus-rich soil, in sun or dappled shade.

Origanum

Lamiacae

Cultivars and hybrids of *Origanum laevigatum* are not culinary herbs. They have tall, wiry stemmed, whorled and airy panicles of pink or purple flowers with darker calyces and bracts, giving each tiny floret pleasing definition. They bloom from late spring or early summer to autumn, with never a day free from the visitations of bees or butterflies. They associate well with silver-leaved plants, and if grown with thymes and lavenders, provide a continuous bee-fest for months on end.

In *O. laevigatum* 'Herrenhausen', flowers are intense pink, and foliage flushed purple when young and in winter cold; *O.* 'Rosenkuppel' retains a dusky purple foliar flush throughout summer, with flowers of intense dark purplish pink; *O. laevigatum* 'Hopleys' is taller, with larger heads of paler pink flowers.

◀ *Origanum*
'Rosenkuppel'

▶ *Panicum virgatum*

Knee to mid thigh high. Fully hardy z5–10. Well-drained, preferably alkaline, poor or not-too-fertile soil in sun.

Panicum

Poaceae ▪ switch grass

A rhizomatous native of tall-grass prairie, marsh, damp and dry woodland, *P. virgatum* has strong vertical line—resolutely erect in habit, but translucent as silk chiffon when in flower in early autumn. The broad, diffuse arrays of tiny red-purple spikelets on hair-fine branchlets form a shimmering haze above the foliage. They stand well: winter-persistent, wind- and weather resistant. Switch grasses are among the finest of grasses for late season colour, often beginning their metamorphosis soon after midsummer, the tints suffusing from the leaf tips downwards in shades of red, burgundy, red-gold and blonde, the flower panicles darkening as they ripen. Natural companions include echinaceas, rudbeckias, *Veronicastrum* and *Verbena hastata*.

Panicum virgatum forms a sheaf of glaucous blue-green or purple-flushed stems sheathed in erect leaves, smooth and green, turning gold in autumn. The flower panicles form an arching plume at first, then a scintillating veil of pale purple, then golden spikelets. It is variable in height. *Panicum virgatum* 'Dallas Blues', at chest to head high, has powdery blue-grey leaves turning foxy copper in autumn, with

▶ *Panicum virgatum*
'Rehbraun'

▶ *Panicum virgatum*
'Shenandoah'

large hazy inflorescences of red-purple spikelets; *P. v.* 'Hänse Herms' is a compact, mid thigh-high fountain of blue-green leaves, suffused first with red, then rich red-purple in autumn; *P. v.* 'Heavy Metal', is very erect, waist high, with metallic blue-grey leaves, blonde in autumn, with pink-toned inflorescences and burgundy seedheads; *P. v.* 'Rehbraun' is chest high, with purple-flushed, grey-green leaves, red-brown at the tips, and foxy russet in autumn; *P. v.* 'Shenandoah', at waist high, has pale green leaves that take on purple-red tones in mid- to late summer, before finally turning rich burgundy in autumn.

Waist to chest high. Fully hardy, z5–9. Full sun, in lean or not-too-fertile, moist but well-drained soil. Drought-tolerant once established.

Polemonium

Polemoniaceae

A traditional cottage garden perennial, *Polemonium caeruleum* is always welcome in early summer, but always gone too soon. Self-sown seedlings flower a little earlier or a little later, prolonging the season. Forming clumps of twice pinnate leaves in the familiar ladder-like arrangement that gives it the common name of Jacob's ladder, it bears loose cymes of bell-shaped lavender blue flowers, giving a pretty, open texture at about mid thigh. I value its self-seeding habit, allowing it to appear randomly and where it will fill gaps.

I use *P. pauciflorum* in the same way. It is shorter than *P. caeruleum*, with trumpet-shaped, soft yellow flowers tinted dusky red; this and *Digitalis grandiflora* 'Carillon', a very slender yellow-belled foxglove, are allowed to thread their way through most of my borders by self-seeding—among the brunneras and pulmonarias and other plants that flower early, leaving good but flowerless foliage behind.

Polemonium caeruleum occurs in the wild in limestone grassland, on scree and rock ledges, and although not often used as a meadow

▶ *Scabiosa caucasica* 'Clive Greaves'

◀ *Polemonium caeruleum* BRIZE D'ANJOU 'Blanjou'

▼ *Polemonium pauciflorum*

plant, it looks lovely with wild blue aquilegias in fine grass or in wild gardens—as does BRISE D'ANJOU 'Blanjou', its neatly variegated form.

Knee to thigh high. Fully hardy, z3–9. Well-drained moisture-retentive soil in sun or dappled shade.

Scabiosa

Dipsacaceae

The tale of a fashion victim: when *Scabiosa atropurpurea* 'Chile Black' hit the show stands, it sold like hotcakes—such a fabulous dark, sanguineous colour, with pincushion flowers on long wiry stems, like a knautia with some-

thing of the night about it...but with nothing of *Knautia*'s staying power. 'Chile Black' flowers from mid- to late summer, but it's not enough; botanically a short-lived perennial or biennial, it invariably behaves as a biennial for me, which is grievous when it costs as much as a long-term perennial does.

Scabiosa caucasica, on the other hand...well, the flowers aren't black, but it has the most beautifully formed pincushions of all. It flowers from midsummer to autumn, with solitary flowers on long stalks above a basal clump of divided grey green leaves; they have a domed pincushion centre, surrounded by two ranks of frilled, slightly crumpled, pale blue or lavender blue petals (florets) with a subdued crystalline sheen. Two of the finest cultivars are *S. c.* 'Clive Greaves' in pure lavender blue and *S. c.* 'Miss Willmott', slightly taller with white flowers. The House Nursery that raised them also grew a range of *S. caucasica* hybrids, still available as House's Hybrids, in shades of blue, white and heliotrope. They're very easily grown from seed and flower the first year. Other pure single colours are found in *S. c.* 'Fama', deep lavender blue with silvery white pincushions, and *S. c.* Stäfa with large, deep-blue-lavender flowers. These plants are hotspots for bees and butterflies especially when associated with blue nepetas and lavenders, *Teucrium fruticans*, *Caryopteris* and *Perovskia*.

Mid thigh high. Fully hardy, z4–9. Well-drained, fertile, preferably alkaline soil in sun.

Selinum
Apiaceae

The great plantsman E. A. Bowles once described *Selinum wallichianum* as the "queen of umbellifers, with almost transparent tender green-ness and the marvellously lacy pattern of its large leaves". It's a tall umbellifer, from Kashmir to Bhutan, a native of meadows and scrub in the foothills of the Himalayas. The bloomed red-purple stems reach head high before branching into flat, white-stalked umbels of starry, pristine white flowers with conspicuous wispy, white-margined bracts, with each umbel rising higher than the next

▲ *Scabiosa atropurpurea* 'Chile Black' with sidalceas

to form exquisite tiers of delicate lace above mounds of ferny, finely divided, lucent green leaves. Blooming from midsummer to autumn, it thrives beneath a high sun-dappling canopy in a woodland garden or shady border, not because it positively needs shade, but because the flowers take on an ethereal glow in diminished light. Where there is room, growing a stand in light woodland would be the finest way to display its exceptional beauty.

Head high. Fully hardy, z7–9. Moist but well-drained, deep, fertile soil in sun or dappled shade.

◀ *Selinum wallichianum*

▼ *Smyrnium perfoliatum*
with forget-me-nots

Smyrnium

Apiaceae

Smyrnium perfoliatum (perfoliate alexanders) is an extraordinary woodland umbellifer in vivid and translucent shades of lime green and gold immediately evocative of the (unrelated) euphorbias. Outstanding in the semi-shade of the woodland garden, where it naturalizes readily, it forms luminous drifts by self-seeding—once it has been established, and providing you don't hoe out the bright seedlings in error. It is a monocarpic perennial, dying after seeding; in the first year it will form two leaves and an incipient tap root, in the second it grows taller and in the third year it flowers. The basal leaves are finely divided and bright green, while those on the erect flowering stems are rounded and lime green. The flower stem grows through the middle of the leaf; at the top of each stem a haze of tiny umbels of minute greenish yellow flowers appears in spring. It is best sown from fresh ripe seed (beg some from a friend), and resents transplanting.

Smyrnium perfoliatum is lovely with blue-flowered woodlanders, such as pulmonarias, and the golden sheaves of *Milium effusum* 'Aureum'. It is an obvious companion for the English bluebell, *Hyacinthoides non-scripta*—but take care that bluebells are not overwhelmed by smyrnium, which tends to rampage about in the damp, woodsy soils that bluebells need.

Thigh to head high (very variable). Fully hardy, z6–10. Humus-rich, moist but well-drained soils in sun or dappled shade.

Stipa
Poaceae

Stipas occur mainly in open habitats, in open woodland, on streambanks, and in more exposed sites in dry, rocky and sandy soils and tend not to enjoy jostling with close neighbours. All have a beautiful textural presence—translucent, transparent and elegantly mobile—and a strength of form that develops to its fullest potential if given space to express it.

Stipa calamagrostis is a deciduous species that could justifiably be used for its arching line. It forms a mound of narrow, blue-green leaves that fountain outwards to form a mound wider than tall, then, in summer, produces a cascading halo of flower at waist height, the purple spikelets giving a pink haze to lax, open silvery plumes.

Stipa gigantea is evergreen or semi-evergreen, forming a dense clump of slender, greyish green leaves of a modesty that belies the fabulous stature of its summer flowers. They rocket to well above head height, bursting into an open panicle of pendulous, long-bristled, silvery pale purple spikelets ageing first to golden brown then to glistening golden blonde. Despite its height, it has such complete transparency that it will not obscure anything that you place behind it—a clear sky, a view of blue distant hills. Give it prime placement as a specimen, on a sweep of gravel or another minimalistic foreground.

Stipa tenuissima forms erect, thigh-high sheaves of deciduous, almost filamentous yellow-green leaves, becoming paler and more golden as it comes into flower—infinitely fine, nodding panicles forming soft, silky clouds in summer, rippling in the breeze as when cats' paws of wind move through fields of barley, creating moving patterns of glistening light and shade. Long drifts or massed plantings afford the best kinetic displays.

◀ *Stipa calamagrostis*

▼ *Stipa gigantea*

▲ *Stipa tenuissima*

Thigh high to sky high. Fully hardy, z7–9. Well-drained, open-textured, moderately fertile soil in full sun.

Thalictrum

Ranunculaceae • meadow rue

The genus *Thalictrum* includes both clouds and transparents. All have very attractive, often glaucous leaves evocative of substantial maidenhair ferns or delicate aquilegias, divided into lobed leaflets. *Thalictrum aquilegiifolium* is a rhizomatous clump-former, with pale green columbine-like leaves and erect, leafy, glaucous stems with terminal flower panicles at waist to chest height in summer. The sepals are soon discarded to leave only flat, crowded clusters of stamens in fluffy lilac-pink clouds. *Thalictrum lucidum* bears cloudy puffs of creamy yellow-green flowers at head height on strong stems, smelling sweetly of roses, and with foliage finely divided into narrowly linear dark green leaflets. Both are beautiful with the dark blue spires of Elatum Group delphiniums.

The flowerheads of *T. delavayi*, on slender purple-flushed stems, are borne in diffuse, wide-branching panicles at chest to head height, with tiny brushes of white stamens hanging beneath a cup of deep lilac sepals, in mid- to late summer or early autumn. *Thalictrum dipterocarpum*, about the same size and height, has flowers of delicate mauve with creamy anthers and blue-green foliage; they're very similar and most plants advertised as *T. dipterocarpum* are *T. delavayi*.

Thalictrum 'Elin' soars well above head height. It has beautifully glaucous, blue-grey foliage, flushed purple on emergence, and strong, stiffly erect, dusky stems bearing open sprays of smoky, rose-purple buds opening to creamy yellow, from early to late summer. I'm told to stake it, but haven't, though it's rather a test of nerve. It towers above the tiered white umbels of *Selinum wallichianum*, or the deep pink *Chaerophyllum hirsutum* 'Roseum', and is exquisite among tall grasses such as *Molinia caerulea* subsp. *arundinacea* 'Sky Racer'. I have done the same silly trick with thalictrums as with gypsophila; they emerge late and are easily hoed during spells of attention deficit unless clearly marked.

▲ *Thalictrum delavayi*   ▲ *Thalictrum* 'Elin'

▲ *Thalictrum lucidum*   ▼ *Thalictrum aquilegiifolium*

Fully hardy, z4–8/9. Light dappled shade, in moist, humusy, moderately fertile soil.

▶ *Tiarella cordifolia*

Tiarella

Saxifragaceae • foam flower

Scarcely reaching knee high even when in flower, the herbaceous tiarellas form creeping mats of palmately lobed leaves, maple-like in outline, often with attractive autumn tints in foxy coppers and bronze reds. They give good dense ground cover, forming a flatter carpet than the related, more mounded heucheras—in fact, there is no reason why they might not be used as a low horizontal line. It is the wands of tiny flowers that lend transparency; erect spikes of slender stems bear a profusion of tiny stars on top, over long periods during spring and summer.

Tiarella cordifolia is sometimes invasive. *Tiarella wherryi*, with sharply lobed pale green leaves with a burgundy flush, is more restrained and refined; it has very light open spikes of white- or pink-flushed flowers on dark stems. Several hybrids have decorative shadings, frecklings and marblings on their foliage: *T. wherryi* 'Heronswood Mist' has pale green leaves freckled with creamy white, with earthy pink stems bearing gauzy spikes of starry flowers in palest pink. *Tiarella* 'Mint Chocolate' has deeply lobed mint green leaves, with a chocolate overlay along the veins forming a star, which take on coral tints in cold weather; the strong spikes of white flowers are buff-pink in bud. *Tiarella* 'Pinwheel' has particularly deeply cut lobed leaves in mid green with deep bronze-maroon markings; its flower spikes are particularly airy, the tiny flowers having very slender petals. For plants that are native to woodlands and damp streambanks, they show unexpected tolerance of dry shade.

Fully hardy, z5/6–9. Sun, part-shade or dappled shade in any good, fertile, well-drained soil with adequate summer moisture.

▶ *Tiarella* 'Mint Chocolate'

▶ *Tiarella* 'Pinwheel'

Photographs appearing on pages (21 top; garden of Sir Richard and Lady Storey), 46 and 61 (top) are by Linden Hawthorne. Line drawings on page 11 and colour wheel on page 25 are by Catriona Stewart. Image of Leonardo da Vinci's Vitruvian Man on page 10 has been provided by Luc Viatour.

All other photos have been provided courtesy of the Garden Collection – www.garden-collection.com / Jonathan Buckley: (18tcl Hatfield House), (19tr Design: Penny Smith), (22cl, 45l, 175bl Design: Paul Picton, Old Court Nurseries), 24bl, 24tr, 24tcr, 24br, (32b Design: Paul Kelly), (37b, 86tr, 91tl, 95cr, 113cl,119cr, 120bl, 139tr,182tr, 187cr, 205, 226bl, 230bl, 236-237tc, 252tl, 268br Christopher Lloyd, Great Dixter), 47tl, 48b, (49c Sticky Wicket, Dorset), 56t, 57c, 63br, (65b,87cr, 165cr Beth Chatto Gardens, Essex), 66t, 67cr, (70bl Design: Pam Schwerdt and Sybyl Kreutzberger), 73tr, 74b, (75tl, 125c, 133r Design: Graham Gough, Marchants Nursery), 87tl, 90t, 95tl, 97tl, 98tl, (102tr, 125t, 156bl, 199t, 245bl Glen Chantry, Essex), 103br, 105br, (114tl Design: Veronica Cross), 115tl, 124tl, 124tr, 127b, 132tr, 133bl, 140t, 140b, (142tr Design: Judy Pearce), 150b, 151, 153bl, 158l, 159l, 165tl, 166, 172tr, 173b, 182tl, 184br, 192cr, 192br, 193, 194tl, 197, 198bl, 207tr, 208br, 223tl, 223tr, 228br, 232l, 243br, 254br, 255tl, 259l, 262cl, 263cl, 271cr, 271br; Torie Chugg: (14tr Marwood Hill Garden, Devon), 58t, 58b, 59tr, 70tl, 71c, 73bl, 80b, 109tl, 113tr, 113cr, 132tl, 136tr, 154br, 177br, 178b, 204t, 206b, 208bl, 247br, 265tl, 266cr, 270b; Liz Eddison: (15tr,17, 20br, 27tr, 27br Prieuré de Notre-Dame d'Orsan, France), (18r Jim Keeling, Whichford Pottery), (22cr Adam Woolcott, RHS Chelsea 07), 24tcl, 56bl, (64cr Design: Reaseheath College, RHS Tatton Park 05), 65c, 78b, 87tr, 97br, 98cr, (100tl Design: Jeremy Salt & Roger Bullock), 115cr, 119tc, 123tl, 134br, 157t, 201b, 212c, 239cr, 242tc, 242tr, 243tr, 247tl, 248bl, 267cr, 268bl; Sam Eddison: 75cr; Derek Harris: (15tl Miserden Park Gardens, Glos), (16tl Holker Hall), (27bl Biddulph Grange), (36tr Bourton House), 60tl, 64tr, 72t, 73tl, 82tl, (90c RHS Gardens, Rosemoor), 102tl, 110t, 119tr, 122tl, 128bl, 138tr, 161tr, 184cl, 217cl, 218bl, 218br, 231t, 231b, 255cl; Andrew Lawson: 11cr, (12 Giverny, France), (13 York Gate, Leeds), (14bc Design: Christopher Bradley-Hole, Bury Court), 16br, (18tl Beth Chatto Gardens, Essex), 18bcl, 18bl, (19tcr, 27tl Design: Mirabel Osler), 19bcr, 19br, (20tl The Dillon Garden, Dublin), (20tr Creche ar Pape), 21br, (24tl, 76t, 227tl Sticky Wicket, Dorset), 24bcr, 27cl, (27tc House of Pitmuies, Tayside), 31cr, (31bl Old Rectory, Sudborough), 32t, (33c, 225tr Barnsley House, Glos), 33b, (36tl Design: Dan Pearson), 41t, 41b, 45r, 47cl, 47br, 49t, 49b, 50t, 51t, 51b, 52br, 53t, (53c Dr Ronald McKenzie), 53b, 54br, 55, 56br, 57t, 59tl, 60br, 61cr, 62tl, 62tr, 62cr, 62br, 63bl, 65t, 67cl, 68, 71tl, 71b, 73br, 74t, 75tr, 76c, (76b Lance Hattatt Design Garden), 77t, 77b, 78c, 79tr, 79bl, 80t, 81tl, 81cl, 81cr, 83tl, 83br, 84tl, 84cl, 84br, 85bl, 85bc, 86tl, 86cr, 87cl, 88tl, 89tl, 89tr, 89cr, 90b, 91tr, 92t, 93tl, 93cr, 93br, 94tl, 95tr, 95br, 96t, 96bc, 96br, 98cl, 99tl, 99tr, 100cl, 100tr, 100c, 100br, 101tl, 101cl, 102bl, 102br, 103cl, 104, 105tl, 105tr, 105bl, 106tl, 106tr, 107tl, 107tr, 107cr, 108, 109tr, 109bl, 109br, 111tl, 111tr, 112tl, 112tr, 112cr, 113tl, 113tc, 114tc, 114tr, 115bl, 116tl, 116tr, 116cl, 117tl, 117tr, 117cr, 117bl, 117br, 118, 119tl, 120tl, 120cr, 121tl, 121tr, 123cr, 124b, 125b, 126tl, 126tr, 126b, 127t, 127c, (128t Design: Tom Sitta, Sydney), 129tl, 129tc, 129bcr, 129br, 130bl, 130br, 131t, 131c, 132bc, 132br, 134tl, 134cl, 134bl, 135tl, 135tr, 135bl, 135br, 136tl, 137tr, 138tl, 138bc, 138br, 139tl, 139br, 142tl, 142br, 143t, 143b, 144, 146r, 147, 148, 149tl, 149tr, 150t, 152l, 152r, 153tl, 153tr, 155, 156cr, 158tr, 158c, 159r, 160l, 160r, 161tl, 161br, 162tl, 162tr, 163tl, 163tr, (164 Bourton House, Glos), 165cl, 167t, 167b, 168bl, 168br, 169bl, 170tl, 170cr, 171, 172tl, 173r, 174, 175tl, 175tr, 176cl, 176bl, 177tl, 177cr, 178t, 179tl, 179tr, 180, 182cr, 184tl, 185tl, 185tr, 186tl, 186cr, 189cr, 189bl, 190tr, 190cr, 192tr, 194bl, 195tl, 195tr, 196tl, 198tl, 201t, 202t, 202b, 203t, 203c, 203b, (204b Design: Isabelle Van Groenigen & Gabriella Pape), 206t, 206c, 207tl, 210cr, 210bl, 210br, 212tc, 212cr, 213, 214, (215tl Hestercombe, Somerset), 215bc, 215br, 216, 217tl, 218tl, 219cr, (220-221t Eastgrove Cottage, Worcs), 221br, 222, 223cr, 224tl, 224br, 225tl, 226tl, 227tr, 228cl, 228bl, 228tr, 230tl, 230r, 232-233tc, 234, 236l, 237r, 238tl, 238cr, 239tr, 239bl, 239br, 240tl, 240br, 241bl, 241bc, 242tl, 242bl, 242br, 244tl, 244tr, 245tl, 245cl, 246tr, 246cr, 247tr, 247cr, 248br, 249tr, 250tr, 251tl, 251tr, 252bc, 252br, 254tr, 256tr, 257tl, 257cl, 258tr, 258cr, 259br, 260, 261tl, 261bl, 262tl, 262cr, 264tl, 264br, 265tr, 265cr, 265br, 266tr, 267tl, 269cr, 269br, 270tc, 270tr, 270c, 271tr; Marie O'Hara: 81br, 88tr, 91cr, (112bl Design: Clare Agnew, RHS Chelsea 08), 191; Gary Rogers: (16bl Design: Reaseheath College, RHS Tatton Park 05), (16cr Design: Mr & Mrs Cesare Settepassi), (31tl Design: Karl Foerster), (42l Design: Jamie Dunstan, RHS Tatton Park 05), 98tr, 120cl, 129tl, 163bl, (210tr Design: Ngaere Macray & David Seeler); Jane Sebire: (31tr Design: Matthew Wilson, Harlow Carr); Derek St Romaine: (31cl, 228cr RHS Gardens, Rosemoor), (31br, 78t ,85br, 92c, 211b, 219tr, 233tr, 245cr Glen Chantry, Essex), (37t Beth Chatto Gardens, Essex), 40, 42r, 44, (48t Bruno Marmiroli, Chaumont 01), 50b, 52bl, 54tl, 59cl, 66b, 70tr, 72c, 81tr, 82tr, 83tr, 84bc, 89br, 93tc, 97tr, 98bl, (101r Design: Piet Oudolf, RHS Wisley), (121bl Mr & Mrs David Way, Southover, Kent), 122tr, 137bl, 146l, 154cr, 156tl, 157b, 170br, (172br Design: Mark Rumary), (183 Mr & Mrs Abbot, Harrogate), 185cr, 187t, (188 Stoney Middleton), 195cr, 196cl, 198tr, 199b, 211t, 215tr, (220b Design: Carol Klein – RHS Chelsea 1999), (227cr Mount Pleasant Farm, East Sussex), 233br, 250bl, 256tcr, 263cr; Nicola Stocken Tomkins: (2 Wayford Manor), 8, (14tl Beth Chatto Gardens, Essex), 15bl, 16tr, (20tcr Ilford Manor), (20bcr East Ruston Old Vicarage, Norfolk), 21cr, 22tr, 22br, 23tl, 23tr, (23cl, 32c Goulters Mill), 23bl, (33t Moleshill), 36bl, 38, 75br, 79tl, 79cl, 92b, 93tr, 94tr, 103tl, 110b, 111cl, 111cr, 111bl, 111br, 117cl, 122cr, 123tr, 123cl, 128cr, 129tcr, 133tl, 141, 149bl, 149br, 154bl, 169br, 170tr, 177cl, 186tr, 196tr, 196cr, 198br, 202c, 207bl, 208tr, 208cr, 218tr, 221tr, 228tl, 243tcr, 243bcr, 250tl, 253, 254tl, 256bcr, 256br, 257br, 258cl, 261tcl, 261bcl, 269tr; Mark Taylor: 11br, 24bcr.